GO!

with Microsoft®

Access 2010

Brief

Shelley Gaskin and Carolyn McLellan

D1558117

Prentice Hall

Boston Columbus Indianapolis New York San Francisco Upper Saddle River
Amsterdam Cape Town Dubai London Madrid Milan Munich Paris Montreal Toronto
Delhi Mexico City Sao Paulo Sydney Hong Kong Seoul Singapore Taipei Tokyo

Associate VP/Executive Acquisitions Editor, Print: Stephanie Wall
Editorial Project Manager: Laura Burgess
Editor in Chief: Michael Payne
Product Development Manager: Eileen Bien Calabro
Development Editor: Ginny Munroe
Editorial Assistant: Nicole Sam
Director of Marketing: Kate Valentine
Marketing Manager: Tori Olson Alves
Marketing Coordinator: Susan Osterlitz
Marketing Assistant: Darshika Vyas
Senior Managing Editor: Cynthia Zonneveld
Associate Managing Editor: Camille Trentacoste
Production Project Manager: Mike Lackey
Operations Director: Alexis Heydt
Operations Specialist: Natacha Moore

Senior Art Director: Jonathan Boylan
Cover Photo: © Ben Durrant
Text and Cover Designer: Blair Brown
Manager, Cover Visual Research & Permissions: Karen Sanatar
Manager, Rights and Permissions: Zina Arabia
AVP/Director of Online Programs, Media: Richard Keaveny
AVP/Director of Product Development, Media: Lisa Strite
Media Project Manager, Editorial: Alana Coles
Media Project Manager, Production: John Cassar
Full-Service Project Management: PreMediaGlobal
Composition: PreMediaGlobal
Printer/Binder: Quebecor World Book Services
Cover Printer: Lehigh-Phoenix Color
Text Font: Bookman Light

Credits and acknowledgments borrowed from other sources and reproduced, with permission, in this textbook appear on appropriate page within text.

Microsoft® and Windows® are registered trademarks of the Microsoft Corporation in the U.S.A. and other countries. Screen shots and icons reprinted with permission from the Microsoft Corporation. This book is not sponsored or endorsed by or affiliated with the Microsoft Corporation.

10 9 8 7 6 5 4 3 2 1

Prentice Hall
is an imprint of

www.pearsonhighered.com

ISBN 10: 0-13-612247-7
ISBN 13: 978-0-13-612247-0

Brief Contents

Contents

Access

Chapter 1 Getting Started with Access Databases 49

GO! System Contributors

We thank the following people for their hard work and support in making the *GO!* System all that it is!

Instructor Resource Authors

Adickes, Erich	Parkland College	Holland, Susan	Southeast Community College-Nebraska
Baray, Carrie	Ivy Tech Community College		
Clausen, Jane	Western Iowa Tech Community College	Landenberger, Toni	Southeast Community College-Nebraska
Crossley, Connie	Cincinnati State Technical and Community College	McMahon, Richard	University of Houston—Downtown
		Miller, Sandra	Wenatchee Valley College
Emrich, Stefanie	Metropolitan Community College of Omaha, Nebraska	Niebur, Katherine	Dakota County Technical College
		Nowakowski, Anthony	Buffalo State
Faix, Dennis	Harrisburg Area Community College	Pierce, Tonya	Ivy Tech Community College
Hadden, Karen	Western Iowa Tech Community College	Roselli, Diane	Harrisburg Area Community College
		St. John, Steve	Tulsa Community College
Hammerle, Patricia	Indiana University/Purdue University at Indianapolis	Sterr, Jody	Blackhawk Technical College
		Thompson, Joyce	Lehigh Carbon Community College
Hines, James	Tidewater Community College	Tucker, William	Austin Community College

Technical Editors

Matthew Bisi	Barbara Edington	Joyce Nielsen	Jan Snyder
Mary Corcoran	Sarah Evans	Janet Pickard	Mara Zebest
Lori Damanti	Adam Layne	Sean Portnoy	

Student Reviewers

Albinda, Sarah Evangeline	Phoenix College	Innis, Tim	Tulsa Community College
Allen, John	Asheville-Buncombe Tech Community College	Jarboe, Aaron	Central Washington University
		Key, Penny	Greenville Technical College
Alexander, Steven	St. Johns River Community College	Klein, Colleen	Northern Michigan University
Alexander, Melissa	Tulsa Community College	Lloyd, Kasey	Ivy Tech Bloomington
Bolz, Stephanie	Northern Michigan University	Moeller, Jeffrey	Northern Michigan University
Berner, Ashley	Central Washington University	Mullen, Sharita	Tidewater Community College
Boomer, Michelle	Northern Michigan University	Nelson, Cody	Texas Tech University
Busse, Brennan	Northern Michigan University	Nicholson, Regina	Athens Tech College
Butkey, Maura	Central Washington University	Niehaus, Kristina	Northern Michigan University
Cates, Concita	Phoenix College	Nisa, Zaibun	Santa Rosa Community College
Charles, Marvin	Harrisburg Area Community College	Nunez, Nohelia	Santa Rosa Community College
		Oak, Samantha	Central Washington University
Christensen, Kaylie	Northern Michigan University	Oberly, Sara	Harrisburg Area Community College Lancaster
Clark, Glen D. III	Harrisburg Area Community College		
		Oertii, Monica	Central Washington University
Cobble, Jan N.	Greenville Technical College	Palenshus, Juliet	Central Washington University
Connally, Brianna	Central Washington University	Pohl, Amanda	Northern Michigan University
Davis, Brandon	Northern Michigan University	Presnell, Randy	Central Washington University
Davis, Christen	Central Washington University	Reed, Kailee	Texas Tech University
De Jesus Garcia, Maria	Phoenix College	Ritner, April	Northern Michigan University
Den Boer, Lance	Central Washington University	Roberts, Corey	Tulsa Community College
Dix, Jessica	Central Washington University	Rodgers, Spencer	Texas Tech University
Moeller, Jeffrey	Northern Michigan University	Rodriguez, Flavia	Northwestern State University
Downs, Elizabeth	Central Washington University	Rogers, A.	Tidewater Community College
Elser, Julie	Harrisburg Area Community College	Rossi, Jessica Ann	Central Washington University
		Rothbauer, Taylor	Trident Technical College
Erickson, Mike	Ball State University	Rozelle, Lauren	Texas Tech University
Frye, Alicia	Phoenix College	Schmadeke, Kimberly	Kirkwood Community College
Gadomski, Amanda	Northern Michigan University	Shafapay, Natasha	Central Washington University
Gassert, Jennifer	Harrisburg Area Community College	Shanahan, Megan	Northern Michigan University
		Sullivan, Alexandra Nicole	Greenville Technical College
Gross, Mary Jo	Kirkwood Community College	Teska, Erika	Hawaii Pacific University
Gyselinck, Craig	Central Washington University	Torrenti, Natalie	Harrisburg Area Community College
Harrison, Margo	Central Washington University		
Hatt, Patrick	Harrisburg Area Community College	Traub, Amy	Northern Michigan University
Heacox, Kate	Central Washington University	Underwood, Katie	Central Washington University
Hedgman, Shaina	Tidewater College	Walters, Kim	Central Washington University
Hill, Cheretta	Northwestern State University	Warren, Jennifer L.	Greenville Technical College
Hochstedler, Bethany	Harrisburg Area Community College Lancaster	Wilson, Kelsie	Central Washington University
		Wilson, Amanda	Green River Community College
Homer, Jean	Greenville Technical College	Wylie, Jimmy	Texas Tech University

Contributors continued

Series Reviewers

Abraham, Reni — Houston Community College
Addison, Paul — Ivy Tech Community College
Agatston, Ann — Agatston Consulting Technical College
Akuna, Valeria, Ph.D. — Estrella Mountain Community College
Alexander, Melody — Ball Sate University
Alejandro, Manuel — Southwest Texas Junior College
Alger, David — Tidewater Community College Chesapeake Campus
Allen, Jackie — Rowan-Cabarrus Community College
Ali, Farha — Lander University
Amici, Penny — Harrisburg Area Community College
Anderson, Patty A. — Lake City Community College
Andrews, Wilma — Virginia Commonwealth College, Nebraska University
Anik, Mazhar — Tiffin University
Armstrong, Gary — Shippensburg University
Arnold, Linda L. — Harrisburg Area Community College
Ashby, Tom — Oklahoma City Community College
Atkins, Bonnie — Delaware Technical Community College
Aukland, Cherie — Thomas Nelson Community College
Bachand, LaDonna — Santa Rosa Community College
Bagui, Sikha — University of West Florida
Beecroft, Anita — Kwantlen University College
Bell, Paula — Lock Haven College
Belton, Linda — Springfield Tech. Community College
Bennett, Judith — Sam Houston State University
Bhatia, Sai — Riverside Community College
Bishop, Frances — DeVry Institute—Alpharetta (ATL)
Blaszkiewicz, Holly — Ivy Tech Community College/Region 1
Boito, Nancy — HACC Central Pennsylvania's Community College
Borger-Boglin, Grietje L. — San Antonio College/Northeast Lakeview College
Branigan, Dave — DeVry University
Bray, Patricia — Allegany College of Maryland
Britt, Brenda K. — Fayetteville Technical Community College
Brotherton, Cathy — Riverside Community College
Brown, Judy — Western Illinois University
Buehler, Lesley — Ohlone College
Buell, C — Central Oregon Community College
Burns, Christine — Central New Mexico Community College
Byars, Pat — Brookhaven College
Byrd, Julie — Ivy Tech Community College
Byrd, Lynn — Delta State University, Cleveland, Mississippi
Cacace, Richard N. — Pensacola Junior College
Cadenhead, Charles — Brookhaven College
Calhoun, Ric — Gordon College
Cameron, Eric — Passaic Community College
Canine, Jill — Ivy Tech Community College of Indiana
Cannamore, Madie — Kennedy King

Cannon, Kim — Greenville Technical College
Carreon, Cleda — Indiana University—Purdue University, Indianapolis
Carriker, Sandra — North Shore Community College
Casey, Patricia — Trident Technical College
Cates, Wally — Central New Mexico Community College
Chaffin, Catherine — Shawnee State University
Chauvin, Marg — Palm Beach Community College, Boca Raton
Challa, Chandrashekar — Virginia State University
Chamlou, Afsaneh — NOVA Alexandria
Chapman, Pam — Wabaunsee Community College
Christensen, Dan — Iowa Western Community College
Clay, Betty — Southeastern Oklahoma State University
Collins, Linda D. — Mesa Community College
Cone, Bill — Northern Arizona University
Conroy-Link, Janet — Holy Family College
Conway, Ronald — Bowling Green State University
Cornforth, Carol G. — WVNCC
Cosgrove, Janet — Northwestern CT Community
Courtney, Kevin — Hillsborough Community College
Coverdale, John — Riverside Community College
Cox, Rollie — Madison Area Technical College
Crawford, Hiram — Olive Harvey College
Crawford, Sonia — Central New Mexico Community College
Crawford, Thomasina — Miami-Dade College, Kendall Campus
Credico, Grace — Lethbridge Community College
Crenshaw, Richard — Miami Dade Community College, North
Crespo, Beverly — Mt. San Antonio College
Crooks, Steven — Texas Tech University
Crossley, Connie — Cincinnati State Technical Community College
Curik, Mary — Central New Mexico Community College
De Arazoza, Ralph — Miami Dade Community College
Danno, John — DeVry University/Keller Graduate School
Davis, Phillip — Del Mar College
Davis, Richard — Trinity Valley Community College
Davis, Sandra — Baker College of Allen Park
Dees, Stephanie D. — Wharton County Junior College
DeHerrera, Laurie — Pikes Peak Community College
Delk, Dr. K. Kay — Seminole Community College
Denton, Bree — Texas Tech University
Dix, Jeanette — Ivy Tech Community College
Dooly, Veronica P. — Asheville-Buncombe Technical Community College
Doroshow, Mike — Eastfield College
Douglas, Gretchen — SUNYCortland
Dove, Carol — Community College of Allegheny
Dozier, Susan — Tidewater Community College, Virginia Beach Campus
Driskel, Loretta — Niagara Community College
Duckwiler, Carol — Wabaunsee Community College
Duhon, David — Baker College
Duncan, Mimi — University of Missouri-St. Louis
Duthie, Judy — Green River Community College
Duvall, Annette — Central New Mexico Community College

Contributors continued

Ecklund, Paula	Duke University	Hotta, Barbara	Leeward Community College
Eilers, Albert	Cincinnati State Technical and Community College	Howard, Bunny	St. Johns River Community
		Howard, Chris	DeVry University
Eng, Bernice	Brookdale Community College	Huckabay, Jamie	Austin Community College
Epperson, Arlin	Columbia College	Hudgins, Susan	East Central University
Evans, Billie	Vance-Granville Community College	Hulett, Michelle J.	Missouri State University
		Humphrey, John	Asheville Buncombe Technical Community College
Evans, Jean	Brevard Community College	Hunt, Darla A.	Morehead State University, Morehead, Kentucky
Feuerbach, Lisa	Ivy Tech East Chicago		
Finley, Jean	ABTCC		
Fisher, Fred	Florida State University	Hunt, Laura	Tulsa Community College
Foster, Nancy	Baker College	Ivey, Joan M.	Lanier Technical College
Foster-Shriver, Penny L.	Anne Arundel Community College	Jacob, Sherry	Jefferson Community College
		Jacobs, Duane	Salt Lake Community College
Foster-Turpen, Linda	CNM	Jauken, Barb	Southeastern Community
Foszcz, Russ	McHenry County College	Jerry, Gina	Santa Monica College
Fry, Susan	Boise State University	Johnson, Deborah S.	Edison State College
Fustos, Janos	Metro State	Johnson, Kathy	Wright College
Gallup, Jeanette	Blinn College	Johnson, Mary	Kingwood College
Gelb, Janet	Grossmont College	Johnson, Mary	Mt. San Antonio College
Gentry, Barb	Parkland College	Jones, Stacey	Benedict College
Gerace, Karin	St. Angela Merici School	Jones, Warren	University of Alabama, Birmingham
Gerace, Tom	Tulane University		
Ghajar, Homa	Oklahoma State University	Jordan, Cheryl	San Juan College
Gifford, Steve	Northwest Iowa Community College	Kapoor, Bhushan	California State University, Fullerton
Glazer, Ellen	Broward Community College	Kasai, Susumu	Salt Lake Community College
Gordon, Robert	Hofstra University	Kates, Hazel	Miami Dade Community College, Kendall
Gramlich, Steven	Pasco-Hernando Community College		
		Keen, Debby	University of Kentucky
Graviett, Nancy M.	St. Charles Community College, St. Peters, Missouri	Keeter, Sandy	Seminole Community College
		Kern-Blystone, Dorothy Jean	Bowling Green State
Greene, Rich	Community College of Allegheny County	Kerwin, Annette	College of DuPage
		Keskin, Ilknur	The University of South Dakota
Gregoryk, Kerry	Virginia Commonwealth State	Kinney, Mark B.	Baker College
Griggs, Debra	Bellevue Community College	Kirk, Colleen	Mercy College
Grimm, Carol	Palm Beach Community College	Kisling, Eric	East Carolina University
Guthrie, Rose	Fox Valley Technical College	Kleckner, Michelle	Elon University
Hahn, Norm	Thomas Nelson Community College	Kliston, Linda	Broward Community College, North Campus
Haley-Hunter, Deb	Bluefield State College	Knuth, Toni	Baker College of Auburn Hills
Hall, Linnea	Northwest Mississippi Community College	Kochis, Dennis	Suffolk County Community College
Hammerschlag, Dr. Bill	Brookhaven College	Kominek, Kurt	Northeast State Technical Community College
Hansen, Michelle	Davenport University		
Hayden, Nancy	Indiana University—Purdue University, Indianapolis	Kramer, Ed	Northern Virginia Community College
		Kretz, Daniel	Fox Valley Technical College
Hayes, Theresa	Broward Community College	Laird, Jeff	Northeast State Community College
Headrick, Betsy	Chattanooga State		
Helfand, Terri	Chaffey College	Lamoureaux, Jackie	Central New Mexico Community College
Helms, Liz	Columbus State Community College		
		Lange, David	Grand Valley State
Hernandez, Leticia	TCI College of Technology	LaPointe, Deb	Central New Mexico Community College
Hibbert, Marilyn	Salt Lake Community College		
Hinds, Cheryl	Norfolk State University	Larsen, Jacqueline Anne	A-B Tech
Hines, James	Tidewater Community College	Larson, Donna	Louisville Technical Institute
Hoffman, Joan	Milwaukee Area Technical College	Laspina, Kathy	Vance-Granville Community College
Hogan, Pat	Cape Fear Community College	Le Grand, Dr. Kate	Broward Community College
Holland, Susan	Southeast Community College	Lenhart, Sheryl	Terra Community College
Holliday, Mardi	Community College of Philadelphia	Leonard, Yvonne	Coastal Carolina Community College
Hollingsworth, Mary Carole	Georgia Perimeter College		
Hopson, Bonnie	Athens Technical College	Letavec, Chris	University of Cincinnati
Horvath, Carrie	Albertus Magnus College	Lewis, Daphne L, Ed.D.	Wayland Baptist University
Horwitz, Steve	Community College of Philadelphia	Lewis, Julie	Baker College-Allen Park
		Liefert, Jane	Everett Community College

Lindaman, Linda — Black Hawk Community College
Lindberg, Martha — Minnesota State University
Lightner, Renee — Broward Community College
Lindberg, Martha — Minnesota State University
Linge, Richard — Arizona Western College
Logan, Mary G. — Delgado Community College
Loizeaux, Barbara — Westchester Community College
Lombardi, John — South University
Lopez, Don — Clovis-State Center Community College District
Lopez, Lisa — Spartanburg Community College
Lord, Alexandria — Asheville Buncombe Tech
Lovering, LeAnne — Augusta Technical College
Lowe, Rita — Harold Washington College
Low, Willy Hui — Joliet Junior College
Lucas, Vickie — Broward Community College
Luna, Debbie — El Paso Community College
Luoma, Jean — Davenport University
Luse, Steven P. — Horry Georgetown Technical College
Lynam, Linda — Central Missouri State University
Lyon, Lynne — Durham College
Lyon, Pat Rajski — Tomball College
Macarty, Matthew — University of New Hampshire
MacKinnon, Ruth — Georgia Southern University
Macon, Lisa — Valencia Community College, West Campus
Machuca, Wayne — College of the Sequoias
Mack, Sherri — Butler County Community College
Madison, Dana — Clarion University
Maguire, Trish — Eastern New Mexico University
Malkan, Rajiv — Montgomery College
Manning, David — Northern Kentucky University
Marcus, Jacquie — Niagara Community College
Marghitu, Daniela — Auburn University
Marks, Suzanne — Bellevue Community College
Marquez, Juanita — El Centro College
Marquez, Juan — Mesa Community College
Martin, Carol — Harrisburg Area Community College
Martin, Paul C. — Harrisburg Area Community College
Martyn, Margie — Baldwin-Wallace College
Marucco, Toni — Lincoln Land Community College
Mason, Lynn — Lubbock Christian University
Matutis, Audrone — Houston Community College
Matkin, Marie — University of Lethbridge
Maurel, Trina — Odessa College
May, Karen — Blinn College
McCain, Evelynn — Boise State University
McCannon, Melinda — Gordon College
McCarthy, Marguerite — Northwestern Business College
McCaskill, Matt L. — Brevard Community College
McClellan, Carolyn — Tidewater Community College
McClure, Darlean — College of Sequoias
McCrory, Sue A. — Missouri State University
McCue, Stacy — Harrisburg Area Community College
McEntire-Orbach, Teresa — Middlesex County College
McKinley, Lee — Georgia Perimeter College
McLeod, Todd — Fresno City College
McManus, Illyana — Grossmont College
McPherson, Dori — Schoolcraft College
Meck, Kari — HACC
Meiklejohn, Nancy — Pikes Peak Community College
Menking, Rick — Hardin-Simmons University

Meredith, Mary — University of Louisiana at Lafayette
Mermelstein, Lisa — Baruch College
Metos, Linda — Salt Lake Community College
Meurer, Daniel — University of Cincinnati
Meyer, Colleen — Cincinnati State Technical and Community College
Meyer, Marian — Central New Mexico Community College
Miller, Cindy — Ivy Tech Community College, Lafayette, Indiana
Mills, Robert E. — Tidewater Community College, Portsmouth Campus
Mitchell, Susan — Davenport University
Mohle, Dennis — Fresno Community College
Molki, Saeed — South Texas College
Monk, Ellen — University of Delaware
Moore, Rodney — Holland College
Morris, Mike — Southeastern Oklahoma State University
Morris, Nancy — Hudson Valley Community College
Moseler, Dan — Harrisburg Area Community College
Nabors, Brent — Reedley College, Clovis Center
Nadas, Erika — Wright College
Nadelman, Cindi — New England College
Nademlynsky, Lisa — Johnson & Wales University
Nagengast, Joseph — Florida Career College
Nason, Scott — Rowan Cabarrus Community College
Ncube, Cathy — University of West Florida
Newsome, Eloise — Northern Virginia Community College Woodbridge
Nicholls, Doreen — Mohawk Valley Community College
Nicholson, John R. — Johnson County Community College
Nielson, Phil — Salt Lake Community College
Nunan, Karen L. — Northeast State Technical Community College
O'Neal, Lois Ann — Rogers State University
Odegard, Teri — Edmonds Community College
Ogle, Gregory — North Community College
Orr, Dr. Claudia — Northern Michigan University South
Orsburn, Glen — Fox Valley Technical College
Otieno, Derek — DeVry University
Otton, Diana Hill — Chesapeake College
Oxendale, Lucia — West Virginia Institute of Technology
Paiano, Frank — Southwestern College
Pannell, Dr. Elizabeth — Collin College
Patrick, Tanya — Clackamas Community College
Paul, Anindya — Daytona State College
Peairs, Deb — Clark State Community College
Perez, Kimberly — Tidewater Community College
Porter, Joyce — Weber State University
Prince, Lisa — Missouri State University-Springfield Campus
Proietti, Kathleen — Northern Essex Community College
Puopolo, Mike — Bunker Hill Community College
Pusins, Delores — HCCC
Putnam, Darlene — Thomas Nelson Community College

Raghuraman, Ram	Joliet Junior College
Rani, Chigurupati	BMCC/CUNY
Reasoner, Ted Allen	Indiana University—Purdue
Reeves, Karen	High Point University
Remillard, Debbie	New Hampshire Technical Institute
Rhue, Shelly	DeVry University
Richards, Karen	Maplewoods Community College
Richardson, Mary	Albany Technical College
Rodgers, Gwen	Southern Nazarene University
Rodie, Karla	Pikes Peak Community College
Roselli, Diane Maie	Harrisburg Area Community College
Ross, Dianne	University of Louisiana in Lafayette
Rousseau, Mary	Broward Community College, South
Rovetto, Ann	Horry-Georgetown Technical College
Rusin, Iwona	Baker College
Sahabi, Ahmad	Baker College of Clinton Township
Samson, Dolly	Hawaii Pacific University
Sams, Todd	University of Cincinnati
Sandoval, Everett	Reedley College
Santiago, Diana	Central New Mexico Community College
Sardone, Nancy	Seton Hall University
Scafide, Jean	Mississippi Gulf Coast Community College
Scheeren, Judy	Westmoreland County Community College
Scheiwe, Adolph	Joliet Junior College
Schneider, Sol	Sam Houston State University
Schweitzer, John	Central New Mexico Community College
Scroggins, Michael	Southwest Missouri State University
Sedlacek, Brenda	Tidewater Community College
Sell, Kelly	Anne Arundel Community College
Sever, Suzanne	Northwest Arkansas Community College
Sewell, John	Florida Career College
Sheridan, Rick	California State University-Chico
Silvers, Pamela	Asheville Buncombe Tech
Sindt, Robert G.	Johnson County Community College
Singer, Noah	Tulsa Community College
Singer, Steven A.	University of Hawai'i, Kapi'olani Community College
Sinha, Atin	Albany State University
Skolnick, Martin	Florida Atlantic University
Smith, Kristi	Allegany College of Maryland
Smith, Patrick	Marshall Community and Technical College
Smith, Stella A.	Georgia Gwinnett College
Smith, T. Michael	Austin Community College
Smith, Tammy	Tompkins Cortland Community Collge
Smolenski, Bob	Delaware County Community College
Smolenski, Robert	Delaware Community College
Southwell, Donald	Delta College
Spangler, Candice	Columbus State
Spangler, Candice	Columbus State Community College
Stark, Diane	Phoenix College
Stedham, Vicki	St. Petersburg College, Clearwater
Stefanelli, Greg	Carroll Community College
Steiner, Ester	New Mexico State University
Stenlund, Neal	Northern Virginia Community College, Alexandria
St. John, Steve	Tulsa Community College
Sterling, Janet	Houston Community College
Stoughton, Catherine	Laramie County Community College
Sullivan, Angela	Joliet Junior College
Sullivan, Denise	Westchester Community College
Sullivan, Joseph	Joliet Junior College
Swart, John	Louisiana Tech University
Szurek, Joseph	University of Pittsburgh at Greensburg
Taff, Ann	Tulsa Community College
Taggart, James	Atlantic Cape Community College
Tarver, Mary Beth	Northwestern State University
Taylor, Michael	Seattle Central Community College
Terrell, Robert L.	Carson-Newman College
Terry, Dariel	Northern Virginia Community College
Thangiah, Sam	Slippery Rock University
Thayer, Paul	Austin Community College
Thompson, Joyce	Lehigh Carbon Community College
Thompson-Sellers, Ingrid	Georgia Perimeter College
Tomasi, Erik	Baruch College
Toreson, Karen	Shoreline Community College
Townsend, Cynthia	Baker College
Trifiletti, John J.	Florida Community College at Jacksonville
Trivedi, Charulata	Quinsigamond Community College, Woodbridge
Tucker, William	Austin Community College
Turgeon, Cheryl	Asnuntuck Community College
Turpen, Linda	Central New Mexico Community College
Upshaw, Susan	Del Mar College
Unruh, Angela	Central Washington University
Vanderhoof, Dr. Glenna	Missouri State University-Springfield Campus
Vargas, Tony	El Paso Community College
Vicars, Mitzi	Hampton University
Villarreal, Kathleen	Fresno
Vitrano, Mary Ellen	Palm Beach Community College
Vlaich-Lee, Michelle	Greenville Technical College
Volker, Bonita	Tidewater Community College
Waddell, Karen	Butler Community College
Wahila, Lori (Mindy)	Tompkins Cortland Community College
Wallace, Melissa	Lanier Technical College
Walters, Gary B.	Central New Mexico Community College
Waswick, Kim	Southeast Community College, Nebraska
Wavle, Sharon M.	Tompkins Cortland Community College
Webb, Nancy	City College of San Francisco
Webb, Rebecca	Northwest Arkansas Community College
Weber, Sandy	Gateway Technical College
Weissman, Jonathan	Finger Lakes Community College
Wells, Barbara E.	Central Carolina Technical College
Wells, Lorna	Salt Lake Community College
Welsh, Jean	Lansing Community College Nebraska
White, Bruce	Quinnipiac University
Willer, Ann	Solano Community College
Williams, Mark	Lane Community College
Williams, Ronald D.	Central Piedmont Community College
Wilms, Dr. G. Jan	Union University
Wilson, Kit	Red River College
Wilson, MaryLou	Piedmont Technical College
Wilson, Roger	Fairmont State University
Wimberly, Leanne	International Academy of Design and Technology

Contributors continued

Winters, Floyd	Manatee Community College	Yip, Thomas	Passaic Community College
Worthington, Paula	Northern Virginia Community College	Zavala, Ben	Webster Tech
		Zaboski, Maureen	University of Scranton
Wright, Darrell	Shelton State Community College	Zlotow, Mary Ann	College of DuPage
Wright, Julie	Baker College	Zudeck, Steve	Broward Community College, North
Yauney, Annette	Herkimer County Community College	Zullo, Matthew D.	Wake Technical Community College

About the Authors

Shelley Gaskin, Series Editor, is a professor in the Business and Computer Technology Division at Pasadena City College in Pasadena, California. She holds a bachelor's degree in Business Administration from Robert Morris College (Pennsylvania), a master's degree in Business from Northern Illinois University, and a doctorate in Adult and Community Education from Ball State University. Before joining Pasadena City College, she spent 12 years in the computer industry where she was a systems analyst, sales representative, and Director of Customer Education with Unisys Corporation. She also worked for Ernst & Young on the development of large systems applications for their clients. She has written and developed training materials for custom systems applications in both the public and private sector, and has written and edited numerous computer application textbooks.

This book is dedicated to my students, who inspire me every day.

Carolyn McLellan is the Dean of the Division of Information Technology and Business at Tidewater Community College in Virginia Beach, Virginia. She has a master's degree in Secondary Education from Regent University and a bachelor's degree in Business Education from Old Dominion University. She taught for Norfolk Public Schools for 17 years in Business Education and served as a faculty member at Tidewater Community College for eight years teaching networking, where she developed over 23 new courses and earned the Microsoft Certified Trainer and Microsoft Certified System Engineer industry certifications. In addition to teaching, Carolyn loves to play volleyball, boogie board at the beach, bicycle, crochet, cook, and read.

This book is dedicated to my daughters, Megan and Mandy, who have my eternal love; to my mother, Jean, who always believes in me and encouraged me to become a teacher; to my sister Debbie, who was my first student and who inspires me with her strength in overcoming hardships; to my niece Jenna, for her bravery, composure, and beauty; to my grandsons, Damon and Jordan, who bring me happiness and a renewed joie de vie; and to the students and IT faculty at Tidewater Community College.

Teach the Course You Want in Less Time

A Microsoft® Office textbook designed for student success!

- **Project-Based** – Students learn by creating projects that they will use in the real world.

- **Microsoft Procedural Syntax** – Steps are written to put students in the right place at the right time.

- **Teachable Moment** – Expository text is woven into the steps—at the moment students need to know it—not chunked together in a block of text that will go unread.

- **Sequential Pagination** – Students have actual page numbers instead of confusing letters and abbreviations.

Student Outcomes and Learning Objectives – Objectives are clustered around projects that result in student outcomes.

Project Activities – A project summary stated clearly and quickly.

Project Files – Clearly shows students which files are needed for the project and the names they will use to save their documents.

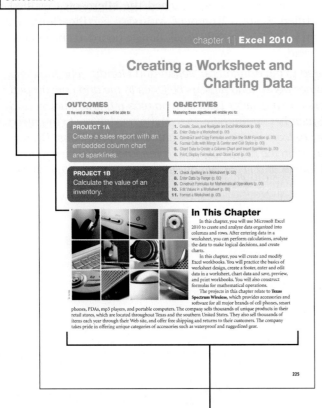

Scenario – Each chapter opens with a story that sets the stage for the projects the student will create.

Project Results – Shows students how their final outcome will appear.

Key Feature

Microsoft Procedural Syntax – Steps are written to put the student in the right place at the right time.

Color Coding – Color variations between the two projects in each chapter make it easy to identify which project students are working on.

Key Feature

Sequential Pagination – Students are given actual page numbers to navigate through the textbook instead of confusing letters and abbreviations.

Key Feature

Teachable Moment – Expository text is woven into the steps—at the moment students need to know it—not chunked together in a block of text that will go unread.

End-of-Chapter

Content-Based Assessments – Assessments with defined solutions.

Objective List - Every project includes a listing of covered objectives from Projects A and B.

End-of-Chapter

Outcomes-Based Assessments – Assessments with open-ended solutions.

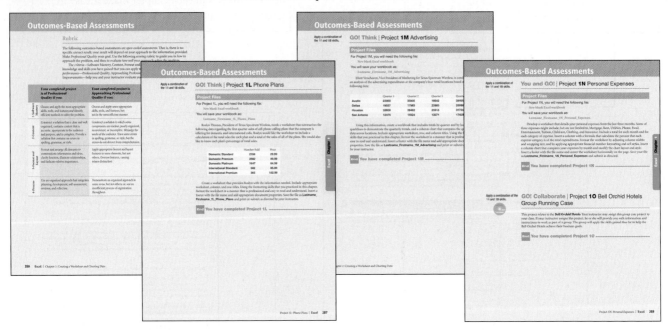

Task-Specific Rubric – A matrix specific to the **GO! Solve It** projects that states the criteria and standards for grading these defined-solution projects.

Outcomes Rubric – A matrix specific to the **GO! Think** projects that states the criteria and standards for grading these open-ended assessments.

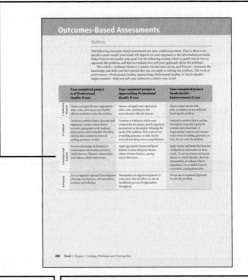

Student CD – All student data files readily available on a CD that comes with the book.

Podcasts – Videos that teach some of the more difficult topics when working with Microsoft applications.

Student Videos – A visual and audio walk-through of every A and B project in the book (see sample images on following page).

Student Videos! – Each chapter comes with two videos that include audio, demonstrating the objectives and activities taught in the chapter.

All Instructor materials available on the IRCD

Instructor Materials

Annotated Instructor Edition - An instructor tool includes a full copy of the student textbook annotated with teaching tips, discussion topics, and other useful pieces for teaching each chapter.

Assignment Sheets – Lists all the assignments for the chapter. Just add in the course information, due dates, and points. Providing these to students ensures they will know what is due and when.

Scripted Lectures – Classroom lectures prepared for you.

Annotated Solution Files – Coupled with the assignment tags, these create a grading and scoring system that makes grading so much easier for you.

PowerPoint Lectures – PowerPoint presentations for each chapter.

Scoring Rubrics – Can be used either by students to check their work or by you as a quick check-off for the items that need to be corrected.

Syllabus Templates - For 8-week, 12-week, and 16-week courses.

Test Bank – Includes a variety of test questions for each chapter.

Companion Website – Online content such as the Online Study Guide, Glossary, and Student Data Files are all at www.pearsonhighered.com/go.

Using the Common Features of Microsoft Office 2010

OUTCOMES

At the end of this chapter you will be able to:

OBJECTIVES

Mastering these objectives will enable you to:

PROJECT 1A
Create, save, and print a Microsoft Office 2010 file.

1. Use Windows Explorer to Locate Files and Folders (p. 3)
2. Locate and Start a Microsoft Office 2010 Program (p. 6)
3. Enter and Edit Text in an Office 2010 Program (p. 9)
4. Perform Commands from a Dialog Box (p. 11)
5. Create a Folder, Save a File, and Close a Program (p. 13)
6. Add Document Properties and Print a File (p. 18)

PROJECT 1B
Use the Ribbon and dialog boxes to perform common commands in a Microsoft Office 2010 file.

7. Open an Existing File and Save It with a New Name (p. 22)
8. Explore Options for an Application (p. 25)
9. Perform Commands from the Ribbon (p. 26)
10. Apply Formatting in Office Programs (p. 32)
11. Use the Microsoft Office 2010 Help System (p. 43)
12. Compress Files (p. 44)

olly/Shutterstock

In This Chapter

In this chapter, you will use Windows Explorer to navigate the Windows folder structure, create a folder, and save files in Microsoft Office 2010 programs. You will also practice using the features of Microsoft Office 2010 that are common across the major programs that comprise the Microsoft Office 2010 suite. These common features include creating, saving, and printing files.

Common features also include the new Paste Preview and Microsoft Office Backstage view. You will apply formatting, perform commands, and compress files. You will see that creating professional-quality documents is easy and quick in Microsoft Office 2010, and that finding your way around is fast and efficient.

The projects in this chapter relate to **Oceana Palm Grill**, which is a chain of 25 casual, full-service restaurants based in Austin, Texas. The Oceana Palm Grill owners plan an aggressive expansion program. To expand by 15 additional restaurants in North Carolina and Florida by 2018, the company must attract new investors, develop new menus, and recruit new employees, all while adhering to the company's quality guidelines and maintaining its reputation for excellent service. To succeed, the company plans to build on its past success and maintain its quality elements.

Project 1A PowerPoint File

Project Activities

In Activities 1.01 through 1.06, you will create a PowerPoint file, save it in a folder that you create by using Windows Explorer, and then print the file or submit it electronically as directed by your instructor. Your completed PowerPoint slide will look similar to Figure 1.1.

Project Files

For Project 1A, you will need the following file:

New blank PowerPoint presentation

You will save your file as:

Lastname_Firstname_1A_Menu_Plan

Project Results

Oceana Palm Grill Menu Plan

Prepared by Firstname Lastname

For Laura Hernandez

Figure 1.1
Project 1A Menu Plan

Objective 1 | Use Windows Explorer to Locate Files and Folders

A *file* is a collection of information stored on a computer under a single name, for example, a Word document or a PowerPoint presentation. Every file is stored in a *folder*— a container in which you store files—or a *subfolder*, which is a folder within a folder. Your Windows operating system stores and organizes your files and folders, which is a primary task of an operating system.

You *navigate*—explore within the organizing structure of Windows—to create, save, and find your files and folders by using the *Windows Explorer* program. Windows Explorer displays the files and folders on your computer, and is at work anytime you are viewing the contents of files and folders in a *window*. A window is a rectangular area on a computer screen in which programs and content appear; a window can be moved, resized, minimized, or closed.

Activity 1.01 | Using Windows Explorer to Locate Files and Folders

1 Turn on your computer and display the Windows *desktop*—the opening screen in Windows that simulates your work area.

Note | Comparing Your Screen with the Figures in This Textbook

Your screen will match the figures shown in this textbook if you set your screen resolution to 1024 × 768. At other resolutions, your screen will closely resemble, but not match, the figures shown. To view your screen's resolution, on the Windows 7 desktop, right-click in a blank area, and then click Screen resolution. In Windows Vista, right-click a blank area, click Personalize, and then click Display Settings. In Windows XP, right-click the desktop, click Properties, and then click the Settings tab.

---

2 In your CD/DVD tray, insert the **Student CD** that accompanies this textbook. Wait a few moments for an **AutoPlay** window to display. Compare your screen with Figure 1.2.

> *AutoPlay* is a Windows feature that lets you choose which program to use to start different kinds of media, such as music CDs, or CDs and DVDs containing photos; it displays when you plug in or insert media or storage devices.

Note | If You Do Not Have the Student CD

If you do not have the Student CD, consult the inside back flap of this textbook for instructions on how to download the files from the Pearson Web site.

Figure 1.2

AutoPlay window ──

Close button ──

Windows desktop (yours
may vary in color
and arrangement) ──

3 In the upper right corner of the **AutoPlay** window, move your mouse over—*point* to—the **Close** button ![Close button], and then *click*—press the left button on your mouse pointing device one time.

4 On the left side of the **Windows taskbar**, click the **Start** button ⊕ to display the **Start menu**. Compare your screen with Figure 1.3.

The *Windows taskbar* is the area along the lower edge of the desktop that contains the *Start button* and an area to display buttons for open programs. The Start button displays the *Start menu*, which provides a list of choices and is the main gateway to your computer's programs, folders, and settings.

Figure 1.3

Computer on Start menu
Start menu (your array of programs may vary)
Windows 7 taskbar
Start button

5 On the right side of the **Start menu**, click **Computer** to see the disk drives and other hardware connected to your computer. Compare your screen with Figure 1.4, and then take a moment to study the table in Figure 1.5.

The *folder window* for *Computer* displays. A folder window displays the contents of the current folder, *library*, or device, and contains helpful parts so that you can navigate within Windows.

In Windows 7, a library is a collection of items, such as files and folders, assembled from *various locations*; the locations might be on your computer, an external hard drive, removable media, or someone else's computer.

The difference between a folder and a library is that a library can include files stored in *different locations*—any disk drive, folder, or other place that you can store files and folders.

Figure 1.4

Back and Forward
Address bar
File list
Navigation pane
Folder window toolbar
Views button
Search box
Preview pane button
Details pane

Window Part	Use to:
Address bar	Navigate to a different folder or library, or go back to a previous one.
Back and Forward buttons	Navigate to other folders or libraries you have already opened without closing the current window. These buttons work in conjunction with the address bar; that is, after you use the address bar to change folders, you can use the Back button to return to the previous folder.
Details pane	Display the most common file properties—information about a file, such as the author, the date you last changed the file, and any descriptive **tags**, which are custom file properties that you create to help find and organize your files.
File list	Display the contents of the current folder or library. In Computer, the file list displays the disk drives.
Folder window for *Computer*	Display the contents of the current folder, library, or device. The Folder window contains helpful features so that you can navigate within Windows.
Folder window toolbar	Perform common tasks, such as changing the view of your files and folders or burning files to a CD. The buttons available change to display only relevant tasks.
Navigation pane	Navigate to, open, and display favorites, libraries, folders, saved searches, and an expandable list of drives.
Preview pane button	Display (if you have chosen to open this pane) the contents of most files without opening them in a program. To open the preview pane, click the Preview pane button on the toolbar to turn it on and off.
Search box	Look for an item in the current folder or library by typing a word or phrase in the search box.
Views button	Choose how to view the contents of the current location.

Figure 1.5

6 On the toolbar of the **Computer** folder window, click the **Views button arrow** 🗾 ▾ — the small arrow to the right of the Views button—to display a list of views that you can apply to the file list. If necessary, on the list, click **Tiles**.

The Views button is a **split button**; clicking the main part of the button performs a **command** and clicking the arrow opens a menu or list. A command is an instruction to a computer program that causes an action to be carried out.

When you open a folder or a library, you can change how the files display in the file list. For example, you might prefer to see large or small **icons**—pictures that represent a program, a file, a folder, or some other object—or an arrangement that lets you see various types of information about each file. Each time you click the Views button, the window changes, cycling through several views—additional view options are available by clicking the Views button arrow.

Another Way

Point to the CD/DVD drive, right-click, and then click Open.

7 In the **file list**, under **Devices with Removable Storage**, point to your **CD/DVD Drive**, and then **double-click**—click the left mouse button two times in rapid succession—to display the list of folders on the CD. Compare your screen with Figure 1.6.

When double-clicking, keep your hand steady between clicks; this is more important than the speed of the two clicks.

Figure 1.6

Views button indicates
Details view

List of folders on the
CD in Details view

Views button arrow

8 In the **file list**, point to the folder **01_student_data_files** and double-click to display the list of subfolders in the folder. Double-click to open the folder **01_common_ features**. Compare your screen with Figure 1.7.

The Student Resource CD includes files that you will use to complete the projects in this textbook. If you prefer, you can also copy the **01_student_data_files** folder to a location on your computer's hard drive or to a removable device such as a ***USB flash drive***, which is a small storage device that plugs into a computer USB port. Your instructor might direct you to other locations where these files are located; for example, on your learning management system.

Figure 1.7

Address bar displays
sequence of folders

One folder in the
01_common_features
folder

9 In the upper right corner of the **Computer** window, click the **Close** button to redisplay your desktop.

Objective 2 | Locate and Start a Microsoft Office 2010 Program

Microsoft Office 2010 includes programs, servers, and services for individuals, small organizations, and large enterprises. A ***program***, also referred to as an ***application***, is a set of instructions used by a computer to perform a task, such as word processing or accounting.

Activity 1.02 | Locating and Starting a Microsoft Office 2010 Program

1 On the **Windows taskbar**, click the **Start** button 🔵 to display the **Start** menu.

2 From the displayed **Start** menu, locate the group of **Microsoft Office 2010** programs on your computer—the Office program icons from which you can start the program may be located on your Start menu, in a Microsoft Office folder on the **All Programs** list, on your desktop, or any combination of these locations; the location will vary depending on how your computer is configured.

> *All Programs* is an area of the Start menu that displays all the available programs on your computer system.

3 Examine Figure 1.8, and notice the programs that are included in the Microsoft Office Professional Plus 2010 group of programs. (Your group of programs may vary.)

> *Microsoft Word* is a word processing program, with which you create and share documents by using its writing tools.

> *Microsoft Excel* is a spreadsheet program, with which you calculate and analyze numbers and create charts.

> *Microsoft Access* is a database program, with which you can collect, track, and report data.

> *Microsoft PowerPoint* is a presentation program, with which you can communicate information with high-impact graphics and video.

> Additional popular Office programs include *Microsoft Outlook* to manage e-mail and organizational activities, *Microsoft Publisher* to create desktop publishing documents such as brochures, and *Microsoft OneNote* to manage notes that you make at meetings or in classes and to share notes with others on the Web.

> The Professional Plus version of Office 2010 also includes *Microsoft SharePoint Workspace* to share information with others in a team environment and *Microsoft InfoPath Designer and Filler* to create forms and gather data.

Figure 1.8

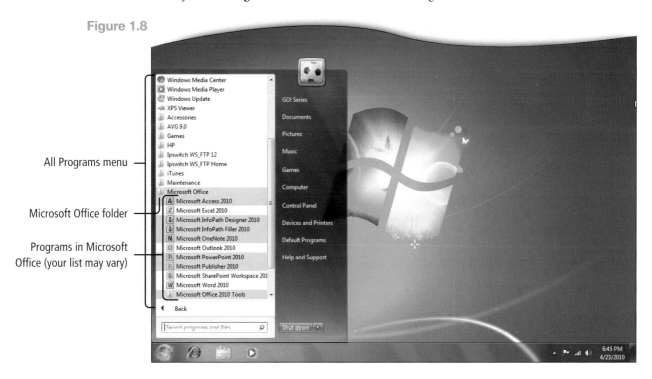

All Programs menu

Microsoft Office folder

Programs in Microsoft Office (your list may vary)

4 Click to open the program **Microsoft PowerPoint 2010**. Compare your screen with Figure 1.9, and then take a moment to study the description of these screen elements in the table in Figure 1.10.

Figure 1.9

Screen Element	Description
File tab	Displays Microsoft Office Backstage view, which is a centralized space for all of your file management tasks such as opening, saving, printing, publishing, or sharing a file—all the things you can do *with* a file.
Group names	Indicate the name of the groups of related commands on the displayed tab.
PowerPoint Slide pane	Displays a large image of the active slide in the PowerPoint program.
Program-level control buttons	Minimizes, restores, or closes the program window.
Quick Access Toolbar	Displays buttons to perform frequently used commands and resources with a single click. The default commands include Save, Undo, and Redo. You can add and delete buttons to customize the Quick Access Toolbar for your convenience.
Ribbon	Displays a group of task-oriented tabs that contain the commands, styles, and resources you need to work in an Office 2010 program. The look of your Ribbon depends on your screen resolution. A high resolution will display more individual items and button names on the Ribbon.
Ribbon tabs	Display the names of the task-oriented tabs relevant to the open program.
Slides/Outline pane	Displays either thumbnails of the slides in a PowerPoint presentation (Slides tab) or the outline of the presentation's content (Outline tab). In each Office 2010 program, different panes display in different ways to assist you.
Status bar	Displays file information on the left and View and Zoom on the right.
Title bar	Displays the name of the file and the name of the program. The program window control buttons—Minimize, Maximize/Restore Down, and Close—are grouped on the right side of the title bar.

Figure 1.10

Objective 3 | Enter and Edit Text in an Office 2010 Program

All of the programs in Office 2010 require some typed text. Your keyboard is still the primary method of entering information into your computer. Techniques to *edit*—make changes to—text are similar among all of the Office 2010 programs.

Activity 1.03 | Entering and Editing Text in an Office 2010 Program

1 In the middle of the PowerPoint Slide pane, point to the text *Click to add title* to display the I pointer, and then click one time.

The *insertion point*—a blinking vertical line that indicates where text or graphics will be inserted—displays.

In Office 2010 programs, the mouse *pointer*—any symbol that displays on your screen in response to moving your mouse device—displays in different shapes depending on the task you are performing and the area of the screen to which you are pointing.

2 Type **Oceana Grille Info** and notice how the insertion point moves to the right as you type. Point slightly to the right of the letter *e* in *Grille* and click to place the insertion point there. Compare your screen with Figure 1.11.

Figure 1.11

Insertion point —

3 On your keyboard, locate and press the Backspace key to delete the letter *e*.

Pressing Backspace removes a character to the left of the insertion point.

4 Point slightly to the left of the *I* in *Info* and click one time to place the insertion point there. Type **Menu** and then press Spacebar one time. Compare your screen with Figure 1.12.

By *default*, when you type text in an Office program, existing text moves to the right to make space for new typing. Default refers to the current selection or setting that is automatically used by a program unless you specify otherwise.

Figure 1.12

Menu inserted —

5 Press `Del` four times to delete *Info* and then type **Plan**

> Pressing `Del` removes—deletes—a character to the right of the insertion point.

6 With your insertion point blinking after the word *Plan*, on your keyboard, hold down the `Ctrl` key. While holding down `Ctrl`, press `←` three times to move the insertion point to the beginning of the word *Grill*.

> This is a ***keyboard shortcut***—a key or combination of keys that performs a task that would otherwise require a mouse. This keyboard shortcut moves the insertion point to the beginning of the previous word.

> A keyboard shortcut is commonly indicated as `Ctrl` + `←` (or some other combination of keys) to indicate that you hold down the first key while pressing the second key. A keyboard shortcut can also include three keys, in which case you hold down the first two and then press the third. For example, `Ctrl` + `Shift` + `←` selects one word to the left.

7 With the insertion point blinking at the beginning of the word *Grill*, type **Palm** and press `Spacebar`.

8 Click anywhere in the text *Click to add subtitle*. With the insertion point blinking, type the following and include the spelling error: **Prepered by Annabel Dunham**

9 With your mouse, point slightly to the left of the *A* in *Annabel*, hold down the left mouse button, and then ***drag***—hold down the left mouse button while moving your mouse—to the right to select the text *Annabel Dunham*, and then release the mouse button. Compare your screen with Figure 1.13.

> The ***Mini toolbar*** displays commands that are commonly used with the selected object, which places common commands close to your pointer. When you move the pointer away from the Mini toolbar, it fades from view.

> To ***select*** refers to highlighting, by dragging with your mouse, areas of text or data or graphics so that the selection can be edited, formatted, copied, or moved. The action of dragging includes releasing the left mouse button at the end of the area you want to select. The Office programs recognize a selected area as one unit, to which you can make changes. Selecting text may require some practice. If you are not satisfied with your result, click anywhere outside of the selection, and then begin again.

Figure 1.13

Mini toolbar displays

Annabel Dunham selected

Oceana Palm Grill Menu Plan

10 With the text *Annabel Dunham* selected, type your own firstname and lastname.

In any Windows-based program, such as the Microsoft Office 2010 programs, selected text is deleted and then replaced when you begin to type new text. You will save time by developing good techniques to select and then edit or replace selected text, which is easier than pressing the [Del] key numerous times to delete text that you do not want.

11 Notice that the misspelled word *Prepered* displays with a wavy red underline; additionally, all or part of your name might display with a wavy red underline.

Office 2010 has a dictionary of words against which all entered text is checked. In Word and PowerPoint, words that are *not* in the dictionary display a wavy red line, indicating a possible misspelled word or a proper name or an unusual word—none of which are in the Office 2010 dictionary.

In Excel and Access, you can initiate a check of the spelling, but wavy red underlines do not display.

12 Point to *Prepered* and then ***right-click***—click your right mouse button one time.

The Mini toolbar and a ***shortcut menu*** display. A shortcut menu displays commands and options relevant to the selected text or object—known as ***context-sensitive commands*** because they relate to the item you right-clicked.

Here, the shortcut menu displays commands related to the misspelled word. You can click the suggested correct spelling *Prepared*, click Ignore All to ignore the misspelling, add the word to the Office dictionary, or click Spelling to display a ***dialog box***. A dialog box is a small window that contains options for completing a task. Whenever you see a command followed by an ***ellipsis*** (...), which is a set of three dots indicating incompleteness, clicking the command will always display a dialog box.

13 On the displayed shortcut menu, click **Prepared** to correct the misspelled word. If necessary, point to any parts of your name that display a wavy red underline, right-click, and then on the shortcut menu, click Ignore All so that Office will no longer mark your name with a wavy underline in this file.

More Knowledge | **Adding to the Office Dictionary**

The main dictionary contains the most common words, but does not include all proper names, technical terms, or acronyms. You can add words, acronyms, and proper names to the Office dictionary by clicking Add to Dictionary when they are flagged, and you might want to do so for your own name and other proper names and terms that you type often.

Objective 4 | Perform Commands from a Dialog Box

In a dialog box, you make decisions about an individual object or topic. A dialog box also offers a way to adjust a number of settings at one time.

Activity 1.04 | Performing Commands from a Dialog Box

1 Point anywhere in the blank area above the title *Oceana Palm Grill Menu Plan* to display the ⬉ pointer.

2 Right-click to display a shortcut menu. Notice the command *Format Background* followed by an ellipsis (…). Compare your screen with Figure 1.14.

Recall that a command followed by an ellipsis indicates that a dialog box will display if you click the command.

Figure 1.14

Shortcut menu ⎯⎯⎯⎯

Ellipsis following command ⎯⎯⎯⎯

3 Click **Format Background** to display the **Format Background** dialog box, and then compare your screen with Figure 1.15.

Figure 1.15

Fill selected ⎯⎯⎯⎯

Format Background dialog box ⎯⎯⎯⎯

Options related to the background fill ⎯⎯⎯⎯

4 On the left, if necessary, click **Fill** to display the **Fill** options.

Fill is the inside color of an object. Here, the dialog box displays the option group names on the left; some dialog boxes provide a set of tabs across the top from which you can display different sets of options.

5 On the right, under **Fill**, click the **Gradient fill** option button.

The dialog box displays additional settings related to the gradient fill option. An *option button* is a round button that enables you to make one choice among two or more options. In a gradient fill, one color fades into another.

6 Click the **Preset colors arrow**—the arrow in the box to the right of the text *Preset colors*—and then in the gallery, in the second row, point to the fifth fill color to display the ScreenTip *Fog*.

A *gallery* is an Office feature that displays a list of potential results. A *ScreenTip* displays useful information about mouse actions, such as pointing to screen elements or dragging.

7 Click **Fog**, and then notice that the fill color is applied to your slide. Click the **Type arrow**, and then click **Rectangular** to change the pattern of the fill color. Compare your screen with Figure 1.16.

Figure 1.16

Gradient fill option
button selected

Rectangular displays

Close button

8 At the bottom of the dialog box, click **Close**.

> As you progress in your study of Microsoft Office, you will practice using many dialog boxes and applying dramatic effects such as this to your Word documents, Excel spreadsheets, Access databases, and PowerPoint slides.

Objective 5 | Create a Folder, Save a File, and Close a Program

A *location* is any disk drive, folder, or other place in which you can store files and folders. Where you store your files depends on how and where you use your data. For example, for your classes, you might decide to store primarily on a removable USB flash drive so that you can carry your files to different locations and access your files on different computers.

If you do most of your work on a single computer, for example your home desktop system or your laptop computer that you take with you to school or work, store your files in one of the Libraries—Documents, Music, Pictures, or Videos—provided by your Windows operating system.

Although the Windows operating system helps you to create and maintain a logical folder structure, take the time to name your files and folders in a consistent manner.

Activity 1.05 | Creating a Folder, Saving a File, and Closing a Program

A PowerPoint presentation is an example of a file. Office 2010 programs use a common dialog box provided by the Windows operating system to assist you in saving files. In this activity, you will create a folder on a USB flash drive in which to store files. If you prefer to store on your hard drive, you can use similar steps to store files in your My Documents folder in your Documents library.

1 Insert a USB flash drive into your computer, and if necessary, **Close** the **AutoPlay** dialog box. If you are not using a USB flash drive, go to Step 2.

As the first step in saving a file, determine where you want to save the file, and if necessary, insert a storage device.

2 At the top of your screen, in the title bar, notice that *Presentation1 – Microsoft PowerPoint* displays.

Most Office 2010 programs open with a new unsaved file with a default name—*Presentation1, Document1*, and so on. As you create your file, your work is temporarily stored in the computer's memory until you initiate a Save command, at which time you must choose a file name and location in which to save your file.

3 In the upper left corner of your screen, click the **File tab** to display **Microsoft Office Backstage** view. Compare your screen with Figure 1.17.

Microsoft Office *Backstage view* is a centralized space for tasks related to *file* management; that is why the tab is labeled *File*. File management tasks include, for example, opening, saving, printing, publishing, or sharing a file. The *Backstage tabs*—*Info, Recent, New, Print, Save & Send*, and *Help*—display along the left side. The tabs group file-related tasks together.

Above the Backstage tabs, *Quick Commands*—*Save, Save As, Open*, and *Close*—display for quick access to these commands. When you click any of these commands, Backstage view closes and either a dialog box displays or the active file closes.

Here, the *Info tab* displays information—*info*—about the current file. In the center panel, various file management tasks are available in groups. For example, if you click the Protect Presentation button, a list of options that you can set for this file that relate to who can open or edit the presentation displays.

On the Info tab, in the right panel, you can also examine the *document properties*. Document properties, also known as *metadata*, are details about a file that describe or identify it, such as the title, author name, subject, and keywords that identify the document's topic or contents. On the Info page, a thumbnail image of the current file displays in the upper right corner, which you can click to close Backstage view and return to the document.

More Knowledge | Deciding Where to Store Your Files

Where should you store your files? In the libraries created by Windows 7 (Documents, Pictures, and so on)? On a removable device like a flash drive or external hard drive? In Windows 7, it is easy to find your files, especially if you use the libraries. Regardless of where you save a file, Windows 7 will make it easy to find the file again, even if you are not certain where it might be.

In Windows 7, storing all of your files within a library makes sense. If you perform most of your work on your desktop system or your laptop that travels with you, you can store your files in the libraries created by Windows 7 for your user account—Documents, Pictures, Music, and so on. Within these libraries, you can create folders and subfolders to organize your data. These libraries are a good choice for storing your files because:

- From the Windows Explorer button on the taskbar, your libraries are always just one click away.
- The libraries are designed for their contents; for example, the Pictures folder displays small images of your digital photos.
- You can add new locations to a library; for example, an external hard drive, or a network drive. Locations added to a library behave just like they are on your hard drive.
- Other users of your computer cannot access your libraries.
- The libraries are the default location for opening and saving files within an application, so you will find that you can open and save files with fewer navigation clicks.

Figure 1.17

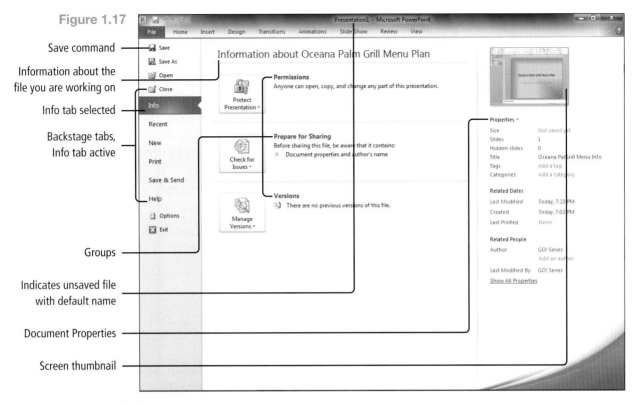

- Save command
- Information about the file you are working on
- Info tab selected
- Backstage tabs, Info tab active
- Groups
- Indicates unsaved file with default name
- Document Properties
- Screen thumbnail

4 Above the **Backstage tabs**, click **Save** to display the **Save As** dialog box.

Backstage view closes and the Save As dialog box, which includes a folder window and an area at the bottom to name the file and set the file type, displays.

When you are saving something for the first time, for example a new PowerPoint presentation, the Save and Save As commands are identical. That is, the Save As dialog box will display if you click Save or if you click Save As.

Note | Saving Your File

After you have named a file and saved it in your desired location, the Save command saves any changes you make to the file without displaying any dialog box. The Save As command will display the Save As dialog box and let you name and save a new file based on the current one—in a location that you choose. After you name and save the new document, the original document closes, and the new document—based on the original one—displays.

---

5 In the **Save As** dialog box, on the left, locate the **navigation pane**; compare your screen with Figure 1.18.

By default, the Save command opens the Documents library unless your default file location has been changed.

Figure 1.18

- Save As dialog box
- Address bar
- Default save location
- Navigation pane
- File list (yours will vary)
- File name box
- Save as type defaults to *PowerPoint Presentation*

6 On the right side of the **navigation pane**, point to the **scroll bar**. Compare your screen with Figure 1.19.

A *scroll bar* displays when a window, or a pane within a window, has information that is not in view. You can click the up or down scroll arrows—or the left and right scroll arrows in a horizontal scroll bar—to scroll the contents up or down or left and right in small increments. You can also drag the *scroll box*—the box within the scroll bar—to scroll the window in either direction.

Figure 1.19

Vertical scroll arrows

Vertical scroll box

Vertical scroll bar

Horizontal scroll bar

Horizontal scroll arrows

Horizontal scroll box

7 Click the **down scroll arrow** as necessary so that you can view the lower portion of the **navigation pane**, and then click the icon for your USB flash drive. Compare your screen with Figure 1.20. (If you prefer to store on your computer's hard drive instead of a USB flash drive, in the navigation pane, click Documents.)

Figure 1.20

Drive letter of your USB flash drive (yours will vary)

New folder button

File list on USB flash drive (yours may contain files or folders)

USB flash drive selected (yours will vary)

8 On the toolbar, click the **New folder** button.

In the file list, a new folder is created, and the text *New folder* is selected.

9 Type **Common Features Chapter 1** and press ⏎. Compare your screen with Figure 1.21.

In Windows-based programs, the ⏎ key confirms an action.

Figure 1.21

New folder

10 In the **file list**, double-click the name of your new folder to open it and display its name in the **address bar**.

11 In the lower portion of the dialog box, click in the **File name** box to select the existing text. Notice that Office inserts the text at the beginning of the presentation as a suggested file name.

12 On your keyboard, locate the ⎵ key. Notice that the Shift of this key produces the underscore character. With the text still selected, type **Lastname_Firstname_1A_Menu_Plan** Compare your screen with Figure 1.22.

> You can use spaces in file names, however some individuals prefer not to use spaces. Some programs, especially when transferring files over the Internet, may not work well with spaces in file names. In general, however, unless you encounter a problem, it is OK to use spaces. In this textbook, underscores are used instead of spaces in file names.

Figure 1.22

File name box indicates
your file name

Save as type box indicates
PowerPoint Presentation

Save button

13 In the lower right corner, click **Save**; or press ⏎. See Figure 1.23.

> Your new file name displays in the title bar, indicating that the file has been saved to a location that you have specified.

Figure 1.23

File name in title bar

14 In the text that begins *Prepared by*, click to position the insertion point at the end of your name, and then press ⏎ to move to a new line. Type **For Laura Hernandez**

15 Click the **File tab** to display **Backstage** view. At the top of the center panel, notice that the path where your file is stored displays. Above the Backstage tabs, click **Close** to close the file. In the message box, click **Save** to save the changes you made and close the file. Leave PowerPoint open.

> PowerPoint displays a message asking if you want to save the changes you have made. Because you have made additional changes to the file since your last Save operation, an Office program will always prompt you to save so that you do not lose any new data.

Objective 6 | Add Document Properties and Print a File

The process of printing a file is similar in all of the Office applications. There are differences in the types of options you can select. For example, in PowerPoint, you have the option of printing the full slide, with each slide printing on a full sheet of paper, or of printing handouts with small pictures of slides on a page.

Activity 1.06 | Adding Document Properties and Printing a File

> **Alert! | Are You Printing or Submitting Your Files Electronically?**
>
> If you are submitting your files electronically only, or have no printer attached, you can still complete this activity. Complete Steps 1-9, and then submit your file electronically as directed by your instructor.

1 In the upper left corner, click the **File tab** to display **Backstage** view. Notice that the **Recent tab** displays.

Because no file was open in PowerPoint, Office applies predictive logic to determine that your most likely action will be to open a PowerPoint presentation that you worked on recently. Thus, the Recent tab displays a list of PowerPoint presentations that were recently open on your system.

2 At the top of the **Recent Presentations** list, click your **Lastname_Firstname_1A_Menu_Plan** file to open it.

3 Click the **File tab** to redisplay **Backstage** view. On the right, under the screen thumbnail, click **Properties**, and then click **Show Document Panel**. In the **Author** box, delete the existing text, and then type your firstname and lastname. Notice that in PowerPoint, some variation of the slide title is automatically inserted in the Title box. In the **Subject** box, type your Course name and section number. In the **Keywords** box, type **menu plan** and then in the upper right corner of the **Document Properties** panel, click the **Close the Document Information Panel** button [×].

Adding properties to your documents will make them easier to search for in systems such as Microsoft SharePoint.

Another Way

Press [Ctrl] + [P] or [Ctrl] + [F2] to display the Print tab in Backstage view.

4 Redisplay **Backstage** view, and then click the **Print tab**. Compare your screen with Figure 1.24.

On the Print tab in Backstage view, in the center panel, three groups of printing-related tasks display—Print, Printer, and Settings. In the right panel, the *Print Preview* displays, which is a view of a document as it will appear on the paper when you print it.

At the bottom of the Print Preview area, on the left, the number of pages and arrows with which you can move among the pages in Print Preview display. On the right, *Zoom* settings enable you to shrink or enlarge the Print Preview. Zoom is the action of increasing or decreasing the viewing area of the screen.

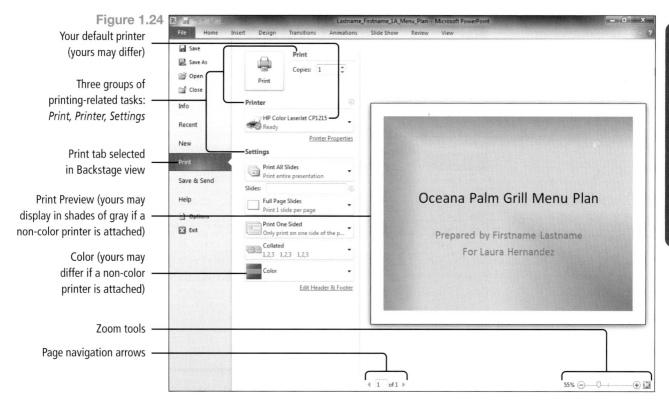

Figure 1.24

Your default printer (yours may differ)

Three groups of printing-related tasks: *Print, Printer, Settings*

Print tab selected in Backstage view

Print Preview (yours may display in shades of gray if a non-color printer is attached)

Color (yours may differ if a non-color printer is attached)

Zoom tools

Page navigation arrows

5 Locate the **Settings group**, and notice that the default setting is to **Print All Slides** and to print **Full Page Slides**—each slide on a full sheet of paper.

6 Point to **Full Page Slides**, notice that the button glows orange, and then click the button to display a gallery of print arrangements. Compare your screen with Figure 1.25.

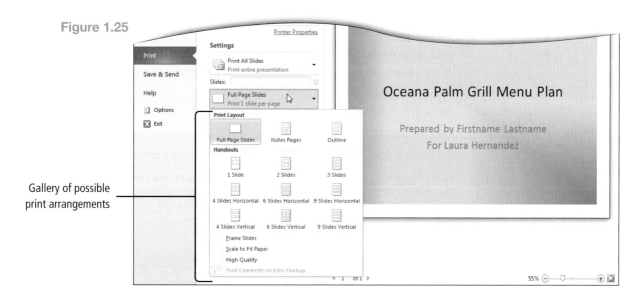

Figure 1.25

Gallery of possible print arrangements

7 In the displayed gallery, under **Handouts**, click **1 Slide**, and then compare your screen with Figure 1.26.

The Print Preview changes to show how your slide will print on the paper in this arrangement.

Figure 1.26

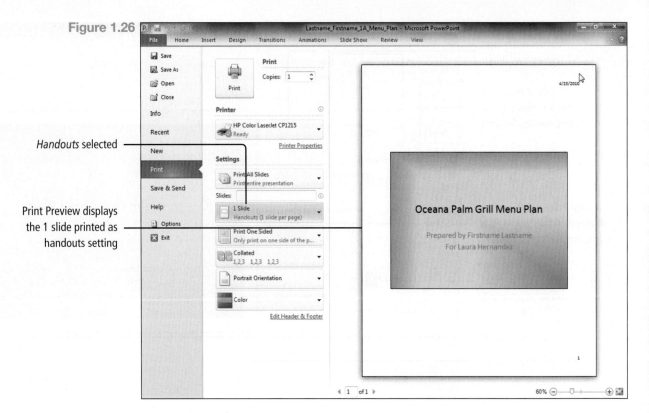

Handouts selected

Print Preview displays
the 1 slide printed as
handouts setting

8 To submit your file electronically, skip this step and move to Step 9. To print your slide, be sure your system is connected to a printer, and then in the **Print group**, click the **Print** button. On the Quick Access Toolbar, click **Save** 🔲, and then move to Step 10.

> The handout will print on your default printer—on a black and white printer, the colors will print in shades of gray. Backstage view closes and your file redisplays in the PowerPoint window.

9 To submit your file electronically, above the **Backstage tabs**, click **Close** to close the file and close **Backstage** view, click **Save** in the displayed message, and then follow the instructions provided by your instructor to submit your file electronically.

Another Way

In the upper right corner of your PowerPoint window, click the red Close button.

10 Display **Backstage** view, and then below the **Backstage tabs**, click **Exit** to close your file and close PowerPoint.

More Knowledge | Creating a PDF as an Electronic Printout

From Backstage view, you can save an Office file as a *PDF file*. *Portable Document Format* (PDF) creates an image of your file that preserves the look of your file, but that cannot be easily changed. This is a popular format for sending documents electronically, because the document will display on most computers. From Backstage view, click Save & Send, and then in the File Types group, click Create PDF/XPS Document. Then in the third panel, click the Create PDF/XPS button, navigate to your chapter folder, and then in the lower right corner, click Publish.

End You have completed Project 1A ————————————————

Project 1B Word File

Project Activities

In Activities 1.07 through 1.16, you will open, edit, save, and then compress a Word file. Your completed document will look similar to Figure 1.27.

Project Files

For Project 1B, you will need the following file:

cf01B_Cheese_Promotion

You will save your Word document as:

Lastname_Firstname_1B_Cheese_Promotion

Project Results

Memo

TO: Laura Mabry Hernandez, General Manager

FROM: Donna Jackson, Executive Chef

DATE: December 17, 2014

SUBJECT: Cheese Specials on Tuesdays

To increase restaurant traffic between 4:00 p.m. and 6:00 p.m., I am proposing a trial cheese event in one of the restaurants, probably Orlando. I would like to try a weekly event on Tuesday evenings where the focus is on a good selection of cheese.

I envision two possibilities: a selection of cheese plates or a cheese bar—or both. The cheeses would have to be matched with compatible fruit and bread or crackers. They could be used as appetizers, or for desserts, as is common in Europe. The cheese plates should be varied and diverse, using a mixture of hard and soft, sharp and mild, unusual and familiar.

I am excited about this new promotion. If done properly, I think it could increase restaurant traffic in the hours when individuals want to relax with a small snack instead of a heavy dinner.

The promotion will require that our employees become familiar with the types and characteristics of both foreign and domestic cheeses. Let's meet to discuss the details and the training requirements, and to create a flyer that begins something like this:

Oceana Palm Grill Tuesday Cheese Tastings

Lastname_Firstname_1B_Cheese_Promotion

Figure 1.27
Project 1B Cheese Promotion

Objective 7 | Open an Existing File and Save It with a New Name

In any Office program, use the Open command to display the *Open dialog box*, from which you can navigate to and then open an existing file that was created in that same program.

The Open dialog box, along with the Save and Save As dialog boxes, are referred to as *common dialog boxes*. These dialog boxes, which are provided by the Windows programming interface, display in all of the Office programs in the same manner. Thus, the Open, Save, and Save As dialog boxes will all look and perform the same in each Office program.

Activity 1.07 | Opening an Existing File and Saving it with a New Name

In this activity, you will display the Open dialog box, open an existing Word document, and then save it in your storage location with a new name.

1 Determine the location of the student data files that accompany this textbook, and be sure you can access these files.

> For example:
>
> If you are accessing the files from the Student CD that came with this textbook, insert the CD now.
>
> If you copied the files from the Student CD or from the Pearson Web site to a USB flash drive that you are using for this course, insert the flash drive in your computer now.
>
> If you copied the files to the hard drive of your computer, for example in your Documents library, be sure you can locate the files on the hard drive.

2 Determine the location of your **Common Features Chapter 1** folder you created in Activity 1.05, in which you will store your work from this chapter, and then be sure you can access that folder.

> For example:
>
> If you created your chapter folder on a USB flash drive, insert the flash drive in your computer now. This can be the same flash drive where you have stored the student data files; just be sure to use the chapter folder you created.
>
> If you created your chapter folder in the Documents library on your computer, be sure you can locate the folder. Otherwise, create a new folder at the computer at which you are working, or on a USB flash drive.

3 Using the technique you practiced in Activity 1.02, locate and then start the **Microsoft Word 2010** program on your system.

Another Way

In the Word (or other program) window, press [Ctrl] + [F12] to display the Open dialog box.

4 On the Ribbon, click the **File tab** to display **Backstage** view, and then click **Open** to display the **Open** dialog box.

5 In the **navigation pane** on the left, use the scroll bar to scroll as necessary, and then click the location of your student data files to display the location's contents in the **file list**. Compare your screen with Figure 1.28.

> For example:
>
> If you are accessing the files from the Student CD that came with your book, under Computer, click the CD/DVD.
>
> If you are accessing the files from a USB flash drive, under Computer, click the flash drive name.
>
> If you are accessing the files from the Documents library of your computer, under Libraries, click Documents.

Figure 1.28

Open dialog box

Scroll bar in navigation pane

Navigation pane

CD/DVD selected (or location of your student files)

Another Way

Point to a folder name, right-click, and then from the shortcut menu, click Open.

6 Point to the folder **01_student_data_files** and double-click to open the folder. Point to the subfolder **01_common_features**, double-click, and then compare your screen with Figure 1.29.

Figure 1.29

File list displays the contents of the *01_common_features* folder

Another Way

Click one time to select the file, and then press Enter or click the Open button in the lower right corner of the dialog box.

7 In the **file list**, point to the **chapter_01** subfolder and double-click to open it. In the **file list**, point to Word file **cf01B_Cheese_Promotion** and then double-click to open and display the file in the Word window. On the Ribbon, on the **Home tab**, in the **Paragraph group**, if necessary, click the **Show/Hide** button ¶ so that it is active—glowing orange. Compare your screen with Figure 1.30.

On the title bar at the top of the screen, the file name displays. If you opened the document from the Student CD, (*Read-Only*) will display. If you opened the document from another source to which the files were copied, (*Read-Only*) might not display. ***Read-Only*** is a property assigned to a file that prevents the file from being modified or deleted; it indicates that you cannot save any changes to the displayed document unless you first save it with a new name.

Figure 1.30

File name displays in the title bar (*Read-only* will display if opened from the CD)

Show/Hide button active

Word document displays in the Word window

> **Alert!** | Do You See a Message to Enable Editing or Enable Content?
>
> In Office 2010, some files open in *Protected View* if the file appears to be from a potentially risky location, such as the Internet. Protected View is a new security feature in Office 2010 that protects your computer from malicious files by opening them in a restricted environment until you enable them. *Trusted Documents* is another security feature that remembers which files you have already enabled. You might encounter these security features if you open a file from an e-mail or download files from the Internet; for example, from your college's learning management system or from the Pearson Web site. So long as you trust the source of the file, click Enable Editing or Enable Content—depending on the type of file you receive—and then go ahead and work with the file.

Another Way

Press F12 to display the Save As dialog box.

8 Click the **File tab** to display **Backstage** view, and then click the **Save As** command to display the **Save As** dialog box. Compare your screen with Figure 1.31.

The Save As command displays the Save As dialog box where you can name and save a *new* document based on the currently displayed document. After you name and save the new document, the original document closes, and the new document—based on the original one—displays.

Figure 1.31

Save As dialog box

Navigation pane

Current file name selected

Default type is *Word Document*

9 In the **navigation pane**, click the location in which you are storing your projects for this chapter—the location where you created your **Common Features Chapter 1** folder; for example, your USB flash drive or the Documents library.

10 In the **file list**, double-click the necessary folders and subfolders until your **Common Features Chapter 1** folder displays in the **address bar**.

11 Click in the **File name** box to select the existing file name, or drag to select the existing text, and then using your own name, type **Lastname_Firstname_1B_Cheese_Promotion** Compare your screen with Figure 1.32.

As you type, the file name from your 1A project might display briefly. Because your 1A project file is stored in this location and you began the new file name with the same text, Office predicts that you might want the same or similar file name. As you type new characters, the suggestion is removed.

Figure 1.32

Your folder name in address bar

File name box displays your new file name

Save button

12 In the lower right corner of the **Save As** dialog box, click **Save**; or press Enter. Compare your screen with Figure 1.33.

The original document closes, and your new document, based on the original, displays with the name in the title bar.

Figure 1.33

New document name in title bar

Insertion point at beginning of document

Objective 8 | Explore Options for an Application

Within each Office application, you can open an *Options dialog box* where you can select program settings and other options and preferences. For example, you can set preferences for viewing and editing files.

Activity 1.08 | Viewing Application Options

1 Click the **File tab** to display **Backstage** view. Under the **Help tab**, click **Options**.

2 In the displayed **Word Options** dialog box, on the left, click **Display**, and then on the right, locate the information under **Always show these formatting marks on the screen**.

When you press Enter, Spacebar, or Tab on your keyboard, characters display to represent these keystrokes. These screen characters do not print, and are referred to as *formatting marks* or *nonprinting characters*.

Office | Chapter 1

3 Under **Always show these formatting marks on the screen**, be sure the last check box, **Show all formatting marks**, is selected—select it if necessary. Compare your screen with Figure 1.34.

Figure 1.34

Word Options dialog box

Display selected

Information about formatting marks

Check box selected

4 In the lower right corner of the dialog box, click **OK**.

Objective 9 | Perform Commands from the Ribbon

The *Ribbon*, which displays across the top of the program window, groups commands and features in a manner that you would most logically use them. Each Office program's Ribbon is slightly different, but all contain the same three elements: *tabs*, *groups*, and *commands*.

Tabs display across the top of the Ribbon, and each tab relates to a type of activity; for example, laying out a page. Groups are sets of related commands for specific tasks. Commands—instructions to computer programs—are arranged in groups, and might display as a button, a menu, or a box in which you type information.

You can also minimize the Ribbon so only the tab names display. In the minimized Ribbon view, when you click a tab the Ribbon expands to show the groups and commands, and then when you click a command, the Ribbon returns to its minimized view. Most Office users, however, prefer to leave the complete Ribbon in view at all times.

Activity 1.09 | Performing Commands from the Ribbon

1 Take a moment to examine the document on your screen.

This document is a memo from the Executive Chef to the General Manager regarding a new restaurant promotion.

2 On the Ribbon, click the **View tab**. In the **Show group**, if necessary, click to place a check mark in the **Ruler** check box, and then compare your screen with Figure 1.35.

> When working in Word, display the rulers so that you can see how margin settings affect your document and how text aligns. Additionally, if you set a tab stop or an indent, its location is visible on the ruler.

Figure 1.35

Quick Access Toolbar

Ruler selected

Button to minimize Ribbon

Rulers

3 On the Ribbon, click the **Home tab**. In the **Paragraph group**, if necessary, click the **Show/Hide** button ¶ so that it glows orange and formatting marks display in your document. Point to the button to display information about the button, and then compare your screen with Figure 1.36.

> When the Show/Hide button is active—glowing orange—formatting marks display. Because formatting marks guide your eye in a document—like a map and road signs guide you along a highway—these marks will display throughout this instruction. Many expert Word users keep these marks displayed while creating documents.

Figure 1.36

Show/Hide button glows orange

Paragraph group

ScreenTip for Show/Hide button

Paragraph mark

Tab mark

4 In the upper left corner of your screen, above the Ribbon, locate the **Quick Access Toolbar**.

> The *Quick Access Toolbar* contains commands that you use frequently. By default, only the commands Save, Undo, and Redo display, but you can add and delete commands to suit your needs. Possibly the computer at which you are working already has additional commands added to the Quick Access Toolbar.

5 At the end of the Quick Access Toolbar, click the **Customize Quick Access Toolbar** button ▾.

6 Compare your screen with Figure 1.37.

> A list of commands that Office users commonly add to their Quick Access Toolbar displays, including *Open*, *E-mail*, and *Print Preview and Print*. Commands already on the Quick Access Toolbar display a check mark. Commands that you add to the Quick Access Toolbar are always just one click away.

> Here you can also display the More Commands dialog box, from which you can select any command from any tab to add to the Quick Access Toolbar.

Figure 1.37

Customize Quick Access Toolbar

Popular commands to add

Existing commands checked

Displays *More Commands* dialog box

Another Way

Right-click any command on the Ribbon, and then on the shortcut menu, click Add to Quick Access Toolbar.

7 On the displayed list, click **Print Preview and Print**, and then notice that the icon is added to the **Quick Access Toolbar**. Compare your screen with Figure 1.38.

> The icon that represents the Print Preview command displays on the Quick Access Toolbar. Because this is a command that you will use frequently while building Office documents, you might decide to have this command remain on your Quick Access Toolbar.

Figure 1.38

Icon for Print Preview command added to Quick Access Toolbar

8 In the first line of the document, be sure your insertion point is blinking to the left of the *O* in *Oceana*. Press Enter one time to insert a blank paragraph, and then click to the left of the new paragraph mark (¶) in the new line.

> The ***paragraph symbol*** is a formatting mark that displays each time you press Enter.

9 On the Ribbon, click the **Insert tab**. In the **Illustrations group**, point to the **Clip Art** button to display its ScreenTip.

> Many buttons on the Ribbon have this type of ***enhanced ScreenTip***, which displays more descriptive text than a normal ScreenTip.

10 Click the **Clip Art** button.

> The Clip Art ***task pane*** displays. A task pane is a window within a Microsoft Office application that enables you to enter options for completing a command.

11 In the **Clip Art** task pane, click in the **Search for** box, delete any existing text, and then type **cheese grapes** Under **Results should be:**, click the arrow at the right, if necessary click to *clear* the check mark for **All media types** so that no check boxes are selected, and then click the check box for **Illustrations**. Compare your screen with Figure 1.39.

Figure 1.39

Search term ——

Blank paragraph ——

12 Click the **Results should be arrow** again to close the list, and then if necessary, click to place a check mark in the **Include Office.com content** check box.

> By selecting this check box, the search for clip art images will include those from Microsoft's online collections of clip art at www.office.com.

13 At the top of the **Clip Art** task pane, click **Go**. Wait a moment for clips to display, and then locate the clip indicated in Figure 1.40.

Figure 1.40

Check box selected ——

Locate this image ——

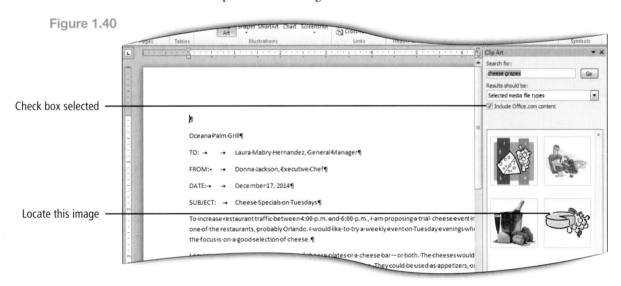

14 Click the image indicated in Figure 1.40 one time to insert it at the insertion point, and then in the upper right corner of the **Clip Art** task pane, click the **Close** ☒ button.

Alert! | If You Cannot Locate the Image

If the image shown in Figure 1.40 is unavailable, select a different cheese image that is appropriate.

---

15 With the image selected—surrounded by a border—on the Ribbon, click the **Home tab**, and then in the **Paragraph group**, click the **Center** button ≡ . Click anywhere outside of the bordered picture to *deselect*—cancel the selection. Compare your screen with Figure 1.41.

Figure 1.41

Center button

Image inserted in
document and
centered horizontally

Oceana·Palm·Grill¶

TO: →   →   Laura·Mabry·Hernandez,·General·Manager¶

16 Point to the inserted clip art image, and then watch the last tab of the Ribbon as you click the image one time to select it.

> The *Picture Tools* display and an additional tab—the *Format* tab—is added to the Ribbon. The Ribbon adapts to your work and will display additional tabs—referred to as **contextual tabs**—when you need them.

17 On the Ribbon, under **Picture Tools**, click the **Format tab**.

Alert! | The Size of Groups on the Ribbon Varies with Screen Resolution

Your monitor's screen resolution might be set higher than the resolution used to capture the figures in this book. In Figure 1.42 below, the resolution is set to 1024 × 768, which is used for all of the figures in this book. Compare that with Figure 1.43 below, where the screen resolution is set to 1280 × 1024.

At a higher resolution, the Ribbon expands some groups to show more commands than are available with a single click, such as those in the Picture Styles group. Or, the group expands to add descriptive text to some buttons, such as those in the Arrange group. Regardless of your screen resolution, all Office commands are available to you. In higher resolutions, you will have a more robust view of the commands.

Figure 1.42

Figure 1.43

Picture Styles group at
1024 x 768 resolution

Arrange group at
1024 x 768 resolution

More styles show

Picture Styles at
1280 x 1024

Arrange group at
1280 x 1024

Expanded buttons

---

18 In the **Picture Styles group**, point to the first style to display the ScreenTip *Simple Frame, White*, and notice that the image displays with a white frame.

19 Watch the image as you point to the second picture style, and then to the third, and then to the fourth.

This is *Live Preview*, a technology that shows the result of applying an editing or formatting change as you point to possible results—*before* you actually apply it.

20 In the **Picture Styles group**, click the fourth style—**Drop Shadow Rectangle**—and then click anywhere outside of the image to deselect it. Notice that the Picture Tools no longer display on the Ribbon. Compare your screen with Figure 1.44.

Contextual tabs display only when you need them.

Figure 1.44

Picture Tools no longer display on the Ribbon

Drop Shadow Rectangle picture style applied to image

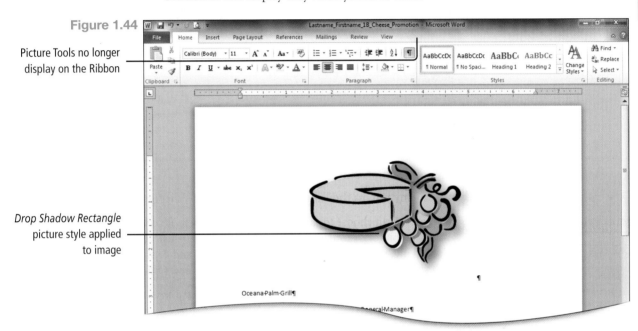

21 In the upper left corner of your screen, on the Quick Access Toolbar, click the **Save** button to save the changes you have made.

Activity 1.10 | Minimizing and Using the Keyboard to Control the Ribbon

Instead of a mouse, some individuals prefer to navigate the Ribbon by using keys on the keyboard. You can activate keyboard control of the Ribbon by pressing the [Alt] key. You can also minimize the Ribbon to maximize your available screen space.

1 On your keyboard, press the [Alt] key, and then on the Ribbon, notice that small labels display. Press [N] to activate the commands on the **Insert tab**, and then compare your screen with Figure 1.45.

Each label represents a *KeyTip*—an indication of the key that you can press to activate the command. For example, on the Insert tab, you can press [F] to activate the Clip Art task pane.

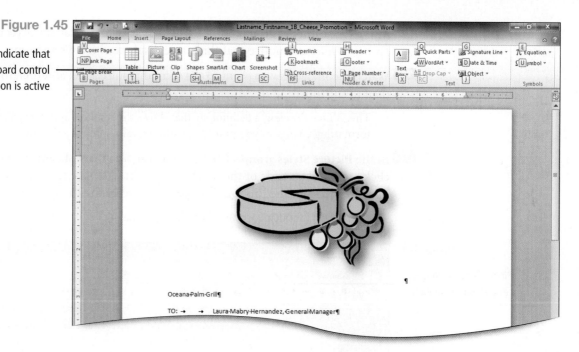

Figure 1.45

KeyTips indicate that keyboard control of the Ribbon is active

2 Press [Esc] to redisplay the KeyTips for the tabs. Then, press [Alt] again to turn off keyboard control of the Ribbon.

3 Point to any tab on the Ribbon and right-click to display a shortcut menu.

Here you can choose to display the Quick Access Toolbar below the Ribbon or minimize the Ribbon to maximize screen space. You can also customize the Ribbon by adding, removing, renaming, or reordering tabs, groups, and commands on the Ribbon, although this is not recommended until you become an expert Office user.

Another Way

Double-click the active tab; or, click the Minimize the Ribbon button at the right end of the Ribbon.

4 Click **Minimize the Ribbon**. Notice that only the Ribbon tabs display. Click the **Home tab** to display the commands. Click anywhere in the document, and notice that the Ribbon reverts to its minimized view.

Another Way

Double-click any tab to redisplay the full Ribbon.

5 Right-click any Ribbon tab, and then click **Minimize the Ribbon** again to turn the minimize feature off.

Most expert Office users prefer to have the full Ribbon display at all times.

6 Point to any tab on the Ribbon, and then on your mouse device, roll the mouse wheel. Notice that different tabs become active as your roll the mouse wheel.

You can make a tab active by using this technique, instead of clicking the tab.

Objective 10 | Apply Formatting in Office Programs

Formatting is the process of establishing the overall appearance of text, graphics, and pages in an Office file—for example, in a Word document.

Activity 1.11 | Formatting and Viewing Pages

In this activity, you will practice common formatting techniques used in Office applications.

1 On the Ribbon, click the **Insert tab**, and then in the **Header & Footer group**, click the **Footer** button.

2 At the top of the displayed gallery, under **Built-In**, click **Blank**. At the bottom of your document, with *Type text* highlighted in blue, using your own name type the file name of this document **Lastname_Firstname_1B_Cheese_Promotion** and then compare your screen with Figure 1.46.

> Header & Footer Tools are added to the Ribbon. A *footer* is a reserved area for text or graphics that displays at the bottom of each page in a document. Likewise, a *header* is a reserved area for text or graphics that displays at the top of each page in a document. When the footer (or header) area is active, the document area is inactive (dimmed).

Figure 1.46

Design tab added

Header & Footer Tools active

Document area inactive (dimmed) when footer area is active

Close Header and Footer button

Your file name

Footer area displays

3 On the Ribbon, on the **Design tab**, in the **Close group**, click the **Close Header and Footer** button.

4 On the Ribbon, click the **Page Layout tab**. In the **Page Setup group**, click the **Orientation** button, and notice that two orientations display—*Portrait* and *Landscape*. Click **Landscape**.

> In *portrait orientation*, the paper is taller than it is wide. In *landscape orientation*, the paper is wider than it is tall.

5 In the lower right corner of the screen, locate the **Zoom control** buttons.

> To *zoom* means to increase or decrease the viewing area. You can zoom in to look closely at a section of a document, and then zoom out to see an entire page on the screen. You can also zoom to view multiple pages on the screen.

6 Drag the **Zoom slider** to the left until you have zoomed to approximately *60%*. Compare your screen with Figure 1.47.

Figure 1.47

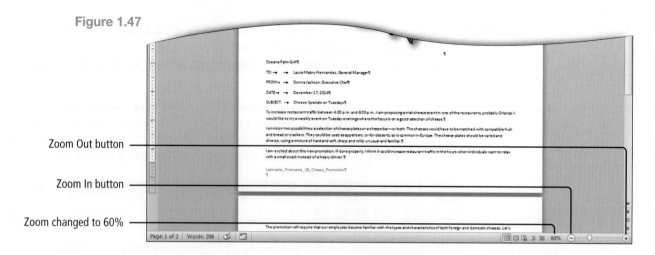

Zoom Out button ———

Zoom In button ———

Zoom changed to 60% ———

7 On the **Page Layout tab**, in the **Page Setup group**, click the **Orientation** button, and then click **Portrait**.

Portrait orientation is commonly used for business documents such as letters and memos.

8 In the lower right corner of your screen, click the **Zoom In** button ⊕ as many times as necessary to return to the **100%** zoom setting.

Use the zoom feature to adjust the view of your document for editing and for your viewing comfort.

9 On the Quick Access Toolbar, click the **Save** button 🖫 to save the changes you have made to your document.

Activity 1.12 | Formatting Text

1 To the left of *Oceana Palm Grill*, point in the margin area to display the 🔏 pointer and click one time to select the entire paragraph. Compare your screen with Figure 1.48.

Use this technique to select complete paragraphs from the margin area. Additionally, with this technique you can drag downward to select multiple-line paragraphs—which is faster and more efficient than dragging through text.

Figure 1.48

Paragraph selected ———

2 On the Ribbon, click the **Home tab**, and then in the **Paragraph group**, click the **Center** button ☰ to center the paragraph.

Alignment refers to the placement of paragraph text relative to the left and right margins. *Center alignment* refers to text that is centered horizontally between the left and right margins. You can also align text at the left margin, which is the default alignment for text in Word, or at the right margin.

3 On the **Home tab**, in the **Font group**, click the **Font button arrow** `Calibri (Body) ▾`. At the top of the list, point to **Cambria**, and as you do so, notice that the selected text previews in the Cambria font.

A *font* is a set of characters with the same design and shape. The default font in a Word document is Calibri, which is a *sans serif* font—a font design with no lines or extensions on the ends of characters.

The Cambria font is a *serif* font—a font design that includes small line extensions on the ends of the letters to guide the eye in reading from left to right.

The list of fonts displays as a gallery showing potential results. For example, in the Font gallery, you can see the actual design and format of each font as it would look if applied to text.

4 Point to several other fonts and observe the effect on the selected text. Then, at the top of the **Font** gallery, under **Theme Fonts**, click **Cambria**.

A *theme* is a predesigned set of colors, fonts, lines, and fill effects that look good together and that can be applied to your entire document or to specific items.

A theme combines two sets of fonts—one for text and one for headings. In the default Office theme, Cambria is the suggested font for headings.

5 With the paragraph *Oceana Palm Grill* still selected, on the **Home tab**, in the **Font group**, click the **Font Size button arrow** `11 ▾`, point to **36**, and then notice how Live Preview displays the text in the font size to which you are pointing. Compare your screen with Figure 1.49.

Figure 1.49

Font Size button

Font button

Font Size list

Pointing to 36 pt font size

Oceana Palm Grill centered,
Cambria font applied

6 On the displayed list of font sizes, click **20**.

Fonts are measured in *points*, with one point equal to 1/72 of an inch. A higher point size indicates a larger font size. Headings and titles are often formatted by using a larger font size. The word *point* is abbreviated as *pt*.

7 With *Oceana Palm Grill* still selected, on the **Home tab**, in the **Font group**, click the **Font Color button arrow** `A ▾`. Under **Theme Colors**, in the seventh column, click the last color—**Olive Green, Accent 3, Darker 50%**. Click anywhere to deselect the text.

8 To the left of *TO:*, point in the left margin area to display the 🔏 pointer, hold down the left mouse button, and then drag down to select the four memo headings. Compare your screen with Figure 1.50.

Use this technique to select complete paragraphs from the margin area—dragging downward to select multiple-line paragraphs—which is faster and more efficient than dragging through text.

Figure 1.50

Title formatted in green 20 pt font size

Mini toolbar

Four memo heading lines selected

9 With the four paragraphs selected, on the Mini toolbar, click the **Font Color** button ⌐A·⌐, which now displays a dark green bar instead of a red bar.

The font color button retains its most recently used color—Olive Green, Accent 3, Darker 50%. As you progress in your study of Microsoft Office, you will use other buttons that behave in this manner; that is, they retain their most recently used format.

The purpose of the Mini toolbar is to place commonly used commands close to text or objects that you select. By selecting a command on the Mini toolbar, you reduce the distance that you must move your mouse to access a command.

10 Click anywhere in the paragraph that begins *To increase*, and then ***triple-click***—click the left mouse button three times—to select the entire paragraph. If the entire paragraph is not selected, click in the paragraph and begin again.

11 With the entire paragraph selected, on the Mini toolbar, click the **Font Color button arrow** ⌐A·⌐, and then under **Theme Colors**, in the sixth column, click the first color— **Red, Accent 2**.

It is convenient to have commonly used commands display on the Mini toolbar so that you do not have to move your mouse to the top of the screen to access the command from the Ribbon.

12 Select the text *TO:* and then on the displayed Mini toolbar, click the **Bold** button ⌐B⌐ and the **Italic** button ⌐I⌐.

Font styles include bold, italic, and underline. Font styles emphasize text and are a visual cue to draw the reader's eye to important text.

13 On the displayed Mini toolbar, click the **Italic** button ⌐I⌐ again to turn off the Italic formatting. Notice that the Italic button no longer glows orange.

A button that behaves in this manner is referred to as a ***toggle button***, which means it can be turned on by clicking it once, and then turned off by clicking it again.

14 With *TO:* still selected, on the Mini toolbar, click the **Format Painter** button. Then, move your mouse under the word *Laura*, and notice the mouse pointer. Compare your screen with Figure 1.51.

> You can use the ***Format Painter*** to copy the formatting of specific text or of a paragraph and then apply it in other locations in your document.

> The pointer takes the shape of a paintbrush, and contains the formatting information from the paragraph where the insertion point is positioned. Information about the Format Painter and how to turn it off displays in the status bar.

Figure 1.51

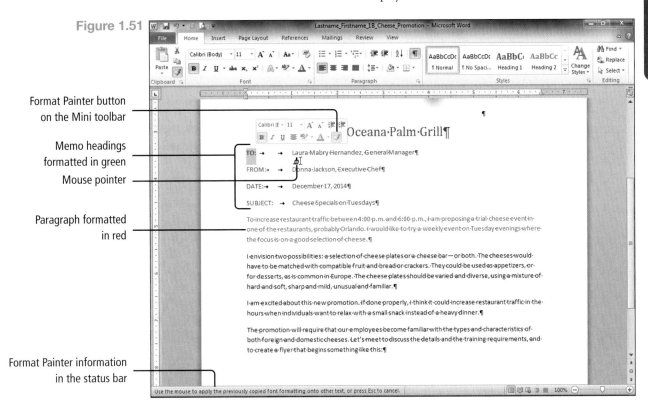

Format Painter button on the Mini toolbar

Memo headings formatted in green

Mouse pointer

Paragraph formatted in red

Format Painter information in the status bar

15 With the pointer, drag to select the text *FROM:* and notice that the Bold formatting is applied. Then, point to the selected text *FROM:* and on the Mini toolbar, *double-click* the **Format Painter** button.

16 Select the text *DATE:* to copy the Bold formatting, and notice that the pointer retains the shape.

> When you *double-click* the Format Painter button, the Format Painter feature remains active until you either click the Format Painter button again, or press Esc to cancel it—as indicated on the status bar.

17 With Format Painter still active, select the text *SUBJECT:*, and then on the Ribbon, on the **Home tab**, in the **Clipboard group**, notice that the **Format Painter** button is glowing orange, indicating that it is active. Compare your screen with Figure 1.52.

Figure 1.52

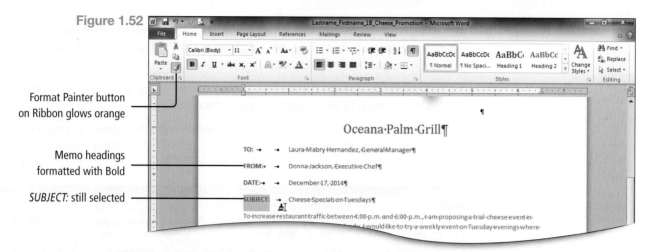

Format Painter button on Ribbon glows orange

Memo headings formatted with Bold

SUBJECT: still selected

18 Click the **Format Painter** button 🖌 on the Ribbon to turn the command off.

19 In the paragraph that begins *To increase*, triple-click again to select the entire paragraph. On the displayed Mini toolbar, click the **Bold** button B and the **Italic** button I. Click anywhere to deselect.

20 On the Quick Access Toolbar, click the **Save** button 🖫 to save the changes you have made to your document.

Activity 1.13 | Using the Office Clipboard to Cut, Copy, and Paste

The **Office Clipboard** is a temporary storage area that holds text or graphics that you select and then cut or copy. When you **copy** text or graphics, a copy is placed on the Office Clipboard and the original text or graphic remains in place. When you **cut** text or graphics, a copy is placed on the Office Clipboard, and the original text or graphic is removed—cut—from the document.

After cutting or copying, the contents of the Office Clipboard are available for you to **paste**—insert—in a new location in the current document, or into another Office file.

1 Hold down Ctrl and press Home to move to the beginning of your document, and then take a moment to study the table in Figure 1.53, which describes similar keyboard shortcuts with which you can navigate quickly in a document.

To Move	Press
To the beginning of a document	Ctrl + Home
To the end of a document	Ctrl + End
To the beginning of a line	Home
To the end of a line	End
To the beginning of the previous word	Ctrl + ←
To the beginning of the next word	Ctrl + →
To the beginning of the current word (if insertion point is in the middle of a word)	Ctrl + ←
To the beginning of a paragraph	Ctrl + ↑
To the beginning of the next paragraph	Ctrl + ↓
To the beginning of the current paragraph (if insertion point is in the middle of a paragraph)	Ctrl + ↑
Up one screen	PgUp
Down one screen	PageDown

Figure 1.53

Another Way

Right-click the selection, and then click Copy on the shortcut menu; or, use the keyboard shortcut `Ctrl` + `C`.

2 To the left of *Oceana Palm Grill*, point in the left margin area to display the ⟨🔍⟩ pointer, and then click one time to select the entire paragraph. On the **Home tab**, in the **Clipboard group**, click the **Copy** button [📋].

> Because anything that you select and then copy—or cut—is placed on the Office Clipboard, the Copy command and the Cut command display in the Clipboard group of commands on the Ribbon.
>
> There is no visible indication that your copied selection has been placed on the Office Clipboard.

3 On the **Home tab**, in the **Clipboard group**, to the right of the group name *Clipboard*, click the **Dialog Box Launcher** button [▫], and then compare your screen with Figure 1.54.

> The Clipboard task pane displays with your copied text. In any Ribbon group, the **Dialog Box Launcher** displays either a dialog box or a task pane related to the group of commands.
>
> It is not necessary to display the Office Clipboard in this manner, although sometimes it is useful to do so. The Office Clipboard can hold 24 items.

Figure 1.54

Copy button —

Dialog Box Launcher in Clipboard group —

Clipboard task pane displays —

Selected text on the Office Clipboard —

4 In the upper right corner of the **Clipboard** task pane, click the **Close** button [✕].

Another Way

Right-click, on the shortcut menu under Paste Options, click the desired option button.

5 Press `Ctrl` + `End` to move to the end of your document. Press `Enter` one time to create a new blank paragraph. On the **Home tab**, in the **Clipboard group**, point to the **Paste** button, and then click the *upper* portion of this split button.

> The Paste command pastes the most recently copied item on the Office Clipboard at the insertion point location. If you click the lower portion of the Paste button, a gallery of Paste Options displays.

6 Click the **Paste Options** button 📋 that displays below the pasted text as shown in Figure 1.55.

Here you can view and apply various formatting options for pasting your copied or cut text. Typically you will click Paste on the Ribbon and paste the item in its original format. If you want some other format for the pasted item, you can do so from the *Paste Options gallery*.

The Paste Options gallery provides a Live Preview of the various options for changing the format of the pasted item with a single click. The Paste Options gallery is available in three places: on the Ribbon by clicking the lower portion of the Paste button—the Paste button arrow; from the Paste Options button that displays below the pasted item following the paste operation; or, on the shortcut menu if you right-click the pasted item.

Figure 1.55
Upper portion of
Paste button

Paste button arrow
on the Ribbon

Pasted text

Paste Options button

Paste Options gallery

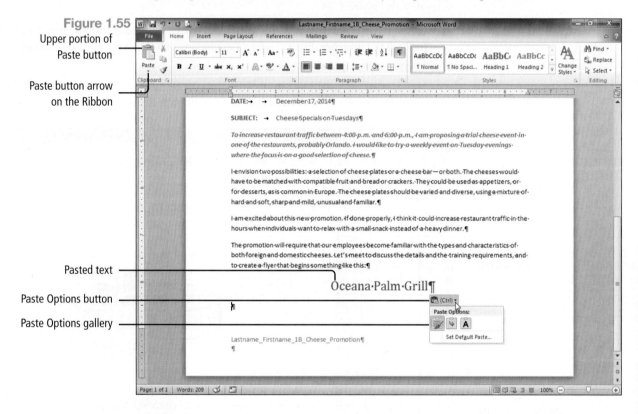

7 In the displayed **Paste Options** gallery, *point* to each option to see the Live Preview of the format that would be applied if you clicked the button.

The contents of the Paste Options gallery are contextual; that is, they change based on what you copied and where you are pasting.

8 Press [Esc] to close the gallery; the button will remain displayed until you take some other screen action.

Another Way

On the Home tab, in the Clipboard group, click the Cut button; or, use the keyboard shortcut [Ctrl] + [X].

9 Press [Ctrl] + [Home] to move to the top of the document, and then click the **cheese image** one time to select it. While pointing to the selected image, right-click, and then on the shortcut menu, click **Cut**.

Recall that the Cut command cuts—removes—the selection from the document and places it on the Office Clipboard.

10 Press (Del) one time to remove the blank paragraph from the top of the document, and then press (Ctrl) + (End) to move to the end of the document.

11 With the insertion point blinking in the blank paragraph at the end of the document, right-click, and notice that the **Paste Options** gallery displays on the shortcut menu. Compare your screen with Figure 1.56.

Figure 1.56

Paste Options on shortcut menu

12 On the shortcut menu, under **Paste Options**, click the first button—**Keep Source Formatting** .

13 Click the picture to select it. On the **Home tab**, in the **Paragraph group**, click the **Center** button .

14 Above the cheese picture, click to position the insertion point at the end of the word *Grill*, press (Spacebar) one time, and then type **Tuesday Cheese Tastings** Compare your screen with Figure 1.57.

Figure 1.57

Heading

Picture inserted and centered

Activity 1.14 | Viewing Print Preview and Printing a Word Document

1 Press (Ctrl) + (Home) to move to the top of your document. Select the text *Oceana Palm Grill*, and then replace the selected text by typing **Memo**

2 Display **Backstage** view, on the right, click **Properties**, and then click **Show Document Panel**. Replace the existing author name with your first and last name. In the **Subject** box, type your course name and section number, and then in the **Keywords** box, type **cheese promotion** and then **Close** the **Document Information Panel**.

Another Way

Press Ctrl + F2 to display Print Preview.

3 On the Quick Access Toolbar, click **Save** 🖫 to save the changes you have made to your document.

4 On the Quick Access Toolbar, click the **Print Preview** button 🔍 that you added. Compare your screen with Figure 1.58.

Figure 1.58

Memo typed

If no printer is attached to your system, OneNote is the default printer

Print tab active in Backstage view

Print Preview (if you have a non-color printer as your default printer, the preview may display in shades of gray)

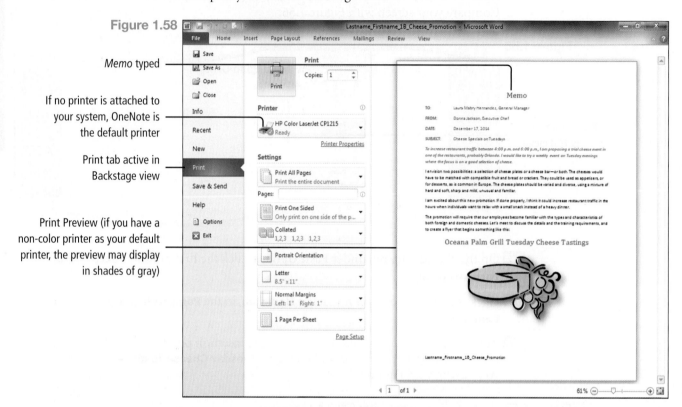

5 Examine the **Print Preview**. Under **Settings**, notice that in **Backstage** view, several of the same commands that are available on the Page Layout tab of the Ribbon also display.

> For convenience, common adjustments to Page Layout display here, so that you can make last-minute adjustments without closing Backstage view.

6 If you need to make any corrections, click the Home tab to return to the document and make any necessary changes.

> It is good practice to examine the Print Preview before printing or submitting your work electronically. Then, make any necessary corrections, re-save, and redisplay Print Preview.

7 If you are directed to do so, click Print to print the document; or, above the Info tab, click Close, and then submit your file electronically according to the directions provided by your instructor.

> If you click the Print button, Backstage view closes and the Word window redisplays.

8 On the Quick Access Toolbar, point to the **Print Preview icon** 🔍 you placed there, right-click, and then click **Remove from Quick Access Toolbar**.

> If you are working on your own computer and you want to do so, you can leave the icon on the toolbar; in a lab setting, you should return the software to its original settings.

9 At the right end of the title bar, click the program **Close** button ⊠ .

10 If a message displays asking if you want the text on the Clipboard to be available after you quit Word, click **No**.

> This message most often displays if you have copied some type of image to the Clipboard. If you click Yes, the items on the Clipboard will remain for you to use.

Objective 11 | Use the Microsoft Office 2010 Help System

Within each Office program, the Help feature provides information about all of the program's features and displays step-by-step instructions for performing many tasks.

Activity 1.15 | Using the Microsoft Office 2010 Help System in Excel

In this activity, you will use the Microsoft Help feature to find information about formatting numbers in Excel.

> **Another Way**
> Press F1 to display Help.

1 **Start** the **Microsoft Excel 2010** program. In the upper right corner of your screen, click the **Microsoft Excel Help** button ❓.

2 In the **Excel Help** window, click in the white box in upper left corner, type **formatting numbers** and then click **Search** or press Enter.

3 On the list of results, click **Display numbers as currency**. Compare your screen with Figure 1.59.

Figure 1.59

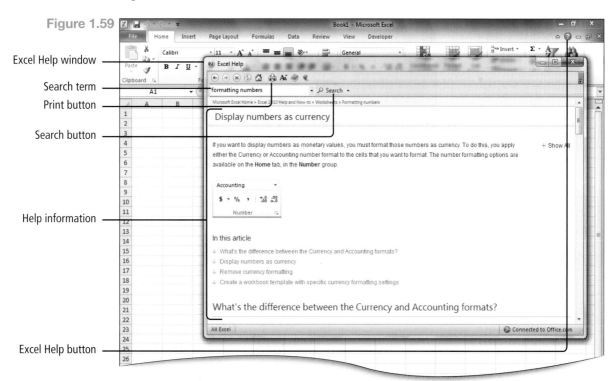

Excel Help window
Search term
Print button
Search button
Help information
Excel Help button

4 If you want to do so, on the toolbar at the top of the **Excel Help** window, click the Print 🖨 button to print a copy of this information for your reference.

Office | Chapter 1

5 On the title bar of the Excel Help window, click the **Close** button. On the right side of the Microsoft Excel title bar, click the **Close** button to close Excel.

Objective 12 | Compress Files

A *compressed file* is a file that has been reduced in size. Compressed files take up less storage space and can be transferred to other computers faster than uncompressed files. You can also combine a group of files into one compressed folder, which makes it easier to share a group of files.

Activity 1.16 | Compressing Files

In this activity, you will combine the two files you created in this chapter into one compressed file.

1 On the Windows taskbar, click the **Start** button, and then on the right, click **Computer**.

2 On the left, in the **navigation pane**, click the location of your two files from this chapter—your USB flash drive or other location—and display the folder window for your **Common Features Chapter 1** folder. Compare your screen with Figure 1.60.

Figure 1.60

Address bar displays path ——

Your chapter files in file list (your name displays) ——

Folder window for your chapter folder ——

Location selected in navigation pane (your location may vary) ——

3 In the **file list**, click your **Lastname_Firstname_1A_Menu_Plan** file one time to select it.

4 Hold down Ctrl, and then click your **Lastname_Firstname_1B_Cheese_Promotion** file to select both files. Release Ctrl.

In any Windows-based program, holding down Ctrl while selecting enables you to select multiple items.

5 Point anywhere over the two selected files and right-click. On the shortcut menu, point to **Send to**, and then compare your screen with Figure 1.61.

Figure 1.61

Two files selected

Send to submenu

Shortcut menu
(yours may vary)

6 On the shortcut submenu, click **Compressed (zipped) folder**.

Windows creates a compressed folder containing a *copy* of each of the selected files. The folder name is the name of the file or folder to which you were pointing, and is selected— highlighted in blue—so that you can rename it.

7 Using your own name, type **Lastname_Firstname_Common_Features_Ch1** and press Enter.

The compressed folder is now ready to attach to an e-mail or share in some other electronic format.

8 **Close** ❌ the folder window. If directed to do so by your instructor, submit your compressed folder electronically.

More Knowledge | **Extracting Compressed Files**

Extract means to decompress, or pull out, files from a compressed form. When you extract a file, an uncompressed copy is placed in the folder that you specify. The original file remains in the compressed folder.

End **You have completed Project 1B**

Content-Based Assessments

Summary

In this chapter, you used Windows Explorer to navigate the Windows file structure. You also used features that are common across the Microsoft Office 2010 programs.

Key Terms

Content-Based Assessments

Matching

Match each term in the second column with its correct definition in the first column by writing the letter of the term on the blank line in front of the correct definition.

A Address bar

B Command

C File

D Folder

E Folder window

F Icons

G Keyboard shortcut

H Library

I Microsoft Excel

J Program

K Ribbon

L Start menu

M Subfolder

N Title bar

O Windows Explorer

_____ 1. A collection of information stored on a computer under a single name.

_____ 2. A container in which you store files.

_____ 3. A folder within a folder.

_____ 4. The program that displays the files and folders on your computer.

_____ 5. The Windows menu that is the main gateway to your computer.

_____ 6. In Windows 7, a window that displays the contents of the current folder, library, or device, and contains helpful parts so that you can navigate.

_____ 7. In Windows, a collection of items, such as files and folders, assembled from various locations that might be on your computer.

_____ 8. The bar at the top of a folder window with which you can navigate to a different folder or library, or go back to a previous one.

_____ 9. An instruction to a computer program that carries out an action.

_____ 10. Small pictures that represent a program, a file, a folder, or an object.

_____ 11. A set of instructions that a computer uses to perform a specific task.

_____ 12. A spreadsheet program used to calculate numbers and create charts.

_____ 13. The user interface that groups commands on tabs at the top of the program window.

_____ 14. A bar at the top of the program window displaying the current file and program name.

_____ 15. One or more keys pressed to perform a task that would otherwise require a mouse.

Multiple Choice

Circle the correct answer.

1. A small toolbar with frequently used commands that displays when selecting text or objects is the:
    A. Quick Access Toolbar   B. Mini toolbar   C. Document toolbar

2. In Office 2010, a centralized space for file management tasks is:
    A. a task pane   B. a dialog box   C. Backstage view

3. The commands Save, Save As, Open, and Close in Backstage view are located:
    A. above the Backstage tabs   B. below the Backstage tabs   C. under the screen thumbnail

4. The tab in Backstage view that displays information about the current file is the:
    A. Recent tab   B. Info tab   C. Options tab

5. Details about a file, including the title, author name, subject, and keywords are known as:
    A. document properties   B. formatting marks   C. KeyTips

6. An Office feature that displays a list of potential results is:
    A. Live Preview   B. a contextual tab   C. a gallery

7. A type of formatting emphasis applied to text such as bold, italic, and underline, is called:

   A. a font style **B.** a KeyTip **C.** a tag

8. A technology showing the result of applying formatting as you point to possible results is called:

   A. Live Preview **B.** Backstage view **C.** gallery view

9. A temporary storage area that holds text or graphics that you select and then cut or copy is the:

   A. paste options gallery **B.** ribbon **C.** Office clipboard

10. A file that has been reduced in size is:

   A. a compressed file **B.** an extracted file **C.** a PDF file

Getting Started with Access Databases

OUTCOMES
At the end of this chapter you will be able to:

OBJECTIVES
Mastering these objectives will enable you to:

PROJECT 1A
Create a new database.

1. Identify Good Database Design (p. 51)
2. Create a Table and Define Fields in a New Database (p. 52)
3. Change the Structure of Tables and Add a Second Table (p. 64)
4. Create and Use a Query, Form, and Report (p. 74)
5. Save and Close a Database (p. 80)

PROJECT 1B
Create a database from a template.

6. Create a Database Using a Template (p. 82)
7. Organize Objects in the Navigation Pane (p. 86)
8. Create a New Table in a Database Created with a Template (p. 88)
9. Print a Report and a Table in a Database Created with a Template (p. 90)

Joy Brown/Shutterstock

In This Chapter

In this chapter, you will use Microsoft Access 2010 to organize a collection of related information. Access is a powerful program that enables you to organize, search, sort, retrieve, and present information in a professional-looking manner. You will create new databases, enter data into Access tables, and create a query, form, and report—all of which are Access objects that make a database useful. In this chapter, you will also create a database from a template provided with the Access program. The template creates a complete database that you can use as provided, or you can modify it to suit your needs. Additional templates are available from the Microsoft Online Web site. For your first attempt at a database, consider using a template.

The projects in this chapter relate to **Capital Cities Community College**, which is located in the Washington D. C. metropolitan area. The college provides high-quality education and professional training to residents in the cities surrounding the nation's capital. Its four campuses serve over 50,000 students and offer more than 140 certificate programs and degrees at the associate's level. CapCCC has a highly acclaimed Distance Education program and an extensive Workforce Development program. The college makes positive contributions to the community through cultural and athletic programs and partnerships with businesses and non-profit organizations.

Project 1A Contact Information Database with Two Tables

Project Activities

In Activities 1.01 through 1.17, you will assist Dr. Justin Mitrani, Vice President of Instruction at Capital Cities Community College, in creating a new database for tracking the contact information for students and faculty members. Your completed database objects will look similar to Figure 1.1.

Project Files

For Project 1A, you will need the following files:

New blank Access database
a01A_Students (Excel workbook)
a01A_Faculty (Excel workbook)

You will save your database as:

Lastname_Firstname_1A_Contacts

Project Results

Figure 1.1
Project 1A Contacts

Objective 1 | Identify Good Database Design

A *database* is an organized collection of *data*—facts about people, events, things, or ideas—related to a specific topic or purpose. *Information* is data that is organized in a useful manner. Your personal address book is a type of database, because it is a collection of data about one topic—the people with whom you communicate. A simple database of this type is called a *flat database* because it is not related or linked to any other collection of data. Another example of a simple database is a list of movie DVDs. You do not keep information about your DVDs in your address book because the data is not related to your addresses.

A more sophisticated type of database is a *relational database*, because multiple collections of data in the database are related to one another; for example, data about the students, the courses, and the faculty members at a college. Microsoft Access 2010 is a relational *database management system*—also referred to as a *DBMS*—which is software that controls how related collections of data are stored, organized, retrieved, and secured.

Activity 1.01 | Using Good Design Techniques to Plan a Database

The first step in creating a new database is to determine the information you want to keep track of, and then ask yourself, *What questions should this database be able to answer for me?* The purpose of a database is to store the data in a manner that makes it easy for you to get the information you need by asking questions. For example, in the Contacts database for Capital Cities Community College, the questions to be answered might include:

How many students are enrolled at Capital Cities Community College?

How many faculty members teach in the Accounting Department?

Which and how many students live in Arlington, Virginia?

Which and how many students have a balance owed?

Which and how many students are majoring in Information Systems Technology?

Tables are the foundation of an Access database because all of the data is stored in one or more tables. A table is similar in structure to an Excel worksheet; that is, data is organized into rows and columns. Each table row is a *record*—all of the categories of data pertaining to one person, place, thing, event, or idea. Each table column is a *field*—a single piece of information for every record. For example, in a table storing student contact information, each row forms a record for only one student. Each column forms a field for a single piece of information for every record; for example, the student ID number for all students.

When organizing the fields of information in your database, break each piece of information into its smallest useful part. For example, create three fields for the name of a student—one field for the last name, one field for the first name, and one field for the middle name or initial.

The *first principle of good database design* is to organize data in the tables so that *redundant*—duplicate—data does not occur. For example, record the contact information for students in only *one* table, because if the address for a student changes, the change can be made in just one place. This conserves space, reduces the likelihood of errors when recording the new data, and does not require remembering all of the different places where the address is stored.

The *second principle of good database design* is to use techniques that ensure the accuracy of data when it is entered into the table. Typically, many different people enter data into a database—think of all the people who enter data at your college. When entering a state in a contacts database, one person might enter the state as *Virginia* and another might enter the state as *VA*. Use design techniques to help those who enter data into a database do so in a consistent and accurate manner.

Normalization is the process of applying design rules and principles to ensure that your database performs as expected. Taking the time to plan and create a database that is well designed will ensure that you can retrieve meaningful information from the database.

The tables of information in a relational database are linked or joined to one another by a *common field*—a field in one or more tables that stores the same data. For example, the Student Contacts table includes the Student ID, name, and address of every student. The Student Activities table includes the name of each club, and the Student ID—but not the name or address—of each student in each club. Because the two tables share a common field—Student ID—you can create a list of names and addresses of all the students in the Photography Club. The names and addresses are stored in the Student Contacts table, and the Student IDs of the Photography Club members are stored in the Student Activities table.

Objective 2 | Create a Table and Define Fields in a New Blank Database

There are two methods to create a new Access database: create a new database using a *database template*—a preformatted database designed for a specific purpose—or create a new database from a blank database. A blank database has no data and has no database tools; you create the data and the tools as you need them.

Regardless of the method you use, you must name and save the database before you can create any **objects** in it. Objects are the basic parts of a database; you create objects to store your data and to work with your data. The most common database objects are tables, forms, and reports. Think of an Access database as a container for the objects that you will create.

Activity 1.02 | Starting with a New Database

1 **Start** Access. Take a moment to compare your screen with Figure 1.2 and study the parts of the Microsoft Access window described in the table in Figure 1.3.

From this Access starting point in Backstage view, you can open an existing database, create a new blank database, or create a new database from a template.

Figure 1.2

Available Templates panel

Title bar

Blank database selected

Blank database panel

New tab

Office.com online
Templates (yours may differ)

Browse for a location button

Figure 1.3

Microsoft Access Opening Window	
Window Part	**Description**
Available Templates panel	Displays alternative methods of creating a database.
Blank database	Starts a new blank database.
Blank database panel	Displays when *Blank database* button is selected under Available Templates.
Browse for location button	Enables you to select a storage location for the database.
New tab	Displays, when active in Backstage view, the various methods by which you can create a new database.
Office.com Templates	Displays template categories available from the Office.com Web site.
Title bar	Displays the Quick Access Toolbar, program name, and program-level buttons.

2 On the right, under **Blank database**, to the right of the **File Name** box, click the **Browse** button 📂. In the **File New Database** dialog box, navigate to the location where you are saving your databases for this chapter, create a new folder named **Access Chapter 1** and then notice that *Database1* displays as the default file name—the number at the end of your file name might differ if you have saved a database previously with the default name. In the **File New Database** dialog box, click **Open**.

3 In the **File name** box, replace the existing text with **Lastname_Firstname_1A_Contacts** Press Enter, and then compare your screen with Figure 1.4.

> On the right, the name of your database displays in the File Name box, and the drive and folder where the database is stored displays under the File Name box. An Access database has the file extension *.accdb*.

Figure 1.4

File name with your name and underscores between words

Drive and folder where your database is stored (yours may differ)

Create button

.accdb file extension

4 Under the **File Name** box, click the **Create** button, compare your screen with Figure 1.5, and then take a moment to study the screen elements described in the table in Figure 1.6.

> Access creates the new database and opens *Table1*. Recall that a *table* is an Access object that stores your data in columns and rows, similar to the format of an Excel worksheet. Table objects are the foundation of a database because tables store the actual data.

Figure 1.5

Ribbon with command groups arranged on tabs

Object tab

Table Tools active

Title bar with database name

Object window

Navigation Pane

Object window Close button

Status bar

Parts of the Access Database Window

Window Part	Description
Navigation Pane	Displays the database objects; from here you open the database objects to display in the object window at the right.
Object tab	Identifies and enables you to select the open object.
Object window	Displays the active or open object (table, query, or other object).
Object window Close button	Closes the active object (table, query, or other object).
Ribbon with command groups arranged on tabs	Groups the commands for performing related database tasks on tabs.
Status bar	Indicates the active view and the status of actions occurring within the database on the left; provides buttons to switch between Datasheet view and Design view on the right.
Table Tools	Provides tools for working with a table object; Table Tools are available only when a table is displayed.
Title bar	Displays the name of your database.

Figure 1.6

Activity 1.03 | Assigning the Data Type and Name to Fields

After you have saved and named your database, the next step is to consult your database plan, and then create the tables in which to enter your data. Limit the data in each table to *one* subject. For example, in this project, your database will have two tables—one for student contact information and one for faculty contact information.

Recall that each column in a table is a field and that field names display at the top of each column of the table. Recall also that each row in a table is a record—all of the data pertaining to one person, place, thing, event, or idea. Each record is broken up into its smallest usable parts—the fields. Use meaningful names to name fields; for example, *Last Name*.

1 Notice the new blank table that displays in Datasheet view, and then take a moment to study the elements of the table's object window. Compare your screen with Figure 1.7.

The table displays in *Datasheet view*, which displays the data as columns and rows similar to the format of an Excel worksheet. Another way to view a table is in *Design view*, which displays the underlying design—the *structure*—of the table's fields. The *object window* displays the open object—in this instance, the table object.

In a new blank database, there is only one object—a new blank table. Because you have not yet named this table, the object tab displays a default name of *Table1*. Access creates the first field and names it *ID*. In the ID field, Access assigns a unique sequential number—each number incremented by one—to each record as it is entered into the table.

Figure 1.7

Navigation Pane Close button
Field names row
New record row
Object tab with default table name
First field is *ID*
Navigation Pane
Fields tab on the Ribbon

2 In the **Navigation Pane**, click the **Open/Close** button 〔«〕 to collapse the **Navigation Pane** to a narrow bar on the left and to display more of the table.

The *Navigation Pane* is an area of the Access window that displays and organizes the names of the objects in a database. From the Navigation Pane, you can open objects for use.

Another Way
To the right of *Click to Add*, click the arrow.

3 In the field names row, click anywhere in the text *Click to Add* to display a list of data types. Compare your screen with Figure 1.8.

Data type is the characteristic that defines the kind of data that you can type in a field, such as numbers, text, or dates. A field in a table can have only one data type. Part of your database design should include deciding on the data type of each field. After you have selected the data type, you can name the field.

Figure 1.8

Click to display data types

Navigation Pane closed

List of data types

4 In the list of data types, click **Text**, and notice that in the second column, *Click to Add* changes to *Field1*, which is selected. Type **Last Name** and then press Enter.

The second column displays *Last Name* as the field name, and the data type list displays in the third column. The ***Text data type*** describes text, a combination of text and numbers, or numbers that are not used in calculations, such as a ZIP code.

Another Way

With the list of data types displayed, type *T* to select Text.

5 In the third field name box, click **Text**, type **First Name** and then press Enter. In the fourth field name box, click **Text**, type **Middle Initial** and then press Enter.

6 Using the technique you just practiced, create the remaining fields as follows by first selecting the data type, then typing the field name, and then pressing Enter. The field names in the table will display on one line.

The ZIP/Postal Code field is assigned a data type of Text because the number is never used in a calculation. The Amount Owed field is assigned a data type of Currency; the ***Currency data type*** describes monetary values and numeric data used in mathematical calculations involving data with one to four decimal places. Access automatically adds a U.S. dollar sign ($) and two decimal places to all of the numbers in the fields with a data type of *Currency*.

Data Type		Text	Text	Text	**Text**	**Text**	**Text**	**Text**	**Text**	**Text**	**Text**	**Currency**
Field Name	ID	Last Name	First Name	Middle Initial	**Address**	**City**	**State/ Region**	**ZIP/Postal Code**	**Phone Number**	**E-mail**	**Faculty Advisor ID**	**Amount Owed**

7 If necessary, by using the horizontal scroll bar at the bottom of the screen, scroll to the left to bring the first column into view. Compare your screen with Figure 1.9.

Access automatically created the ID field, and you created 11 additional fields in the table. The horizontal scroll bar indicates that there are additional fields that are not displayed on the screen—your screen width may vary.

Access | Chapter 1

Figure 1.9

Twelve fields created—scroll
to the left to display *ID* and
Last Name fields

Activity 1.04 | Renaming Fields and Changing Data Types in a Table

Another Way

Right-click the field name, and then on the shortcut menu, click Rename Field.

1 Click anywhere in the text *ID*. In the **Properties group**, click the **Name & Caption** button. In the **Enter Field Properties** dialog box, in the **Name** box, change *ID* to **Student ID** and then click **OK**.

The field name *Student ID* is a better description of the data in this field. In the Enter Field Properties dialog box, the *Caption* property is used to display a name for a field other than that listed as the field name. Many database designers do not use spaces in field names; instead, they might name a field LastName—with no spaces—and then create a caption for that field so it displays with spaces in tables, forms, and reports. In the Enter Field Properties dialog box, you can also provide a description for the field if you want to do so.

2 In the **Formatting group**, notice that the **Data Type** for the **Student ID** field is *AutoNumber*. Click the **Data Type arrow**, click **Text**, and then compare your screen with Figure 1.10.

In the new record row, the Student ID field is selected. By default, Access creates an ID field for all new tables and sets the data type for the field to AutoNumber. The *AutoNumber data type* describes a unique sequential or random number assigned by Access as each record is entered. By changing the data type of this field from *AutoNumber* to *Text*, you can enter a custom student ID number.

When records in a database have *no* unique value, for example the names in your address book, the AutoNumber data type is a useful way to automatically create a unique number so that you have a way to ensure that every record is different from the others.

Figure 1.10

Field renamed

New record row—indicated by asterisk

Selected field

Data type indicates *Text*

Activity 1.05 | Adding a Record to a Table

A new address book is not useful until you fill it with names, addresses, and phone numbers. Likewise, a new database is not useful until you **populate** it—fill one or more tables with data. You can populate a table with records by typing data directly into the table.

Another Way

Press Tab to move to the next field.

1 In the new record row, click in the **Student ID** field to display the insertion point, type **1238765** and then press Enter. Compare your screen with Figure 1.11.

The pencil icon ✎ in the **record selector box**—the small box at the left of a record in Datasheet view that, when clicked, selects the entire record—indicates that a record is being entered or edited.

Figure 1.11

Pencil icon indicates record being entered or edited

Record selector box

First student ID is *1238765*

Insertion point in Last Name field

2 With the insertion point positioned in the **Last Name** field, type **Fresch** and then press Enter.

> **Note | Correct Typing Errors**
>
> Correct typing errors by using the techniques you have practiced in other Office applications. For example, use Backspace to remove characters to the left, Del to remove characters to the right, or select the text you want to replace and type the correct information. Press Esc to exit out of a record that has not been completely entered.

3 In the **First Name** field, type **Michael** and then press Enter.

4 In the **Middle Initial** field, type **B** and then press Enter.

5 In the **Address** field, type **7550 Douglas Ln** and then press Enter.

> Do not be concerned if the data does not completely display in the column. As you progress in your study of Access, you will adjust the column widths so that you can view all of the data.

6 Continue entering data in the fields as indicated below, pressing Enter to move to the next field.

City	State/Region	ZIP/Postal Code	Phone Number	E-mail	Faculty Advisor ID
Alexandria	**VA**	**22336**	**(571) 555-0234**	**mfresch@capccc.edu**	**FAC-2289**

> **Note | Format for Typing Telephone Numbers in Access**
>
> Access does not require any specific format for typing telephone numbers in a database. The examples in this project use the format of Microsoft Outlook. Using such a format facilitates easy transfer of Outlook information to and from Access.

Access | Chapter 1

7 In the **Amount Owed** field, type **150** and then press [Enter]. Compare your screen with Figure 1.12.

Pressing [Enter] or [Tab] in the last field moves the insertion point to the next row to begin a new record. As soon as you move to the next row, Access saves the record—you do not have to take any specific action to save a record.

Figure 1.12

First record entered and saved

Insertion point blinking in first field of new record row

8 To give your table a meaningful name, on the Quick Access Toolbar, click the **Save** button [📷]. In the **Save As** dialog box, in the **Table Name** box, using your own name, replace the highlighted text by typing **Lastname Firstname 1A Students**

Save each database object with a name that identifies the data that it contains. When you save objects within a database, it is not necessary to use underscores. Your name is included as part of the object name so that you and your instructor can identify your printouts or electronic files.

9 In the **Save As** dialog box, click **OK**, and then notice that the object tab displays the new table name you just typed.

More Knowledge | Renaming a Table

To change the name of a table, close the table, display the Navigation Pane, right-click the table name, and then on the shortcut menu, click Rename. Type the new name or edit as you would any selected text.

Activity 1.06 │ Adding Additional Records to a Table

1 In the new record row, click in the **Student ID** field, and then enter the contact information for the following two additional students, pressing [Enter] or [Tab] to move from field to field. The data in each field will display on one line in the table.

Student ID	Last Name	First Name	Middle Initial	Address	City	State/ Region	ZIP/ Postal Code	Phone Number	E-mail	Faculty Advisor ID	Amount Owed
2345677	Ingram	Joseph	S	1 Casa Del Sol	Potomac	MD	20854	(240) 555-0177	jingram@ capccc.edu	FAC-2377	378.5
3456689	Bass	Amanda	J	1446 Yellow Rose Ln	Fairfax	VA	22030	(703) 555-0192	abass@ capccc.edu	FAC-9005	0

---

2 Compare your screen with Figure 1.13.

Figure 1.13

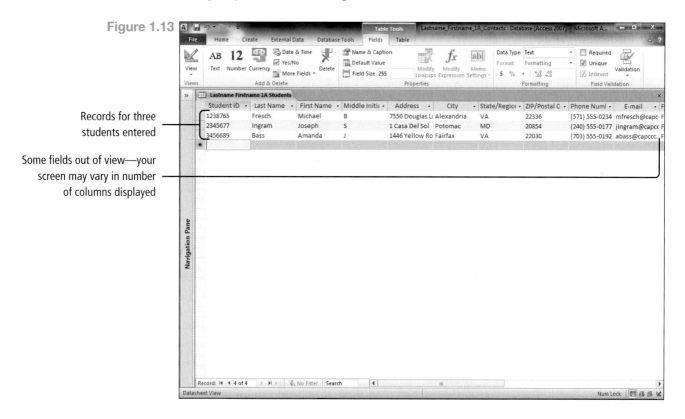

Records for three
students entered

Some fields out of view—your
screen may vary in number
of columns displayed

Activity 1.07 │ Importing Data from an Excel Workbook into an Existing Access Table

When you create a database table, you can type the records directly into a table. You can also *import* data from a variety of sources. Importing is the process of copying data from one source or application to another application. For example, you can import data from a Word table or an Excel worksheet into an Access database because the data is arranged in columns and rows, similar to a table in Datasheet view.

In this activity, you will *append*—add on—data from an Excel spreadsheet to your *1A Students* table. To append data, the table must already be created, and it must be closed.

1 In the upper right corner of the table, below the Ribbon, click the **Object Close** ☒ button to close your **1A Students** table. Notice that no objects are open.

2 On the Ribbon, click the **External Data tab**. In the **Import & Link group**, click the **Excel** button. In the **Get External Data - Excel Spreadsheet** dialog box, click the **Browse** button.

> **Another Way**
>
> Select the file name, and in the lower right area of the dialog box, click Open.

3 In the **File Open** dialog box, navigate to your student files, locate and double-click the Excel file **a01A_Students**, and then compare your screen with Figure 1.14.

The path to the *source file*—the file being imported—displays in the File name box. There are three options for importing data from an Excel workbook—import the data into a *new* table in the current database, append a copy of the records to an existing table, or link the data from Excel to a linked table. A *link* is a connection to data in another file. When linking, Access creates a table that maintains a link to the source data.

Access │ Chapter 1

Figure 1.14

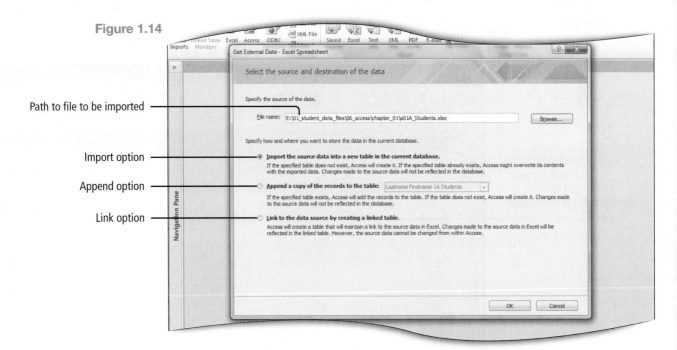

Path to file to be imported ———

Import option ———

Append option ———

Link option ———

4 Click the **Append a copy of the records to the table** option button, and then in the box to its right, click the **arrow**.

> Currently your database has only one table, so no other tables display on the list. However, when a database has multiple tables, here you can select the table to which you want to append records. The table into which you import or append data is referred to as the *destination table*.

5 Press Esc to cancel the list, and then in the lower right corner of the dialog box, click **OK**. Compare your screen with Figure 1.15.

> The first screen of the Import Spreadsheet Wizard displays, and the presence of scroll bars indicates that records and fields are out of view in this window. To append records from an Excel worksheet to an existing database table, the field names in the Excel worksheet must be identical to the field names in the table, and that is true in this table.

Figure 1.15

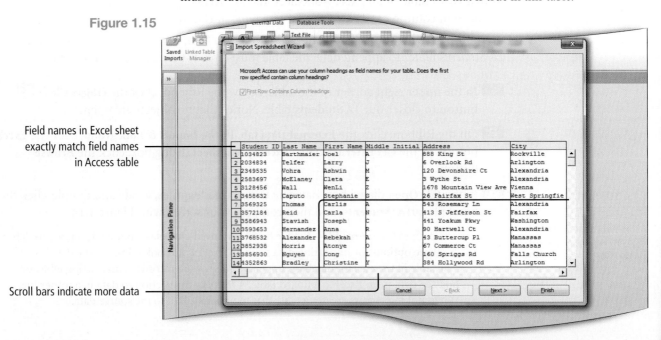

Field names in Excel sheet
exactly match field names
in Access table ———

Scroll bars indicate more data ———

6 In the lower right corner, click **Next**. Notice that the name of your table displays under **Import to Table**. In the lower right corner, click **Finish**.

7 In the **Get External Data - Excel Spreadsheet** dialog box, click **Close**, and then Open [»] the **Navigation Pane**.

8 Point to the right edge of the **Navigation Pane** to display the [↔] pointer. Drag to the right to widen the pane to display the entire table name, and then compare your screen with Figure 1.16.

Figure 1.16

Table in the database

Width of Navigation Pane increased

Another Way

To open an object from the Navigation Pane, right-click the object name, and then on the shortcut menu, click Open.

9 In the **Navigation Pane**, double-click your **1A Students** table to open the table in Datasheet view, and then **Close** [«] the **Navigation Pane**.

10 At the bottom left corner of your screen, locate the navigation area, and notice that there are a total of **26** records in the table—you created three records and imported 23 additional records. Compare your screen with Figure 1.17.

The records from the Excel worksheet display in your table, and the first record is selected. The *navigation area* indicates the number of records in the table and contains controls (arrows) with which you can navigate among the records.

Figure 1.17

Three records you entered

26 total records

Navigation area

Current view indicated

Access | Chapter 1

Objective 3 | Change the Structure of Tables and Add a Second Table

Recall that the structure of a table is the underlying design, including field names and data types. You can create a table or modify a table in Datasheet view. To define and modify fields, many database experts prefer to work in Design view, where you have many additional options for defining the fields in a table.

Activity 1.08 | Deleting a Table Field in Design View

In this activity, you will delete the *Middle Initial* field from the table.

1 Click the **Home tab**, and then in the **Views group**, click the **View button arrow**.

There are four common views in Access, but two that you will use often are Datasheet view and Design view. On the displayed list, Design view is represented by a picture of a pencil, a ruler, and an angle. When one of these four icons is displayed on the View button, clicking the View button will display the table in the view represented by the icon. Datasheet view displays the table data in rows and columns.

2 On the list, click **Design View**, and then compare your screen with Figure 1.18.

Design view displays the underlying design—the structure—of the table and its fields. In Design view, you cannot view the data; you can view only the information about each field's characteristics. Each field name is listed, along with its data type. A column to add a Description—information about the data in the field—is provided.

In the Field Properties area, you can make additional decisions about how each individual field looks and behaves. For example, you can set a specific field size.

Figure 1.18

Delete Rows button

Data Type column

Field Name column

Row selector box for Middle Initial field

Space to add field description

Field Properties area

3 In the **Field Name** column, to the left of **Middle Initial**, point to the row selector box to display the ➡ pointer, and then click one time to select the entire row.

Another Way

Right-click the selected row and click Delete Rows.

4 On the **Design tab**, in the **Tools group**, click the **Delete Rows** button, read the message in the message box, and then click **Yes**.

Deleting a field deletes both the field and its data; you cannot undo this action. Thus, Access prompts you to be sure you want to proceed. If you change your mind after deleting a field, you must add the field back into the table and then reenter the data in that field for every record.

Activity 1.09 | Modifying a Field Size and Adding a Description

Typically, many individuals enter data into a table. For example, at your college many Registration Assistants enter and modify student and course information daily. Two ways to help reduce errors are to restrict what can be typed in a field and to add descriptive information.

1 With your table still displayed in **Design** view, in the **Field Name** column, click anywhere in the **State/Region** field name.

2 In the lower portion of the screen, under **Field Properties**, click **Field Size** to select the text *255*, type **2** and then compare your screen with Figure 1.19.

This action limits the size of the State/Region field to no more than two characters—the size of the two-letter state abbreviations provided by the United States Postal Service. *Field properties* control how the field displays and how data can be entered in the field. You can define properties for every field in the Field Properties area.

The default field size for a text field is 255. Limiting the field size property to 2 ensures that only two characters can be entered for each state. However, this does not prevent someone from entering two characters that are incorrect. Setting the proper data type for the field and limiting the field size are two ways to *help* to reduce errors.

Figure 1.19

State/Region field selected ——

Field Size indicates *2* ——

3 In the **State/Region** row, click in the **Description** box, type **Two-character state abbreviation** and then press ⏎.

> Descriptions for fields in a table are optional. Include a description if the field name does not provide an obvious explanation of the field. Information typed in the description area displays on the left side of the status bar in Datasheet view when the field is active, providing additional information to individuals who are entering data.
>
> When you enter a description for a field, a Property Update Options button displays below the text you typed, which enables you to copy the description for the field to all other database objects that use this table as an underlying source.

4 Click in the **Student ID** field name box. Using the technique you practiced, in the **Field Properties** area, change the **Field Size** to **7**

> By limiting the field size to seven characters, which is the maximum number of characters in a Student ID, you help to ensure the accuracy of the data.

5 In the **Student ID** row, click in the **Description** box, and then type **Seven-digit Student ID number**

6 Click in the **Faculty Advisor ID** field name box. In the **Field Properties** area, change the **Field Size** to **8** In the **Description** box for this field, type **Eight-character ID of faculty member assigned as advisor** and then press ⏎.

7 On the Quick Access Toolbar, click the **Save** button 🖫 to save the design changes to your table, and then notice the message.

> The message indicates that the field size property of one or more fields has changed to a shorter size. If more characters are currently present in the Student ID, State/Region, or Faculty Advisor ID than you have allowed, the data could be *truncated*—cut off or shortened—because the fields were not previously restricted to a specific number of characters.

8 In the message box, click **Yes**.

Activity 1.10 | Viewing a Primary Key in Design View

Primary key refers to the field in the table that uniquely identifies a record. For example, in a college registration database, your Student ID number uniquely identifies you—no other student at the college has your exact student number. In the 1A Students table, the Student ID uniquely identifies each student.

When you create a table using the Blank database command, by default Access designates the first field as the primary key field. It is good database design practice to establish a primary key for every table, because doing so ensures that you do not enter the same record more than once. You can imagine the confusion if another student at your college had the same Student ID number as you do.

1 With your table still displayed in Design view, in the **Field Name** column, click in the **Student ID** box. To the left of the box, notice the small icon of a key, as shown in Figure 1.20.

> Access automatically designates the first field as the primary key field, but you can set any field as the primary key by clicking in the box to the left of the field name, and then clicking the Primary Key button.

Figure 1.20

Primary Key button

Primary Key icon

Property Update Options button

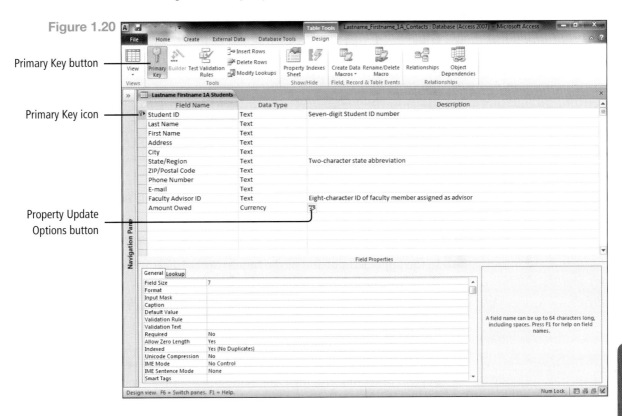

2 On the **Design tab**, in the **Views group**, notice that the **View** button contains a picture of a Datasheet, indicating that clicking the button will return you to Datasheet view. Click the **View** button.

Activity 1.11 | Adding a Second Table to a Database by Importing an Excel Spreadsheet

Many Microsoft Office users track data in an Excel spreadsheet. The sorting and filtering capabilities of Excel are useful for a simple database where all the information resides in one large Excel spreadsheet. However, Excel is limited as a database management tool because it cannot *relate* the information in multiple spreadsheets in a way in which you could ask a question and get a meaningful result. Data in an Excel spreadsheet can easily become an Access table by importing the spreadsheet, because Excel's format of columns and rows is similar to that of an Access table.

1 On the Ribbon, click the **External Data tab**, and then in the **Import & Link group**, click the **Excel** button. In the **Get External Data – Excel Spreadsheet** dialog box, to the right of the **File name** box, click **Browse**.

2 In the **File Open** dialog box, navigate to your student files, and then double-click **a01A_Faculty**. Compare your screen with Figure 1.21.

Access | Chapter 1

Figure 1.21

Get External Data – Excel Spreadsheet dialog box

Browse button

Path to Excel file (yours may differ)

Import option button selected

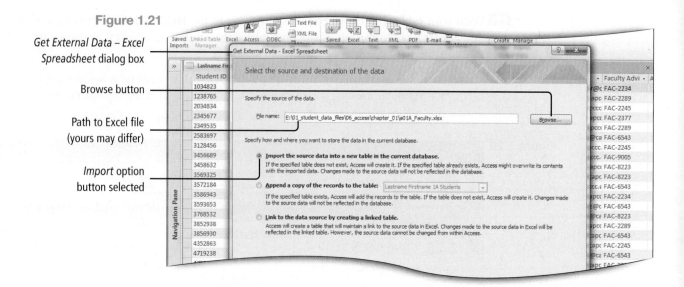

---

3 Be sure that the **Import the source data into a new table in the current database** option button is selected, and then click **OK**.

The Import Spreadsheet Wizard opens and displays the spreadsheet data.

4 In the upper left portion of the **Import Spreadsheet Wizard** dialog box, select the **First Row Contains Column Headings** check box.

The Excel data is framed, indicating that the first row of Excel column titles will become the Access table field names, and the remaining rows will become the individual records in the new Access table.

5 Click **Next**. Notice that the first column—*Faculty ID*—is selected, and in the upper portion of the Wizard, the **Field Name** and the **Data Type** display. Compare your screen with Figure 1.22.

Here you can review and change the field properties for each field (column). You can also identify fields in the spreadsheet that you do not want to import into the Access table by selecting the Do not import field (Skip) check box.

Figure 1.22

Import Spreadsheet Wizard dialog box

Excel column titles

Spreadsheet data—Excel rows become records

Next button

---

6 Click **Next**. In the upper portion of the Wizard, click the **Choose my own primary key** option button, and then be sure that **Faculty ID** displays.

> In the new table, Faculty ID will be the primary key. No two faculty members have the same Faculty ID. By default, Access selects the first field as the primary key, but you can click the arrow to select a different field.

7 Click **Next**. In the **Import to Table** box, type **Lastname Firstname 1A Faculty** and then click **Finish**.

8 In the **Get External Data – Excel Spreadsheet** dialog box, click **Close**, and then **Open** ⟩⟩ the **Navigation Pane**.

9 In the **Navigation Pane**, double-click your **1A Faculty** table to open it in Datasheet view, and then **Close** ⟨⟨ the **Navigation Pane**.

10 Click in the **ZIP/Postal Code** field, and then on the Ribbon, click the **Fields tab**. In the **Formatting group**, change the **Data Type** to **Text**. Compare your screen with Figure 1.23.

> The data from the *a01A_Faculty* worksheet displays in your *1A Faculty* table in the database. The navigation area indicates that there are 30 records in the table. Recall that if a field contains numbers that are not used in calculations, the data type should be set to Text. When you import data from an Excel spreadsheet, check the data types of all fields to ensure they are correct.

Figure 1.23

ZIP/Postal Code data type changed to Text

Table created by importing Excel spreadsheet

Activity 1.12 | Adjusting Column Widths

By using techniques similar to those you use for Excel worksheets, you can adjust the widths of Access fields that display in Datasheet view.

1 In the object window, click the **object tab** for your **1A Students** table.

> Clicking the object tabs along the top of the object window enables you to display open objects to work with them. All of the columns are the same width regardless of the amount of data in the field, the field size that was set, or the length of the field name. If you print the table as currently displayed, some of the data or field names will not fully print until you adjust the column widths.

2 In the field names row, point to the right edge of the **Address** field to display the ⬌ pointer, and then compare your screen with Figure 1.24.

Figure 1.24

Pointer positioned on right edge of Address field

3 With your ⬌ pointer positioned as shown in Figure 1.24, double-click the right edge of the **Address** field.

> The column width of the Address field widens to fully display the longest entry in the field. In this manner, the width of a column can be increased or decreased to fit its contents in the same manner as a column in an Excel worksheet. In Access this is referred to as *Best Fit*.

4 Point to the **Phone Number** field name to display the ↓ pointer, right-click to select the entire column and display a shortcut menu, and then click **Field Width**. In the **Column Width** dialog box, click **Best Fit**.

5 Scroll to the right until the last three fields display. Point to the **E-mail** field name to display the ↓ pointer, hold down the left mouse button, and then drag to the right to select this column, the **Faculty Advisor ID** column, and the **Amount Owed** column. By double-clicking the ⬌ pointer on the right boundary of any of the selected columns, or by displaying the Field Width dialog box from the shortcut menu, apply **Best Fit** to the selected columns.

6 Scroll all the way to the left to view the **Student ID** field. To the left of the *Student ID* field name, click the **Select All** button ▢. Click the **Home tab**, and in the **Records group**, click the **More** button. Click **Field Width**, and in the **Column Width** dialog box, click **Best Fit**. In the first record, scroll to the right as necessary, click in the **Amount Owed** field, and then compare your screen with Figure 1.25.

> In this manner, you can adjust all of the column widths at one time. After applying Best Fit, be sure to click in any field to remove the selection from all of the records; otherwise, the layout changes will not be saved with the table. Adjusting the width of columns does not change the data in the table's records; it changes only the *display* of the data.

Figure 1.25

Select All button

More button

City	State/Region	ZIP/Postal Code	Phone Number	E-mail	Faculty Advisor ID	Amount Owed	Click to Add
Rockville	MD	20857	(301) 555-2320	jbarthmaier@capccc.edu	FAC-2234	$3,210.00	
Alexandria	VA	22336	(571) 555-0234	mfresch@capccc.edu	FAC-2289	$150.00	
Arlington	VA	22226	(571) 555-2017	ltelfer@capccc.edu	FAC-2245	$402.50	
Potomac	MD	20854	(240) 555-0177	jingram@capccc.edu	FAC-2377	$378.50	
Alexandria	VA	22336	(571) 555-0302	avohra@capccc.edu	FAC-2289	$0.00	
Alexandria	VA	22336	(571) 555-0305	cmcelaney@capccc.edu	FAC-6543	$15.15	
Vienna	VA	22180	(703) 555-2329	wwall@capccc.edu	FAC-2245	$0.00	
Fairfax	VA	22030	(703) 555-0192	abass@capccc.edu	FAC-9005	$0.00	
West Springfield	VA	22152	(703) 555-2330	scaputo@capccc.edu	FAC-8223	$0.00	
Alexandria	VA	22334	(703) 555-0301	cthomas@capccc.edu	FAC-8223	$0.00	
Fairfax	VA	22031	(571) 555-2026	creid@capccc.edu	FAC-6543	$1,232.00	
Washington	DC	20262	(202) 555-9360	jstavish@capccc.edu	FAC-2234	$26.25	
Alexandria	VA	22302	(703) 555-0301	ahernandez@capccc.edu	FAC-6543	$896.25	
Manassas	VA		(703) 555-1017	ralexander@capccc.edu	FAC-8223	$0.00	
				amorris@capccc.edu	FAC-2289		

> **Note** | Adjusting Column Widths
>
> If you adjust column widths individually, scroll to the right and scroll down to be sure that all of the data displays in all of the fields. Access adjusts the column widths to fit the screen size based on the displayed data. If data is not displayed on the screen when you adjust a column width, the column may not be adjusted adequately to display all of the data in the field. For that reason, select all of the columns and apply Best Fit to be sure that all of the data displays when scrolling or printing. Click in any field after applying Best Fit to remove the selection, and then save the table before performing other tasks.

7 On the Quick Access Toolbar, click the **Save** button 🖫 to save the table design changes—changing the column widths.

> If you do not save the table after making design changes, Access will prompt you to save when you close the table.

Activity 1.13 | Printing a Table

Although a printed table does not look as professional as a printed report, there are times when you will want to print a table. For example, you may need a quick reference or want to proofread the data that has been entered.

1 On the Ribbon, click the **File tab** to display **Backstage** view, click the **Print** tab, click **Print Preview**, and then compare your screen with Figure 1.26.

Figure 1.26

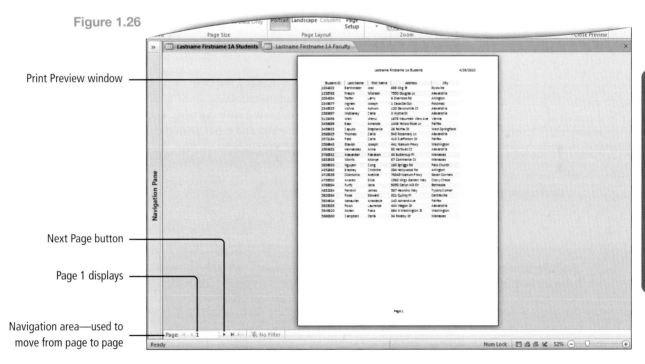

Print Preview window

Navigation Pane

Next Page button

Page 1 displays

Navigation area—used to move from page to page

2 In the lower left corner, click the **Next Page** button ▶ two times. Point to the top of the page to display the 🔍 pointer, click one time to zoom in, and then compare your screen with Figure 1.27.

> The display enlarges, and the Zoom Out pointer displays. The third page of the table displays the last two field columns. The Next Page button is dimmed, indicating there are no more pages. The Previous Page button is darker, indicating that pages exist before this page.

Figure 1.27

Zoom Out pointer

Last two fields display
on a third page

Page 3 displays

Previous page button

Another Way
Click the 🔍 pointer
to zoom back to Fit to
Window view.

▶ ▶ **3** On the Ribbon, in the **Zoom group**, click the **Zoom** button to zoom back to Fit to
Window view.

4 In the **Page Layout group**, click the **Landscape** button. In the navigation area, click
the **Previous Page** button ◀ to display **Page 1**, and then compare your screen
with Figure 1.28.

The orientation of the printout changes, the table name and current date display at the
top of the page, and the page number displays at the bottom. The change in orientation
from portrait to landscape is not saved with the table. Each time you print, you must
check the margins, page orientation, and other print parameters to print as you intend.

Figure 1.28

Landscape button

First page displays in
landscape orientation

Note | Headers and Footers in Access Objects

The headers and footers in Access tables and queries are controlled by default settings; you cannot add additional information or edit the information. The object name displays in the center of the header area with the date on the right—that is why adding your own name to the object name is helpful to identify your paper or electronic results. The page number displays in the center of the footer area. The headers and footers in Access reports and forms, however, are more flexible; you can add to and edit the information.

5 On the **Print Preview tab**, in the **Print group**, click the **Print** button. In the **Print** dialog box, under **Print Range**, verify that the **All** option button is selected. Under **Copies**, verify that the **Number of Copies** is **1**. Compare your screen with Figure 1.29.

Figure 1.29

Print dialog box

Default printer (yours may differ)

One copy

Print all pages

6 Determine how your instructor wants you to submit your work for this project—on paper or electronically. If submitting electronically, determine if, in addition to submitting your Access database, you are to create and submit electronic printouts of individual database objects.

7 To print on paper, in the **Print** dialog box, click **OK**, and then in the **Close Preview group**, click the **Close Print Preview** button. This printout will have two pages. To create an electronic PDF printout of this table object, in the Print dialog box, click Cancel, and then follow the steps in the following Note—or follow the specific directions provided by your instructor.

Note | To Create a PDF Electronic Printout of an Access Object

Display the object (table, report, and so on) in Print Preview and adjust margins and orientation as desired. On the Print Preview tab, in the Data group, click the PDF or XPS button. In the Publish as PDF or XPS dialog box, navigate to your chapter folder. Use the default file name, or follow your instructor's directions to name the object. In the lower right corner, click Publish—the default setting is PDF. If necessary, close the Adobe Acrobat/Reader window and the Export-PDF dialog box. Click the Close Print Preview button; your electronic printout is saved.

8 At the far right edge of the object window, click the **Close Object** button ☒ to close the **1A Students** table.

9 With your **1A Faculty** table displayed, to the left of the **Faculty ID** field name, click the **Select All** button ☐ to select all of the columns. On the **Home tab**, in the **Records group**, click the **More** button. Click **Field Width**, and in the **Column Width** dialog box, click **Best Fit**. Click in any field in the table to remove the selection, and then **Save** 🖫 the table.

Access | Chapter 1

10 Display the table in **Print Preview**. Change the **Orientation** to **Landscape**. If directed to do so by your instructor, create a paper or electronic printout, and then **Close Print Preview**—two pages result.

11 Click the **Close Object** button [×].

All of your database objects—the *1A Students* table and the *1A Faculty* table—are closed; the object window is empty.

Objective 4 | Create and Use a Query, Form, and Report

A *query* is a database object that retrieves specific data from one or more database objects—either tables or other queries—and then, in a single datasheet, displays only the data that you specify. Because the word *query* means *to ask a question*, think of a query as a question formed in a manner that Access can answer.

A *form* is an Access object with which you can enter data, edit data, or display data from a table or a query. In a form, the fields are laid out in an attractive format on the screen, which makes working with the database easier for those who must enter and look up data.

A *report* is a database object that displays the fields and records from a table or a query in an easy-to-read format suitable for printing. Create reports to *summarize* information in a database in a professional-looking manner.

Activity 1.14 | Using the Simple Query Wizard to Create a Query

A *select query* is one type of Access query. A select query, also called a *simple select query*, retrieves (selects) data from one or more tables or queries and then displays the selected data in a datasheet. A select query creates subsets of data to answer specific questions; for example, *Which students live in Arlington, VA?*

The objects from which a query selects its data are referred to as the query's *data source*. In this activity, you will create a simple select query using a *wizard*. A wizard is a feature in Microsoft Office programs that walks you step by step through a process. The process involves choosing the data source, and then indicating the fields you want to include in the query result. The query—the question that you want to ask—is *What is the name, complete mailing address, and Student ID of every student?*

1 Click the **Create tab**, and then in the **Queries group**, click the **Query Wizard** button. In the **New Query** dialog box, click **Simple Query Wizard**, and then click **OK**. Compare your screen with Figure 1.30.

Figure 1.30

*Simple Query
Wizard* dialog box

Tables/Queries arrow

Add Field button

No database objects
display in object
window—all are closed

2 Click the **Tables/Queries arrow**, and then click your **Table: 1A Students**.

To create a query, first choose the data source—the object from which to select data. The name and complete mailing address of every student is stored in the 1A Students table, so this table will be your data source.

3 Under **Available Fields**, click **Student ID**, and then click the **Add Field** button ▶ to move the field to the **Selected Fields** list on the right. Point to the **Last Name** field, and then double-click to add the field to the **Selected Fields** list.

Use either method to add fields to the Selected Fields list. Fields can be added in any order.

4 By using the **Add Field** button ▶ or by double-clicking the field name, add the following fields to the **Selected Fields** list: **First Name**, **Address**, **City**, **State/Region**, and **ZIP/Postal Code**. Compare your screen with Figure 1.31.

Choosing these seven fields will answer the question, *What is the Student ID, name, and address of every student?*

Figure 1.31

Data source—1A
Students table

Seven fields added to
Selected Fields list

Next button

5 Click **Next**. In the **Simple Query Wizard** dialog box, click in the **What title do you want for your query?** box. Edit as necessary so that the query name, using your own last and first name, is **Lastname Firstname 1A All Students Query** and then compare your screen with Figure 1.32.

Access | Chapter 1

Figure 1.32

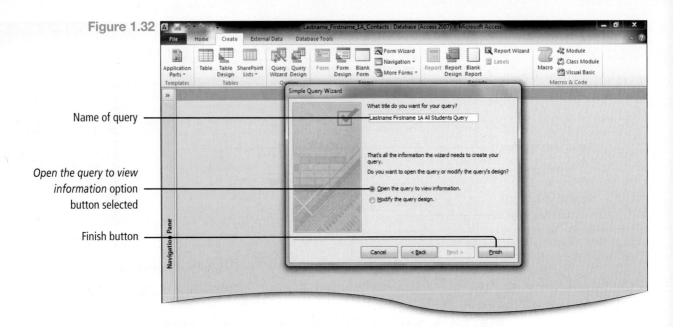

Name of query

Open the query to view
information option
button selected

Finish button

6 Click **Finish**.

Access *runs* the query—performs the actions indicated in your query design by searching the records in the data source you selected, and then finding the records that match specified criteria. The records that match the criteria display in a datasheet. A select query *selects*—pulls out and displays—*only* the information from the data source that you requested, including the specified fields.

In the object window, Access displays every student record in Datasheet view, but displays *only* the seven fields that you moved to the Selected Fields list in the Simple Query Wizard dialog box.

7 If necessary, apply Best Fit to the columns and then Save the query. Display the query in **Print Preview**. Change the **Orientation** to **Landscape**, and then create a paper or electronic printout as instructed. **Close** the **Print Preview**.

8 In the object window, click the **Close Object** button ☒ to close the query.

Activity 1.15 | Creating and Printing a Form

One type of Access form displays only one record in the database at a time. Such a form is useful not only to the individual who performs the data entry—typing in the actual records—but also to anyone who has the job of viewing information in a database. For example, when you visit the Records office at your college to obtain a transcript, someone displays your record on a screen. For the viewer, it is much easier to look at one record at a time, using a form, than to look at all of the student records in the database table.

The Form command on the Ribbon creates a form that displays all of the *fields* from the underlying data source (table)—one record at a time. You can use this new form immediately, or you can modify it. Records that you create or edit in a form are automatically added to or updated in the underlying table or tables.

1 **Open** ⟫ the **Navigation Pane**. Increase the width of the **Navigation Pane** so that all object names display fully. Notice that a table displays a datasheet icon, and a query displays an icon of two overlapping datasheets. Right-click your **1A Students** table to display a menu as shown in Figure 1.33.

Figure 1.33

Navigation Pane Close button

Table icon

1A Students table

Query icon

Shortcut menu

2 On the shortcut menu, click **Open** to display the table in the object window, and then **Close** ⟪ the **Navigation Pane** to maximize your object space.

3 Scroll to the right, and notice that there are 11 fields in the table. On the **Create tab**, in the **Forms group**, click the **Form** button. Compare your screen with Figure 1.34.

> Access creates a form based on the currently selected object—the 1A Students table. Access creates the form in a simple top-to-bottom format, with all 11 fields in the record lined up in a single column.

> The form displays in *Layout view*—the Access view in which you can make changes to a form or to a report while the object is open. Each field displays the data for the first student record in the table—*Joel Barthmaier*.

Figure 1.34

Form object icon

First record, for *Joel Barthmaier*, displays

Layout View button active

Next record button

Total number of records is 26

Navigation buttons to move among records

Access | Chapter 1

4 At the right edge of the status bar, notice that the **Layout View** button ▣ is active, indicating that the form is displayed in Layout view.

Another Way

On the Home tab, in the Views group, click the View button, which displays an icon of a form.

5 At the right edge of the status bar, click the **Form View** button ▦.

In *Form view*, you can view the records, but you cannot change the layout or design of the form.

6 In the navigation area, click the **Next record** button ▶ three times. The fourth record—for *Joseph Ingram*—displays.

You can use the navigation buttons to scroll among the records to display any single record.

7 **Save** 🖫 the form with the default name—*Lastname Firstname 1A Students*. Along the left edge of the record, under ▶, click anywhere in the narrow gray bar—the *record selector bar*—to select only the record for *Joseph Ingram*. Notice that the bar turns black, indicating that the record is selected.

8 To print the form for *Joseph Ingram* only, click the **File tab**, and then click **Print**—do *not* display Print Preview. Instead, click **Print**. In the **Print** dialog box, in the lower left corner, click **Setup**. Click the **Columns tab**, change the **Width** to **7.5** so that the form prints on one page, and then click **OK**. The maximum column width that you can enter is dependent upon the printer that is installed on your system. In the lower left corner of the **Print** dialog box, click the **Selected Record(s)** option button, and then click **OK**.

> **Note** | To Print a Single Form in PDF
>
> To create a PDF electronic printout of a single record in a form, change the column width to 7.5 as described in step 8 above, and then in the Print dialog box, click Cancel. On the left edge of the form, click the Record Selector bar so that it is black—selected. On the Ribbon click the External Data tab. In the Export group, click the PDF or XPS button. Navigate to your chapter folder, and then in the lower left corner of the dialog box, if necessary, select the Open file after publishing check box. In the lower right corner of the dialog box, click the Options button. In the Options dialog box, under Range, click the Selected records option button, click OK, and then click Publish. Close the Adobe Reader or Acrobat window.

9 **Close** ☒ the form. Notice that your **1A Students** table remains open.

Activity 1.16 | Creating, Modifying, and Printing a Report

1 **Open** ⟫ the **Navigation Pane**, and then open your **1A Faculty** table by double-clicking the table name or by right-clicking and clicking Open from the shortcut menu. **Close** ⟪ the **Navigation Pane**.

2 Click the **Create tab**, and then in the **Reports group**, click the **Report** button.

When you click the Report button, Access generates the report in Layout view and includes all of the fields and all of the records in the table, and does so in a format suitable for printing. Dotted lines indicate how the report would break across pages if you print it. In Layout view, you can make quick changes to the report layout.

Another Way

Right-click the field. From the shortcut menu, click Select Entire Column, and then press Del.

3 Click the **Faculty ID** field name, and then on the Ribbon, click the **Arrange tab**. In the **Rows & Columns group**, click the **Select Column** button, and then press Del. Using the same technique, delete the **Rank** field.

The Faculty ID and Rank fields and data are deleted, and the report readjusts the fields.

4 Click the **Address** field name, and then use the scroll bar at the bottom of the screen to scroll to the right to display the **Mobile Phone** field; be careful not to click in the report. Hold down Shift and then click the **Mobile Phone** field name to select all of the fields from *Address* through *Mobile Phone*. With all the field names selected— surrounded by a colored border—in the **Row & Columns group**, click the **Select Column** button, and then press Del.

Use this technique to select and delete multiple columns in Layout view.

5 Scroll to the left, and notice that you can see all of the remaining fields. In any record, click in the **E-mail** field. Point to the right edge of the field box to display the ↔ pointer. Drag to the right slightly to increase the width of the field so that all E-mail addresses display on one line.

6 Click the **Last Name** field name. On the Ribbon, click the **Home tab**. In the **Sort & Filter group**, click the **Ascending** button. Compare your screen with Figure 1.35.

By default, tables are sorted in ascending order by the primary key field, which is the Faculty ID field. You can change the default and sort any field in either ascending order or descending order. The sort order does not change in the underlying table, only in the report.

Figure 1.35

Ascending button selected

Four fields display in report

Report sorted by Last Name field

E-mail addresses display on one line

7 Click the **Save** button 📄. In the **Report Name** box, add **Report** to the end of the suggested name, and then click **OK**.

8 Display the report in **Print Preview**. In the **Zoom group**, click the **Two Pages** button, and then compare your screen with Figure 1.36.

The report will print on two pages because the page number at the bottom of the report is located beyond the right margin of the report.

Figure 1.36

Two Pages button

Page number at bottom of second page

Access | Chapter 1

9 In the **Close Preview group**, click the **Close Print Preview button**. Scroll down to the bottom of the report, and then scroll to the right to display the page number. Click the page number—**Page 1 of 1**—and then press ⌊Del⌋.

10 Display the report in **Print Preview** and notice that the report will print on one page. In the **Zoom group**, click the **One Page** button. **Save** 🖫 the changes to the design of the report, and then create a paper or electronic printout as instructed. At the right end of the Ribbon, click the **Close Print Preview** button.

> The default margins of a report created with the Report tool are 0.25 inch. Some printers require a greater margin so your printed report may result in two pages—you will learn to adjust this later. Also, if a printer is not installed on your system, the report may print on two pages.

11 Along the top of the object window, right-click any object tab, and then click **Close All** to close all of the open objects and leave the object window empty.

Objective 5 | Save and Close a Database

When you close an Access table, any changes made to the records are saved automatically. If you change the design of the table or change the layout of the Datasheet view, such as adjusting the column widths, you will be prompted to save the design changes. At the end of your Access session, close your database and exit Access. If the Navigation Pane is open when you close Access, it will display when you reopen the database.

Activity 1.17 | Closing and Saving a Database

1 **Open** » the **Navigation Pane**. Notice that your report object displays with a green report icon. Compare your screen with Figure 1.37.

Figure 1.37

Navigation Pane open (your selected object may differ)

Two tables

One query

One form

One report

All objects closed—object window empty

Another Way

In the upper right corner of the window, click the Close button.

2 Display **Backstage** view, click **Close Database**, and then click **Exit**. As directed by your instructor, submit your database and the five paper or electronic printouts—two tables, one query, one form, and one report—that are the results of this project.

End You have completed Project 1A _____

Project 1B Student Workshops Database

Project Activities

In Activities 1.18 through 1.23, you will assist Dr. Kirsten McCarty, Vice President of Student Services, by creating a database to store information about student workshops presented by Capital Cities Community College. You will use a database template that tracks event information, add workshop information to the database, and then print the results. Your completed report and table will look similar to Figure 1.38.

Project Files

For Project 1B, you will need the following files:

> New Access database using the Events template
> a01B_Workshops (Excel workbook)

You will save your database as:

> Lastname_Firstname_1B_Student_Workshops

Project Results

Figure 1.38
Project 1B Student Workshops

Objective 6 | Create a Database Using a Template

A *database template* contains pre-built tables, queries, forms, and reports to perform a specific task, such as tracking a large number of events. For example, your college may hold events such as athletic contests, plays, lectures, concerts, and club meetings. Using a predefined template, your college Activities Director can quickly create a database to manage these events. The advantage of using a template to start a new database is that you do not have to create the objects—all you need to do is enter your data and modify the pre-built objects to suit your needs.

The purpose of the database in this project is to track the student workshops offered by Capital Cities Community College. The questions to be answered might include:

What workshops will be offered and when will they be offered?

In what rooms and campus locations will the workshops be held?

Which workshop locations have a computer projector for PowerPoint presentations?

Activity 1.18 | Creating a New Database Using a Template

1 **Start** Access. Under **Available Templates**, click **Sample templates**. If necessary, scroll down to locate and then click **Events**. Compare your screen with Figure 1.39.

Sample templates are stored on your computer; they are included with the Access program.

Figure 1.39

2 On the right side of the screen, to the right of the **File Name** box, click the **Browse** button, and then navigate to your **Access Chapter 1** folder.

3 At the bottom of the **File New Database** dialog box, select the text in the **File name** box. Using your own name, type **Lastname_Firstname_1B_Student_Workshops** and then press Enter.

4 In the lower right corner of your screen, click the **Create** button.

> Access creates the *1B Student Workshops* database, and the database name displays in the title bar. A predesigned *form*—Event List—displays in the object window. Although you can enter events for any date, when you open the database in the future, the Event List will display only those events for the current date and future dates.

5 Under the Ribbon, on the **Message Bar**, a Security Warning displays. On the **Message Bar**, click the **Enable Content** button.

> Databases provided by Microsoft are safe to use on your computer.

Activity 1.19 | Building a Table by Entering Records in a Multiple Items Form

The purpose of a form is to simplify the entry of data into a table—either for you or for others who enter data. In Project 1A, you created a simple form that enabled you to display or enter records in a table one record at a time. The Events template creates a *Multiple Items form*, a form that enables you to display or enter *multiple* records in a table, but still with an easier and simplified layout than typing directly into the table itself.

1 Click in the first empty **Title** field. Type **Your Cyber Reputation** and then press Tab. In the **Start Time** field, type **3/9/16 7p** and then press Tab.

> Access formats the date and time. As you enter dates and times, a small calendar displays to the right of the field, which you can click to select a date instead of typing.

2 In the **End Time** field, type **3/9/16 9p** and then press Tab. In the **Description** field, type **Internet Safety** and then press Tab. In the **Location** field, type **Jefferson Campus** and then press Tab three times to move to the **Title** field in the new record row. Compare your screen with Figure 1.40.

> Because the workshops have no unique value, Access uses the AutoNumber data type of the ID field to assign a unique, sequential number to each record. In the navigation area, each record is identified as a task, rather than a record or page.

Figure 1.40

Multiple items form named as *Event List*

AutoNumber data type creates a unique number

First record entered

Total line displays by default

Access formats date and time

3 Directly above the field names row, click **New Event**.

> A *single-record form* displays, similar to the simple form you created in Project 1A. A single-record form enables you to display or enter one record at a time into a table.

4 Using Tab to move from field to field, enter the following record—press Tab three times to move from the **End Time** field to the **Description** field. Compare your screen with Figure 1.41.

Title	Location	Start Time	End Time	Description
Writing a Research Paper	**Washington Campus**	**3/10/16 4p**	**3/10/16 6p**	**Computer Skills**

Figure 1.41

Save and New button

New Event button

Single-record form

Close button

5 In the upper right corner of the single-record form, click **Close**, and notice that the new record displays in the Multiple Items form.

6 Using either the rows on the Multiple Items form or the New Event single-record form, enter the following records, and then compare your screen with Figure 1.42.

ID	Title	Start Time	End Time	Description	Location
3	**Resume Writing**	**3/18/16 2p**	**3/18/16 4p**	**Job Skills**	**Capital Campus**
4	**Careers in the Legal Profession**	**3/19/16 2p**	**3/19/16 4p**	**Careers**	**Central Campus**

Alert! | Does a Single Record Form Open?

In the Multiple Items form, pressing Enter three times at the end of a row to begin a new record may display the single-record New Event form. If you prefer to use the Multiple Items form, close the single-record form and continue entering records, using the Tab key to move from field to field.

Figure 1.42

Four records entered in form

7 In the upper right corner of the object window, click **Close** ✕ to close the **Event List** form.

8 On the Ribbon, click the **External Data tab**. In the **Import & Link group**, click the **Excel** button.

Recall that you can populate a table by importing data from an Excel workbook.

9 In the **Get External Data – Excel Spreadsheet** dialog box, click the **Browse** button. Navigate to your student files, and then double-click **a01B_Workshops**.

10 Click the second option button—**Append a copy of the records to the table**—and then click **OK**.

11 Click **Next**, click **Finish**, and then **Close** the dialog box.

12 **Open** ⏵ the **Navigation Pane**. Double-click **Event List** to open the form that displays data stored in the Events table, and then **Close** ⏴ the **Navigation Pane**.

13 To the left of the **ID** field name, click the **Select All** button ☐ to select all of the columns.

Another Way

With the columns selected, in the field heading row, point to the right edge of any of the selected columns, and then double-click to apply Best Fit to all of the selected columns.

14 In the field names row, point to any of the selected field names, right-click, and then click **Field Width**. In the **Column Width** dialog box, click **Best Fit**. Notice that the widths of all of the columns are adjusted to accommodate the longest entry in the column.

15 In the first record, click in the **Title** field to deselect the columns. **Save** 🖫 the form, and then compare your screen with Figure 1.43.

Eight additional records display—those imported from the a01B_Workshops Excel workbook.

Access | Chapter 1

Figure 1.43

Eight additional records imported from an Excel workbook

Objective 7 | Organize Objects in the Navigation Pane

Use the Navigation Pane to organize database objects, to open them, and to perform common tasks like renaming an object.

Activity 1.20 | Organizing Database Objects in the Navigation Pane

The Navigation Pane groups and displays your database objects and can do so in predefined arrangements. In this activity, you will group your database objects using the *Tables and Related Views* category, which groups objects by the table to which they are related. This grouping is useful because you can easily determine the data source table of queries, forms, and reports.

1 **Open** 》 the **Navigation Pane**. At the top of the **Navigation Pane**, click the **Navigation arrow** ▾. In the list, under **Navigate To Category**, click **Tables and Related Views**.

2 Confirm that *Events* displays in the bar under the Search box at the top of the **Navigation Pane**. Compare your screen with Figure 1.44.

The icons to the left of the objects listed in the Navigation Pane indicate that the Events template created a number of objects for you—among them, one table titled *Events*, one query, two forms, and five reports. The Event List Multiple Items form, which is currently displayed in the object window, is included in the Navigation Pane. All of the objects were created using the underlying data source, which is the Events table.

Figure 1.44

One table
One query
Two forms
Five reports

Another Way

Double-click the table name to open it in the object window.

3 In the **Navigation Pane**, point to the **Events** *table*, right-click, and then click **Open**.

The Events table is the active object in the object window. Use the Navigation Pane to open objects for use. The 12 records that you entered using the Multiple Items *form* and by importing from an Excel workbook display in the *table*. Tables are the foundation of your database because your data must be stored in a table. You can enter records directly into a table or you can use a form to enter records.

4 In the object window, click the **Event List tab** to bring the form into view and make it the active object.

Recall that a form presents a more user-friendly screen for entering records into a table.

Another Way

Double-click the report name to open it.

5 In the **Navigation Pane**, right-click the *report* (green icon) named **Current Events**, and then click **Open**. Compare your screen with Figure 1.45.

An advantage of using a template to begin a database is that many objects, such as attractively formatted reports, are already designed for you.

Figure 1.45

Three open objects

Current Events report preformatted and designed by the template

Current Events report in Navigation Pane

6 In the object window, **Close** ✕ the **Current Events** report.

7 From the **Navigation Pane**, open the **Events By Week** report.

In this predesigned report, the events are displayed by week. After entering records in the form or table, the preformatted reports are updated with the records from the table.

8 **Close** ✕ the **Events By Week** report, and then **Close** ✕ the remaining two open objects. **Close** « the **Navigation Pane**.

Access | Chapter 1

Objective 8 | Create a New Table in a Database Created with a Template

The Events database template created only one table—the *Events* table. Although the database was started from a template and contains other objects, you can add additional objects as needed.

Activity 1.21 | Creating a New Table and Changing Its Design

Dr. McCarty has information about the various locations where workshops are held. For example, for the Jefferson campus, she has information about the room, seating arrangements, number of seats, and audio-visual equipment. In the Events table, workshops are scheduled in rooms at each of the four campuses. It would not make sense to store information about the campus rooms multiple times in the same table. It is *not* considered good database design to have duplicate information in a table.

When data in a table becomes redundant, it is usually an indication that you need a new table to contain the information about the topic. In this activity, you will create a table to track the workshop locations and the equipment and seating arrangements in each location.

1 On the Ribbon, click the **Create tab**. In the **Tables group**, click the **Table** button.

2 Click the **Click to Add arrow**, click **Text**, type **Campus/Location** and then press Enter.

3 In the third column, click **Text**, type **Room** and then press Enter. In the fourth column, click **Text**, type **Seats** and then press Enter. In the fifth column, click **Text**, type **Room Arrangement** and then press Enter. In the sixth column, click **Text**, type **Equipment** and then press ↓.

The table has six fields. Access creates the first field in the table—the ID field—to ensure that every record has a unique value.

4 Right-click the **ID** field name, and then click **Rename Field**. Type **Room ID** and then press Enter. On the **Fields tab**, in the **Formatting group**, click the **Data Type arrow**, and then click **Text**. In the **Field Validation group**, notice that **Unique** is selected.

Recall that, by default, Access creates the ID field with the AutoNumber data type so that the field can be used as the primary key. Here, this field will store a unique room ID that is a combination of letters, symbols, and numbers, so it is appropriate to change the data type to Text. In Datasheet view, the primary key field is identified by the selection of the Unique check box.

5 In the new record row, click in the **Room ID** field, type **JEFF-01** and then press Tab. In the **Campus/Location** field, type **Jefferson Campus** and then press Tab. In the **Room** field, type **J123** and then press Tab. In the **Seats** field, type **150** and then press Tab. In the **Room Arrangement** field, type **Theater** and then press Tab. In the **Equipment** field, type **Computer Projector, Surround Sound, & Microphones** and then press Tab to move to the new record row. Compare your screen with Figure 1.46.

> Recall that Access saves the record when you move to another row within the table. You can press either Tab or Enter to move to another field in a table.

Figure 1.46

New table

Renamed field

First record entered

Room ID field assigned data type of *Text*

Selected field—Room ID—indicated as primary key field

6 In the **Views group**, click the **View** button to switch to **Design** view. In the **Save As** dialog box, save the table as **Lastname Firstname 1B Workshop Locations** and then click **OK**.

7 In the **Field Name** column, to the left of the **Room ID** box, notice the key icon.

> In Design view, the key icon indicates the field—Room ID—that is identified as the primary key.

8 In the **Views group**, click the **View** button to switch to **Datasheet** view.

9 Enter the following records in the table:

Room ID	Campus/Location	Room	Seats	Room Arrangement	Equipment
WASH-01	**Washington Campus**	**A15**	**35**	**Lecture/Classroom**	**Computer Projector**
CAP-01	**Capital Campus**	**C202**	**50**	**Lecture/Classroom**	**Smart Board**
CEN-01	**Central Campus**	**H248**	**20**	**U-shaped**	**White Board**
JEFF-02	**Jefferson Campus**	**A15**	**25**	**U-shaped**	**25 Computers, Projector**

10 To the left of the **Room ID** field name, click the **Select All** button ☐ to select all of the columns. On the **Home tab**, in the **Records group**, click the **More** button. Click **Field Width**, and in the **Column Width** dialog box, click **Best Fit**. Click in any field to remove the selection, and then **Save** 🖫 the changes to the table. In the object window, **Close** ✕ the **1B Workshop Locations** table.

11 **Open** » the **Navigation Pane**, and then locate the name of your new table. Point to the right edge of the **Navigation Pane** to display the ⬌ pointer. Drag to the right to display the entire table name, and then compare your screen with Figure 1.47.

> Recall that as currently arranged, the Navigation Pane organizes the objects by Tables and Related Views. In Figure 1.47, the Events table is listed first, followed by its related objects, and then the Workshop Locations table is listed. In its current view, the tables are sorted in ascending order by name; therefore, your table may be listed before the Events table depending on your last name.

Figure 1.47

Navigation Pane width increased

Section for Events table and related objects

Section for Workshop Locations table and related objects (your section and table location may differ)

New table

Objective 9 | Print a Report and a Table in a Database Created with a Template

Recall that an advantage to starting a new database with a template, instead of from a blank database, is that many report objects are already created for you.

Activity 1.22 | Viewing and Printing a Report

1 From the **Navigation Pane**, open the **Event Details** *report* (not the form).

The pre-built Event Details report displays in an attractively arranged format.

2 **Close** ⊠ the **Event Details** report. Open the **All Events** report. In the lower right corner of the status bar, click the **Layout View** button ⊞. At the top of the report, click on the text *All Events* to display a colored border, and then click to the left of the letter *A* to place the insertion point there. Using your own name, type **Lastname Firstname** and then press Spacebar. Press Enter, and then **Save** 🖫 the report.

Each report displays the records in the table in different useful formats.

Another Way

Right-click the object tab, and then click Print Preview.

3 Display **Backstage** view, click **Print**, and then click **Print Preview**. In the navigation area, notice that the navigation arrows are dimmed, which indicates that this report will print on one page.

4 Create a paper or electronic printout as instructed, **Close Print Preview**, and then **Close** ⊠ the report.

Activity 1.23 | Printing a Table

When printing a table, use the Print Preview command to determine if the table will print on one page or if you need to adjust column widths, margins, or the orientation. Recall that there will be occasions when you want to print a table for a quick reference or for proofreading. For a more professional-looking format, and for more options to format the output, create and print a report.

1 From the **Navigation Pane**, open your **1B Workshop Locations** table. **Close** [«] the **Navigation Pane**. Display **Backstage** view, click **Print**, and then click **Print Preview**.

> The table displays in the Print Preview window, showing how it will look when it is printed. The name of the table and the date the table is printed display at the top of the page. The navigation area displays *1* in the Pages box, and the right-pointing arrow—the Next Page arrow—is active. Recall that when a table is in the Print Preview window, the navigation arrows are used to navigate from one page to the next, rather than from one record to the next.

2 In the navigation area, click the **Next Page** button [▸].

> The second page of the table displays the last field column. Whenever possible, try to print all of the fields horizontally on one page. Of course, if there are many records, more than one page may be needed to print all of the records.

3 On the **Print Preview tab**, in the **Page Layout group**, click the **Landscape** button, and then compare your screen with Figure 1.48. Notice that the entire table will print on one page.

Figure 1.48

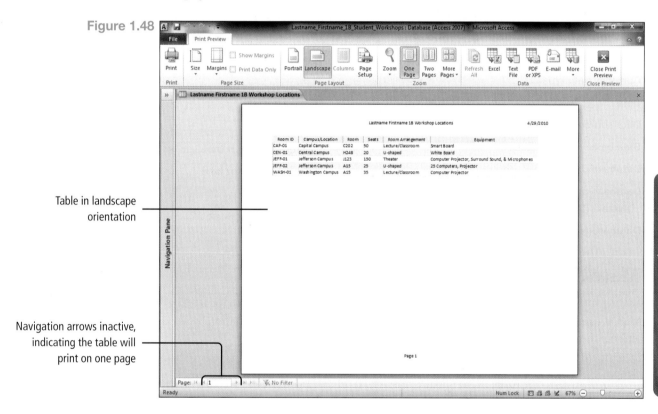

Table in landscape orientation

Navigation arrows inactive, indicating the table will print on one page

4 Create a paper or electronic printout if instructed to do so, and then **Close Print Preview**.

5 **Close** [✕] the **1B Workshop Locations** table. For the convenience of the next person opening the database, **Open** [»] the **Navigation Pane**. In **Backstage** view, click **Close Database**, and then click **Exit** to close the Access program. As directed by your instructor, submit your database and the two paper or electronic printouts—one report and one table—that are the results of this project.

End **You have completed Project 1B** ——————————

Summary

Microsoft Access 2010 is a database management system that uses various objects—tables, forms, queries, reports—to organize information. Data is stored in tables in which you establish fields, set the data type and field size, and create a primary key. Data from a database can be reported and printed.

Key Terms

Append 61	Datasheet view 56	Multiple Items form 83	Run 76
AutoNumber data type 58	DBMS 51	Navigation area 63	Second principle of good database design 52
Best Fit 70	Design view 56	Navigation Pane 56	Select query 74
Blank database................53	Destination table 62	Normalization 52	Simple select query 74
Caption 58	Field.................................51	Object window 56	Single-record form..........84
Common field 52	Field properties 65	Objects 53	Source file.......................61
Currency data type..........57	First principle of good database design 52	Populate 59	Structure 56
Data 51	Flat database 51	Primary key.....................66	Table 51
Data source 74	Form 74	Query...............................74	Tables and Related Views 86
Data type..........................56	Form view 78	Record..............................51	Text data type 57
Database...........................51	Import 61	Record selector bar 78	Truncated 66
Database management system (DBMS) 51	Information 51	Record selector box 59	Wizard 74
Database template..........52	Layout view......................77	Redundant 52	
	Link 61	Relational database 51	
		Report 74	

Matching

Match each term in the second column with its correct definition in the first column by writing the letter of the term on the blank line in front of the correct definition.

_____ 1. An organized collection of facts about people, events, things, or ideas related to a specific topic.

_____ 2. Facts about people, events, things, or ideas.

_____ 3. Data that is organized in a useful manner.

_____ 4. A simple database file that is not related or linked to any other collection of data.

_____ 5. The database object that stores the data, and which is the foundation of an Access database.

_____ 6. A table row that contains all of the categories of data pertaining to one person, place, thing, event, or idea.

_____ 7. A single piece of information that is stored in every record and represented by a column in a table.

_____ 8. A principle stating that data is organized in tables so that there is no redundant data.

_____ 9. A principle stating that techniques are used to ensure the accuracy of data entered into a table.

A Common field

B Data

C Database

D Field

E First principle of good database design

F Flat database

G Information

H Navigation Pane

I Normalization

J Object window

K Objects

L Populate

M Record

N Second principle of good database design

O Table

_____ 10. The process of applying design rules and principles to ensure that a database performs as expected.

_____ 11. A field in one or more tables that stores the same data.

_____ 12. The basic parts of a database; for example tables, forms, queries, and reports.

_____ 13. The window area that organizes the database objects and from which you open objects.

_____ 14. The window area that displays each open object on its own tab.

_____ 15. The action of filling a database with records.

Multiple Choice

Circle the correct answer.

1. The Access view that displays data in columns and rows like an Excel worksheet is:
   A. Datasheet view   B. Design view   C. Layout view

2. The characteristic that defines the kind of data you can enter into a field is the:
   A. data source   B. data type   C. field property

3. The box at the left of a record in Datasheet view that you click to select an entire record is the:
   A. link   B. navigation area   C. record selector box

4. To add on to the end of an object, such as to add records to the end of an existing table, is to:
   A. append   B. import   C. run

5. Characteristics of a field that control how the field displays and how data is entered are:
   A. data sources   B. data types   C. field properties

6. The field that uniquely identifies a record in a table is known as the:
   A. attachments field   B. common field   C. primary key

7. The underlying design of a table is referred to as the:
   A. caption   B. source file   C. structure

8. The object that retrieves specific data and then displays only the data that you specify is a:
   A. form   B. query   C. report

9. The object that displays fields and records from a table or query in a printable format is a:
   A. form   B. query   C. report

10. Information repeated in a database in a manner that indicates poor design is said to be:
    A. relational   B. redundant   C. truncated

Access | Chapter 1

Apply **1A** skills from these Objectives:

1 Identify Good Database Design

2 Create a Table and Define Fields in a New Database

3 Change the Structure of Tables and Add a Second Table

4 Create and Use a Query, Form, and Report

5 Save and Close a Database

Skills Review | Project **1C** Work Study Students Database

In the following Skills Review, you will create a database to store information about the Work Study students and the divisions in which they are employed. Your completed database objects will look similar to Figure 1.49.

Project Files

For Project 1C, you will need the following files:

New blank Access database
a01C_Student_Workers (Excel workbook)
a01C_Divisions (Excel workbook)

You will save your database as:

Lastname_Firstname_1C_Student_Workers

Project Results

Figure 1.49

(Project 1C Work Study Students Database continues on the next page)

Content-Based Assessments

Skills Review | Project 1C Work Study Students Database (continued)

1 **Start** Access. Click **Blank database**, and then in the lower right corner, click the **Browse** button. In the **File New Database** dialog box, navigate to your **Access Chapter 1** folder, and then in the **File name** box, replace the existing text with **Lastname_Firstname_1C_Student_Workers** Press Enter, and then in the lower right corner, click **Create**.

  a. **Close** the **Navigation Pane**. Click in the text *Click to Add*. Click **Text**, type **Last Name** and then press Enter.

  b. In the third field name box, click **Text**, type **First Name** and then press Enter. In the fourth field name box, click **Text**, type **Middle Initial** and then press Enter. Create the remaining fields as shown in **Table 1**, pressing Enter after the last field name.

  c. Scroll as necessary to view the first field. Click the **ID** field name. In the **Properties group**, click the **Name & Caption** button. In the **Enter Field Properties** dialog box, in the **Name** box, change *ID* to **Student ID** and then click **OK**. In the **Formatting group**, click the **Data Type arrow**, and then click **Text**.

  d. In the first record row, click in the **Student ID** field, type **3512784** and press Enter. In the **Last Name** field, type **Elkington** In the **First Name** field, type **Susan** In the **Middle Initial** field, type **A** In the **Address** field, type **185 Kevin Ln**

  e. Continue entering data in the fields as shown in **Table 2**, pressing Enter to move to the next field and to the next row.

  f. Click **Save**, and then in the **Table Name** box, using your own name, replace the selected text by typing **Lastname Firstname 1C Student Workers** and then click **OK**.

2 Scroll, if necessary, to view the first field. In the new record row, click in the **Student ID** field, and then enter the information for two additional students as shown in **Table 3**, pressing Enter to move from field to field.

  a. **Close** your **1C Student Workers** table. On the **External Data tab**, in the **Import & Link group**, click the **Excel** button. In the **Get External Data - Excel Spreadsheet** dialog box, click the **Browse** button. In the **File Open** dialog box, navigate to your student data files, and then double-click the **a01C_Student_Workers** Excel file.

  b. **Append a copy of the records to the table**, and then click **OK**. Click **Next**, click **Finish**, and then click **Close**. **Open** the **Navigation Pane**, and then widen it so that you can view the entire table name. In the **Navigation Pane**, double-click your **1C Student Workers** table to open it, and then **Close** the **Navigation Pane**—30 total records display.

Table 1

Data Type					Text	Text	Text	Text	Text	Text	Currency
Field Name	ID	Last Name	First Name	Middle Initial	Address	City	State/Region	ZIP/Postal Code	Phone Number	Employing Division	Hourly Pay

(Return to Step 1-c)

Table 2

City	State/Region	ZIP/Postal Code	Phone Number	Employing Division	Hourly Pay
Alexandria	VA	22336	(571) 555-5816	DIV-ENLW	15

(Return to Step 1-f)

Table 3

Student ID	Last Name	First Name	Middle Initial	Address	City	State/Region	ZIP/Postal Code	Phone Number	Employing Division	Hourly Pay
3641892	Monroe	Stephen	D	48 Monrovia Rd	Potomac	MD	20854	(240) 555-7701	DIV-ENLD	10.5
4126598	Ludwig	Karen	E	1508 Moonlit Ave	Fairfax	VA	22030	(703) 555-2109	DIV-ENGC	9.75

(Return to Step 2-a)

(Project 1C Work Study Students Database continues on the next page)

Content-Based Assessments

3 Click the **Home tab**, and then in the **Views group**, click the **View** button to switch to **Design** view.

a. To the left of **Middle Initial**, point to the row selector box, and then click to select the entire row. On the **Design tab**, in the **Tools group**, click the **Delete Rows** button, and then click **Yes**.

b. Click anywhere in the **State/Region** field name, and then under **Field Properties**, set the **Field Size** to **2** In the **State/Region** row, click in the **Description** box, and then type **Two-character state abbreviation**

c. Click in the **Student ID** field name box, set the **Field Size** to **7** and in the **Description** box, type **Seven-digit Student ID** Then **Save** the design of your table; click **Yes**. On the **Design tab**, in the **Views group**, click the **View** button to switch to **Datasheet** view.

4 On the Ribbon, click the **External Data tab**, and then in the **Import & Link group**, click the **Excel** button. In the **Get External Data – Excel Spreadsheet** dialog box, click the **Browse** button. Navigate to your student data files, and then double-click **a01C_Divisions**. Be sure that the **Import the source data into a new table in the current database** option button is selected, and then click **OK**.

a. In the **Import Spreadsheet Wizard** dialog box, click to select the **First Row Contains Column Headings** check box, and then click **Next**.

b. Click **Next** again. Click the **Choose my own primary key** option button, and to the right, be sure that *Division ID* displays. Click **Next**. In the **Import to Table** box, type **Lastname Firstname 1C Divisions** and then click **Finish**. Click **Close**, **Open** the **Navigation Pane**, and then open your **1C Divisions** table. **Close** the **Navigation Pane**—22 records display.

c. At the top of the object window, click the **1C Student Workers tab**. To the left of the **Student ID** field name, click the **Select All** button. Click the **Home tab**, and in the **Records group**, click the **More** button. Click **Field Width**, and in the **Column Width** dialog box, click **Best Fit**. Click in any field, and then **Save** the table.

d. Display **Backstage** view, click **Print**, and then click **Print Preview**. In the **Page Layout group**, click the **Landscape** button. Create a paper or electronic printout as directed by your instructor; two pages result. Click **Close Print Preview**, and then **Close** your **1C Student Workers** table.

e. With your **1C Divisions** table displayed, to the left of the **Division ID** field name, click the **Select All** button, and then apply **Best Fit** to all of the columns. Click in any field, **Save** the table, and then display the table in **Print Preview**. Change the **Orientation** to **Landscape**. Create a paper or electronic printout as directed—two pages result. **Close Print Preview**, and then **Close** your **1C Divisions** table.

5 On the **Create tab**, in the **Queries group**, click the **Query Wizard** button. In the **New Query** dialog box, click **Simple Query Wizard**, and then click **OK**. Click the **Tables/Queries arrow**, and then be sure your **Table: 1C Divisions** is selected.

a. Under **Available Fields**, click **Division ID**, and then click the **Add Field** button to move the field to the **Selected Fields** list on the right. Using either the **Add Field** button or by double-clicking, add the following fields to the **Selected Fields** list: **Division Name**, **Campus**, **Dean Last Name**, **Dean First Name**, **Division Phone**, and **Division E-mail**. The query will answer the question, *What is the Division ID, Division Name, Campus, Dean's name, Division Phone number, and Division E-mail address of every division?*

b. Click **Next**. In the **Simple Query Wizard** dialog box, change the query title to **Lastname Firstname 1C All Divisions Query** and then click **Finish** to run the query.

c. Display the query in **Print Preview**. Change the **Orientation** to **Landscape**. In the **Page Size group**, click the **Margins** button, and then click **Normal**. Create a paper or electronic printout as directed— one page results. **Close Print Preview**, and then **Close** the query.

d. **Open** the **Navigation Pane**, open your **1C Student Workers** table, and then **Close** the **Navigation Pane**. The table contains 10 fields. On the **Create tab**, in the **Forms group**, click the **Form** button. Click **Save**, and then in the **Save As** dialog box, accept the default name for the form—*Lastname Firstname 1C Student Workers*—by clicking **OK**. In the navigation area, click the **Next record** button three times to display the record for *James Parkhill*. At the left edge of the form, click the gray **record selector bar** to select only this record. By using the instructions in Activity 1.15, print or create an electronic printout of this record as directed. **Close** the form object. Your **1C Student Workers** table object remains open.

(Project 1C Work Study Students Database continues on the next page)

Content-Based Assessments

6 Open the **Navigation Pane**, open your **1C Divisions** table, and then **Close** the **Navigation Pane**. On the **Create tab**, in the **Reports group**, click the **Report** button. In the field names row at the top of the report, click the **Division ID** field name. On the Ribbon, click the **Arrange tab**. In the **Rows & Columns group**, click the **Select Column** button, and then press Del. Using the same technique, delete the **Campus** field.

a. Scroll to position the **Dean MI** field at the left of your screen, and click the field name **Dean MI**. Hold down Ctrl, and then click the field names for **Address**, **City**, **State/Region**, and **ZIP/Postal Code**. On the **Arrange tab**, in the **Rows & Columns group**, click the **Select Column** button, and then press Del.

b. Scroll to the left, and then click in the **Dean Last Name** field name. By using the ↔ pointer, decrease the width of the field until there is about **0.25 inch** of space between the **Dean Last Name** field and the **Dean First Name** field. Decrease the widths of the **Dean First Name** and **Division Phone** fields in a similar manner. In the **Division E-mail** field, click in the first record—the data in the field displays on two lines. Increase the width of the field slightly so that each record's data in the field displays on one line. Be sure that the width of the report is within the dotted boundaries.

c. Click the **Division Name** field name. On the Ribbon, click the **Home tab**. In the **Sort & Filter group**, click

the **Ascending** button to sort the report in alphabetic order by Division Name.

d. **Save** the report as **Lastname Firstname 1C Divisions Report** and then click **OK**. Display the report in **Print Preview**. In the **Zoom group**, click the **Two Pages** button, and notice that the report will print on two pages because the page number is beyond the right margin of the report. **Close Print Preview**. With the report displayed in **Layout** view, scroll down and to the right to display the page number— **Page 1 of 1**. Click the page number, press Del, and then **Save** the changes to the report.

e. Display the report in **Print Preview**, and notice that the report will print on one page. In the **Zoom group**, click the **One Page** button. Create a paper or electronic printout of the report as directed. Click **Close Print Preview**. Along the top of the object window, right click any **object tab**, and then click **Close All** to close all of the open objects, leaving the object window empty.

f. **Open** the **Navigation Pane**. If necessary, increase the width of the **Navigation Pane** so that all object names display fully. Display **Backstage** view, click **Close Database**, and then click **Exit**. As directed by your instructor, submit your database and the five paper or electronic printouts—two tables, one query, one form, and one report—that are the results of this project.

End You have completed Project **1C**

Apply 1B skills from these Objectives:

6 Create a Database Using a Template

7 Organize Objects in the Navigation Pane

8 Create a New Table in a Database Created with a Template

9 Print a Report and a Table in a Database Created with a Template

Skills Review | Project **1D** Benefits Events

In the following Skills Review, you will create a database to store information about Employee Benefit Events at Capital Cities Community College. Your completed report and table will look similar to Figure 1.50.

Project Files

For Project 1D, you will need the following files:

> New Access database using the Events template
> a01D_Benefits_Events (Excel workbook)

You will save your database as:

> Lastname_Firstname_1D_Benefits_Events

Project Results

Figure 1.50

(Project 1D Benefits Events continues on the next page)

Content-Based Assessments

1 **Start** Access. Under **Available Templates**, click **Sample templates**, and then click **Events**. On the right, to the right of the **File Name** box, click the **Browse** button, and then navigate to your **Access Chapter 1** folder.

a. Select the text in the **File name** box, and then using your own information, type **Lastname_Firstname_ 1D_Benefits_Events** and then press Enter. In the lower right corner of your screen, click the **Create** button. If necessary, click Enable Content.

b. Click in the first empty **Title** field, type **Medical Plan** and then press Tab. In the **Start Time** field, type **5/2/16 8a** and then press Tab.

c. In the **End Time** field, type **5/2/16 1p** and then press Tab. In the **Description** field, type **Health Benefits** and then press Tab. In the **Location** field, type **Jefferson Campus** and then press Tab three times to move to the **Title** field in the new record row.

d. Directly above the field names row, click **New Event**, and then using Tab to move from field to field, enter the record shown in **Table 1** by using the single-record form, which is another way to enter records into a table.

e. **Close** the single-record form. Using either the rows on the Multiple Items form or the New Event single-record form, enter the records shown in **Table 2**.

f. **Close** the **Event List** form. On the Ribbon, click the **External Data tab**, and in the **Import & Link group**, click the **Excel** button. In the **Get External Data – Excel Spreadsheet** dialog box, click the **Browse** button. Navigate to your student data files, and then double-click **a01D_Benefits_Events**. Click the second option button—**Append a copy of the records to the table**—and then click **OK**.

g. Click **Next**, click **Finish**, and then **Close** the dialog box. **Open** the **Navigation Pane**, and then double-click **Event List** to open the form that displays data stored in the Events table—11 total records display.

2 At the top of the **Navigation Pane**, click the **Navigation arrow**. In the list, under **Navigate To Category**, click **Tables and Related Views**.

a. In the **Navigation Pane**, point to the **Events** *table*, right-click, and then click **Open** to display the records in the underlying table.

b. In the **Navigation Pane**, double-click the *report* named **Current Events** to view this predesigned report. From the **Navigation Pane**, open the **Events By Week** report to view this predesigned report.

c. **Close** the **Events By Week** report, and then **Close** the remaining three open objects. **Close** the **Navigation Pane**.

3 On the **Create tab**, in the **Tables group**, click the **Table** button.

a. Click the **Click to Add arrow**, click **Text**, type **Campus/Location** and then press Enter. In the third column, click **Text**, type **Room** and then press Enter. In the fourth column, click **Text**, type **Seats** and then press Enter. In the fifth column, click **Text**, type **Room Arrangement** and then press Enter. In the sixth column, click **Text**, type **Equipment** and then press ↓.

b. Right-click the **ID** field name, and then click **Rename Field**. Type **Room ID** and then press Enter. On the **Fields tab**, in the **Formatting group**, click the **Data Type arrow**, and then click **Text**.

c. In the new record row, click in the **Room ID** field, type **CAP-01** and then press Tab. In the **Campus/Location** field, type **Capital Campus** and then press Tab. In the **Room** field, type **C14** and then press Tab. In the **Seats** field, type **150** and then press Tab. In the **Room Arrangement** field, type **Theater** and then press Tab. In the **Equipment** field, type **Computer Projector, Surround Sound, & Microphones** and then press Tab to move to the new record row.

Table 1

Title	Location	Start Time	End Time	Description	
Eye Care Plan	Washington Campus	5/2/16 2p	5/2/16 4p	Health Benefits	- - - ➤ (Return to Step 1-e)

Table 2

ID	Title	Start Time	End Time	Description	Location	
3	Prescription Plan	5/3/16 8a	5/3/16 10a	Health Benefits	Capital Campus	
4	Pension Plan	5/3/16 2p	5/3/16 4p	Retirement Benefits	Central Campus	- - - ➤ (Return to Step 1-f)

(Project 1D Benefits Events continues on the next page)

Content-Based Assessments

d. In the **Views group**, click the **View** button to switch to **Design** view. In the **Save As** dialog box, save the table as **Lastname Firstname 1D Event Locations** and then click **OK**. Notice that the **Room ID** field is the **Primary Key**.

e. On the **Design tab**, in the **Views group**, click the **View** button to switch to **Datasheet** view. Enter the records in the table as shown in **Table 3**.

f. To the left of the **Room ID** field name, click the **Select All** button to select all of the columns. On the **Home tab**, in the **Records group**, click the **More** button. In the **Column Size** dialog box, click **Best Fit**.

g. Click in any record to cancel the selection of the columns, and then **Save** the table. **Open** the **Navigation Pane**, and then widen the pane to view the full names of all objects.

4 **Open** the **All Events** report, and then **Close** the **Navigation Pane**. In the lower right corner, click the **Layout View** button. At the top of the report, click the text *All Events* to surround the title with a colored border, and then click to the left of the letter *A* to place the insertion

point there. Using your own name, type **Lastname Firstname** and then press Spacebar and Enter. **Save** the report.

a. Display **Backstage** view, click **Print**, and then click **Print Preview**. Notice that the entire report will print on one page in portrait orientation. Create a paper or electronic printout if instructed to do so, and then click **Close Print Preview**. **Close** the **All Events** report.

b. With the **1D Event Locations** table open in **Datasheet** view, display **Backstage** view, click **Print**, and then click **Print Preview**. On the **Print Preview tab**, in the **Page Layout group**, click the **Landscape** button, and then notice that the entire table will print on one page.

c. Create a paper or electronic printout if instructed to do so, and then click **Close Print Preview**. **Close** the **1D Event Locations** table.

d. **Open** the **Navigation Pane**. Display **Backstage** view, click **Close Database**, and then click **Exit**. As directed by your instructor, submit your database and the two paper or electronic printouts—one report and one table—that are the results of this project.

Table 3

Room ID	Campus/Location	Room	Seats	Room Arrangement	Equipment
CEN-01	Central Campus	H212	35	Lecture/Classroom	Computer Projector, 3 screens
JEFF-01	Jefferson Campus	J520	50	Lecture/Classroom	Smart Board
WASH-01	Washington Campus	A150	40	U-shaped	White Board & Computer Projector
CEN-02	Central Campus	C14	25	Computer Lab	25 Computers & Projector

(Return to Step 3-f)

End You have completed Project 1D

Content-Based Assessments

Apply 1A skills from these Objectives:

- 1️⃣ Identify Good Database Design
- 2️⃣ Create a Table and Define Fields in a New Database
- 3️⃣ Change the Structure of Tables and Add a Second Table
- 4️⃣ Create and Use a Query, Form, and Report
- 5️⃣ Save and Close a Database

Mastering Access | Project 1E Kiosk Inventory

In the following Mastering Access project, you will create a database to track information about the inventory of items for sale in the kiosk located on the quad at the Central Campus of Capital Cities Community College. Your completed database objects will look similar to those in Figure 1.51.

Project Files

For Project 1E, you will need the following files:

New blank Access database
a01E_Inventory (Excel workbook)
a01E_Inventory_Storage (Excel workbook)

You will save your database as:

Lastname_Firstname_1E_Inventory

Project Results

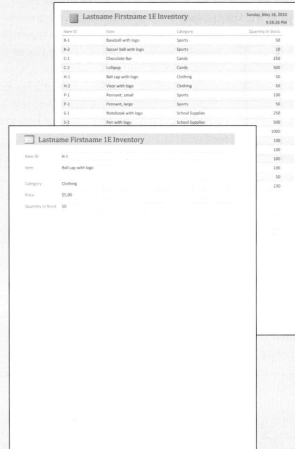

Figure 1.51

(Project 1E Kiosk Inventory continues on the next page)

Content-Based Assessments

1 **Start** Access. Create a new **Blank database** in your **Access Chapter 1** folder. Name the database **Lastname_ Firstname_1E_Inventory** and then **Close** the **Navigation Pane**. Create additional fields as shown in **Table 1**.

2 Change the **Data Type** of the **ID** field to **Text**, rename the field to **Item ID** and then enter the records as shown in **Table 2**.

3 **Save** the table as **Lastname Firstname 1E Inventory** and then **Close** the table. From your student data files, **Import** and then **Append** the **a01E_Inventory** Excel file to the **1E Inventory** table. Then, from the **Navigation Pane**, open your **1E Inventory** table—17 records display. Widen and then **Close** the **Navigation Pane**.

4 In **Design** view, delete the **Storage Location** field. Click in the **Category** field, change the **Field Size** to **25** and in the **Description** box, type **Enter the category of the Item** Click in the **Item ID** field, and then change the **Field Size** to **10 Save** the changes to the design of your table, click **Yes**, and then switch to **Datasheet** view. Apply **Best Fit** to all of the fields in the table, **Save** the table, and then display the table in **Print Preview**—one page results. Create a paper or electronic printout as directed by your instructor. **Close** the table.

5 From your student data files, **Import** the **a01E_Inventory_Storage** Excel file into the database as a new table; use the first row as the column headings and the **Category** field as the primary key. As the last step in the Wizard, name the table **Lastname Firstname 1E Inventory Storage** and then **Open** the **Navigation Pane**. **Open** your **1E Inventory Storage** table, and then **Close** the **Navigation Pane**. Display the new table in **Design** view, click in the **Location Detail** field, change the **Field Size** to

30 and then as the **Description**, type **Enter room and bin numbers or alternate location of inventory item.** In **Datasheet** view, apply **Best Fit** to all of the fields, **Save** the table, and then display the table in **Print Preview**. Create a paper or electronic printout as directed—one page results. **Close** the table.

6 **Create**, by using the **Query Wizard**, a **Simple Query** based on your **1E Inventory** table. Include only the fields that will answer the question *For all Items, what is the Quantity in Stock?* **Save** the query with the default name. Create a paper or electronic printout as directed and then **Close** the query.

7 Display the **1E Inventory** table, and then **Create** a **Form** for this table. **Save** the form as **Lastname Firstname 1E Inventory Form** Display and then select the fifth record. By using the instructions in Activity 1.15, print or create an electronic printout of only this record as directed. **Close** the form object.

8 With the **1E Inventory** table open, **Create** a **Report**. **Delete** the **Price** field, and then sort the records in **Ascending** order by the **Item ID** field. Scroll down to the bottom of the report and delete the page number—**Page 1 of 1**. **Save** the report as **Lastname Firstname 1E Inventory Report** and then create a paper or electronic printout as directed.

9 **Close All** open objects. **Open** the **Navigation Pane**. If necessary, widen the pane so that all of the object names display fully. In **Backstage** view, click **Close Database** and then click **Exit**. As directed by your instructor, submit your database and the five paper or electronic printouts—two tables, one query, one form, and one report—that are the results of this project.

Table 1

Data Type		Text	Text	Text	Currency	Number
Field Name	ID	Item	Category	Storage Location	Price	Quantity in Stock

---> (Return to Step 2)

Table 2

Item ID	Item	Category	Storage Location	Price	Quantity in Stock
C-1	Chocolate Bar	Candy	J100A	.5	250
C-2	Lollipop	Candy	J100A	.25	500
T-1	T-shirt, S	Clothing	J100B	8.5	100

---> (Return to Step 3)

End **You have completed Project 1E**

Content-Based Assessments

Apply **1B** skills from these Objectives:

- **6** Create a Database Using a Template
- **7** Organize Objects in the Navigation Pane
- **8** Create a New Table in a Database Created with a Template
- **9** Print a Report and a Table in a Database Created with a Template

Mastering Access | Project **1F** Recruiting Events

In the following Mastering Access project, you will create a database to store information about the recruiting events that are scheduled to attract new students to Capital Cities Community College. Your completed report and table will look similar to those in Figure 1.52.

Project Files

For Project 1F, you will need the following files:

New Access database using the Events template
a01F_Recruiting_Events (Excel workbook)

You will save your database as:

Lastname_Firstname_1F_Recruiting_Events

Project Results

Figure 1.52

(Project 1F Recruiting Events continues on the next page)

Mastering Access | Project **1F** Recruiting Events (continued)

1 **Start** Access, click **Sample templates**, and then click **Events**. In your **Access Chapter 1** folder, save the database as **Lastname_Firstname_1F_Recruiting_Events** If necessary, enable the content.

2 In the Multiple Items form or the New Event single-record form, enter the records shown in **Table 1** into the Events table.

3 **Close** the **Event List** form, and then click the **External Data tab**. **Import** and **Append** the **Excel** file **a01F_Recruiting_Events** to the **Events** table. **Open** the **Navigation Pane**, organize the objects by **Tables and Related Views**, and then **Open** your **Events** table to view 13 records. **Close** the **Navigation Pane**. Apply **Best Fit** to all of the fields, **Save** the table, and then **Close** the table.

4 **Create** a new table using the **Table** button. Click the **Click to Add arrow**, click **Text**, type **Location** and then press Enter. In the third column, click **Text**, type **Last Name** and then press Enter. In the fourth column, click **Text**, type **First Name** and then press Enter. In the fifth column, click **Text**, type **E-mail Address** and then press Enter. In the sixth column, click **Text**, type **Business Phone** and then press ↓.

5 Right-click the **ID** field name, and then **Rename** the field to **Recruiter ID** Change the **Data Type** to **Text**, and then enter the records as shown in **Table 2**.

6 Apply **Best Fit** to all of the columns. **Save** the table as **Lastname Firstname 1F Recruiting Contacts** and then **Close** the table.

7 From the **Navigation Pane**, open the **Current Events Report**. In the lower right corner of the status bar, click the **Layout View** button, click the title *Current Events*, and then click to position your insertion point to the left of *C*. Type your own name in the format **Lastname Firstname** Display the report in **Print Preview**, and then create a paper or electronic printout if instructed to do so. **Close** the **Print Preview**. **Close** the report and save the changes.

8 From the **Navigation Pane**, open your **1F Recruiting Contacts** table. Display the table in **Print Preview**, change to **Landscape** orientation, and then create a paper or electronic printout if instructed to do so. **Close** the **Print Preview**, and then **Close** the table. **Open** the **Navigation Pane** and, if necessary, increase the width of the pane so that your table name displays fully. From **Backstage** view, click **Close Database**, and then click **Exit**. As directed by your instructor, submit your database and the two paper or electronic printouts—one report and one table—that are the results of this project.

Table 1

ID	Title	Start Time	End Time	Description	Location
1	Health Professions	6/1/16 8a	6/1/16 1p	Science Students	Washington HS
2	New Students	6/1/16 6p	6/1/16 9p	College Fair	Jefferson HS
3	Information Technology	6/2/16 9a	6/2/16 1p	Technical Students	Madison Technical Center
4	New Students	6/2/16 2p	6/2/16 5p	Open House	Central Campus

(Return to Step 3)

Table 2

Recruiter ID	Location	Last Name	First Name	E-mail Address	Business Phone
R-01	Washington HS	Luiz	Penelope	pluiz@washhs.sch	(202) 555-3410
R-02	Jefferson HS	Hart	Robert	rlhart@jeffhs.sch	(571) 555-1938
R-03	Madison Technical Center	Sedlacek	Belinda	bsedlacek@madihs.sch	(703) 555-0471
R-04	Central Campus	Monroe	Stephen	smonroe@capccc.edu	(571) 555-2387

(Return to Step 6)

End **You have completed Project 1F**

Apply **1A** and **1B** skills from these Objectives:

1. Identify Good Database Design
2. Create a Table and Define Fields in a New Database
3. Change the Structure of Tables and Add a Second Table
4. Create and Use a Query, Form, and Report
5. Save and Close a Database
6. Create a Database Using a Template
7. Organize Objects in the Navigation Pane
8. Create a New Table in a Database Created with a Template
9. Print a Report and a Table in a Database Created with a Template

Mastering Access | Project **1G** Campus Expansion

In the following Mastering Access project, you will create one database to store information about the campus expansion for Capital Cities Community College and a second database to store information about the public events related to the expansion projects. Your completed database objects will look similar to Figure 1.53.

Project Files

For Project 1G, you will need the following files:

New blank Access database
a01G_Projects (Excel workbook)
a01G_Contractors (Excel workbook)
New Access database using the Events template

You will save your databases as:

Lastname_Firstname_1G_Campus_Expansion
Lastname_Firstname_1G_Public_Events

Project Results

Figure 1.53

(Project 1G Campus Expansion continues on the next page)

Access | Chapter 1

Content-Based Assessments

1 **Start** Access. Create a new **Blank database** in your **Access Chapter 1** folder. Name the database **Lastname_Firstname_1G_Campus_Expansion** and then **Close** the **Navigation Pane**. Create the additional fields shown in **Table 1**.

2 Change the **ID** field name to **Project ID** and change its **Data Type** to **Text**. Add the three records shown in **Table 2**.

3 **Save** the table as **Lastname Firstname 1G Projects** and then **Close** the table. **Import** and **Append** the **Excel** file **a01G_Projects** to the **1G Projects** table. Then, from the **Navigation Pane**, open your **1G Projects** table—8 total records display. **Close** the **Navigation Pane**.

4 In **Design** view, click in the **Project ID** field, change the **Field Size** to **5** and as the **Description** type **Enter Project ID using the format P-###** Switch to **Datasheet** view, and save by clicking **Yes** two times. Apply **Best Fit** to all of the fields in the table, **Save** the table, and then display it in **Print Preview**. Set the orientation to **Landscape**—one page results. Create a paper or electronic printout as directed by your instructor, and then **Close** the table.

5 From the **External Data tab**, import the **Excel** file **a01G_Contractors** into the database as a new table; use the first row as the column headings and set the **ID** field as the primary key. In the final Wizard dialog box, name the table **Lastname Firstname 1G Contractors** and then **Open** the new table in **Datasheet** view. Apply **Best Fit** to all of the fields, **Save** the table, and then display the table in **Print Preview**. Set the orientation to **Landscape**—one page results. Create a paper or electronic printout as directed, and then **Close** the table.

6 **Create**, by using the **Query Wizard**, a **Simple Query** based on your **1G Projects** table. Include only the appropriate fields to answer the question *For every Building Project, what is the Budget Amount?* Create the query and save it with the default name. Create a paper or electronic printout as directed, and then **Close** the query.

7 Open your **1G Projects** table, and then **Create** a **Form** for this table. Save the form as **Lastname Firstname 1G Projects Form** Display and select the seventh record, and then by using the instructions in Activity 1.15, print or create an electronic printout of this record as directed. **Close** the form object, saving changes to it.

8 With the **1G Projects** table open and active, **Create** a **Report**. **Delete** the **Project ID** field. Sort the records in **Descending** order by the **Budget Amount** field—Access automatically totals this field. Adjust the field widths on the left and right as necessary so that the fields display within the margins of the report. At the bottom of the report, delete the **page number**, and then delete the total that displays in the **Budget Amount** column. **Save** the report as **Lastname Firstname 1G Projects Report** and then create a paper or electronic printout as directed.

9 **Close All** open objects. If necessary, **Open** the **Navigation Pane** and widen the pane so that all object names display fully. Display **Backstage** view, and then click **Close Database**. Do *not* exit Access.

Table 1

Data Type		Text	Text	Text	Currency	
Field Name	ID	Building Project	Site	Contractor	Budget Amount	---➤ (Return to Step 2)

Table 2

Project ID	Building Project	Site	Contractor	Budget Amount
P-356	Student Center, 2-story	Jefferson Campus	Glenmore Construction	61450000
P-823	Student Center, multilevel	Central Campus	Glenmore Construction	41900000
P-157	Regional Health Center	Capital Campus	Wright Rosen Construction	42600000

(Return to Step 3)

(Project 1G Campus Expansion continues on the next page)

Content-Based Assessments

Mastering Access | Project **1G** Campus Expansion (continued)

10 From **Sample templates**, create a new database using the **Events** template. **Save** the database in your **Access Chapter 1** folder, and as the file name, type **Lastname_Firstname_1G_Public_Events** If necessary, enable the content. Enter the records in **Table 3** by using the displayed Multiple Items Event List form or the single-record form, which is available by clicking New Event above the field names row.

11 **Close** the **Event List** form. Open the **Navigation Pane**, and then by using the **Navigation Pane arrow**, arrange the database objects by **Tables and Related Views**. Point to the **Events: Table** object, right-click, click **Rename**, and then using your own name, type **Lastname**

Firstname 1G Events Press Enter and then widen the Navigation Pane if necessary.

12 **Open** the **1G Events** table, **Close** the **Navigation Pane**, and then apply **Best Fit** to all of the columns. **Save** the table, display it in **Print Preview**, change the orientation to **Landscape**, set the **Margins** to **Normal**, and then create a paper or electronic printout as directed. **Close** all open objects. **Open** the **Navigation Pane**, display **Backstage** view, click **Close Database**, and then click **Exit**. As directed by your instructor, submit your database and the six paper or electronic printouts—three tables, one query, one form, and one report—that are the results of this project.

Table 3

ID	Title	Start Time	End Time	Description	Location
1	Groundbreaking	6/13/16 10a	6/13/16 11a	Student Center groundbreaking	Jefferson Campus
2	Dedication	8/26/16 12:30p	8/26/16 2p	Gymnasium building dedication	Washington Campus
3	Community Arts Expo	10/5/16 6p	10/5/16 9p	Book and Art Expo	Joint Use Library

(Return to Step 11)

End You have completed Project 1G

Access | Chapter 1

Content-Based Assessments

GO! Fix It | Project **1H** Scholarships

Project Files

For Project 1H, you will need the following file:

a01H_Scholarships

You will save your database as:

Lastname_Firstname_1H_Scholarships

In this project, you will make corrections to and update an Access database that will store information about scholarships awarded to students. Start Access. In Backstage view, click Open, navigate to your student files, and then open the file a01H_Scholarships. With the database open, display Backstage view. Click Save Database As, and in the Save As dialog box, navigate to your Access Chapter 1 folder, name the file **Lastname_Firstname_1H_Scholarships** and then click Save. In the message bar, click the Enable Content button.

To complete the project you must find and correct errors in field names, data types, data design, and column widths. You should know:

- The table name should be renamed **Lastname Firstname 1H Scholarships**

- In the table, all of the data in the fields and the field names should display fully.

- Three fields in the table have incorrect data types.

- The field that represents the unique value for each record should be set as the primary key.

- In one of the records, there is a data entry error involving an athlete's name; after correcting the entry, be sure to click in another record so that the record you edit is saved.

- When open, the Navigation Pane should fully display the table name.

- A query should be created for the 1H Scholarships table that answers the question *What is the Amount, Sport, First Name, and Last Name of every athlete receiving a scholarship?* Apply Best Fit to the query results.

- Using the table, a report should be created that includes the Amount, Sport, Award Date, and the last and first name of the athlete. Sort the report in descending order by the amount and then adjust the column widths so that the fields display within the margins of the report. At the bottom of the report, delete the total for the Amount field, and then delete the page number and save with the default name.

If directed to do so, create a paper or electronic printout of the table, the query, and the report. The table should use Landscape orientation, and the query and report should use Portrait orientation. Be sure that the report prints on one page.

End You have completed Project 1H _____

Content-Based Assessments

GO! Make It | Project 1I Theater Events

Project Files

For Project 1I, you will need the following file:

New Access database using the Events template

You will save your database as:

Lastname_Firstname_1I_Theater_Events

Using the Events database template, create the table of theater events shown in Figure 1.54 that the Performing Arts department will present or host for April. Name the database **Lastname_Firstname_1I_Theater_Events** Arrange the Navigation Pane by Tables and Related Views, rename the Events table **Lastname Firstname 1I Theater Events** and then widen the Navigation Pane so that all object names display fully. Open the table, apply Best Fit to all the columns, save the table, and then create a paper or electronic printout of the table as directed by your instructor. Use Landscape orientation and Normal margins.

Project Results

Lastname Firstname 1I Theater Events   4/29/2010

ID	Title	Start Time	End Time	Location	Description	@
1	Symphony Orchestra Concert	4/2/2016 7:30:00 PM	4/2/2016 10:00:00 PM	Jefferson Campus	Opera soprano Barbara Botillini	(0)
2	The Big Band Concert	4/4/2016 7:30:00 PM	4/4/2016 9:00:00 PM	Capital Campus	The Ruth Mystic Big Band Concert	(0)
3	Chaos in the House	4/6/2016 3:00:00 PM	4/6/2016 5:00:00 PM	Central Campus	Gospel Show	(0)
4	Tom Sawyer	4/7/2016 7:00:00 PM	4/7/2016 10:00:00 PM	Washington Campus	CapCCC Players	(0)
5	Tom Sawyer	4/8/2016 3:00:00 PM	4/8/2016 6:00:00 PM	Washington Campus	CapCCC Players	(0)
6	Virginia Arts Festival	4/16/2016 8:00:00 PM	4/16/2016 10:00:00 PM	Jefferson Campus	Anika Shankar	(0)
7	Virginia Arts Festival	4/17/2016 7:00:00 PM	4/17/2016 9:00:00 PM	Central Campus	Music from the Crooked Elbow	(0)
8	College Awards Ceremony	4/22/2016 1:00:00 PM	4/22/2016 4:00:00 PM	Washington Campus	CapCCC Faculty and Staff Awards	(0)
9	Virginia Arts Festival	4/23/2016 7:30:00 PM	4/23/2016 10:00:00 PM	Capital Campus	Russian Folk Dance Spectacular	(0)
10	Music in Motion Dance	4/29/2016 1:00:00 PM	4/29/2016 3:00:00 PM	Central Campus	Dancing to Modern Music	(0)

Page 1

Figure 1.54

End You have completed Project 1I

Access | Chapter 1

Content-Based Assessments

GO! Solve It | Project **1J** Student Activities

Project Files

For Project 1J, you will need the following files:

New Access database using the Events template
a01J_Student_Activities (Word document)

You will save your database as:

Lastname_Firstname_1J_Student_Activities

Create a new database from the Events database template and name the database **Lastname_Firstname_1J_Student_Activities** Using the data in the a01J_Student_Activities Word document, enter the data into the Multiple Items form. Each event begins at 7 p.m. and ends at 9 p.m. After entering the records, close the form, arrange the Navigation Pane by Tables and Related Views, rename the table that stores the records as **Lastname Firstname 1J Activities** and then widen the Navigation Pane so that all object names display fully. Open the table, apply Best Fit to the columns, and then save the table. Display the table in Print Preview, and then use the proper commands to be sure that the table prints on one page with the table name at the top of the page. Print the table or submit electronically as directed.

Performance Elements		Performance Level		
		Exemplary: You consistently applied the relevant skills	**Proficient:** You sometimes, but not always, applied the relevant skills	**Developing:** You rarely or never applied the relevant skills
	Create database and enter data	Database was created using the correct template and correct name. Data entered correctly.	Some but not all of the data was entered correctly.	Most of the data was entered incorrectly.
	Rename table and format table	Table named correctly and Best Fit applied to all columns.	Table named incorrectly and/or Best Fit not properly applied.	Incorrect table name and inadequate formatting applied to all columns.
	Create table printout	Printout displays on one page in Landscape orientation and the table name displays at the top.	The printout displays on two pages or the table name does not display at the top.	The printout displays on two pages and the table name does not display at the top of the page.

End You have completed Project 1J ⎯⎯⎯⎯⎯⎯

Content-Based Assessments

GO! Solve It | Project **1K** Media Contacts

Project Files

For Project 1K, you will need the following files:

New blank Access database
a01K_Media_Contacts (Excel workbook)

You will save your database as:

Lastname_Firstname_1K_Media_Contacts

Create a new blank database and name the database **Lastname_Firstname_1K_Media_Contacts** Close the default Table1. Create a table by importing the a01K_Media_Contacts Excel workbook, use the first row as the column headings, and use Media ID as the Primary Key. Name the table **Lastname Firstname 1K Media Contacts** Modify the table design by creating separate fields for the Contact's first name and last name, and then adjust the data accordingly. Apply Best Fit to the columns, and then save the table. Display the table in Print Preview, and then use the Page Layout commands to display the table on one page, being sure the table name prints at the top of the page. Print the table or submit electronically as directed.

Create a simple query that answers the following question: *What are the Publication name, first name, last name, and E-mail address for all of the media contacts?* Accept the default name, apply Best Fit to all of the columns, and then create a paper or electronic printout on one page as directed.

Create a report and delete the Media ID column. Adjust the widths of the remaining fields so that all of the data displays within the margins of the report. Sort the report in ascending order by the Publication field. In Layout View, select the report title, and then on the Format tab, in the Font group, change the font of the title of the report to 14. At the bottom of the report, delete the page number. Save the report as **Lastname Firstname 1K Media Contacts Report** and then create a paper or electronic printout as directed. Arrange the Navigation Pane by Tables and Related Views, and then widen the Navigation Pane so that all object names display fully.

Performance Elements	Performance Level		
	Exemplary: You consistently applied the relevant skills	**Proficient:** You sometimes, but not always, applied the relevant skills	**Developing:** You rarely or never applied the relevant skills
Create database, import data to create a table, and then modify the table design	Table created by importing from an Excel workbook, fields correctly modified, and primary key field identified.	Table created by importing from an Excel workbook, but fields are incorrect, or primary key field is incorrect.	Table created by importing from an Excel workbook, but both fields and primary key are incorrect.
Create query	Query created, named correctly, answers the question, formatted correctly.	Query created, but does not completely answer the question or formatted incorrectly.	Query does not answer the question and also includes errors in formatting.
Create report	Report created, Media ID field deleted, field sizes adjusted, sorted by Publication, correctly named, and formatted.	Report created with some errors in fields, report name, sorting, or formatting.	Report created with numerous errors in fields, report name, sorting, or formatting.

End You have completed Project 1K

Outcomes-Based Assessments

Rubric

The following outcomes-based assessments are *open-ended assessments*. That is, there is no specific correct result; your result will depend on your approach to the information provided. Make *Professional Quality* your goal. Use the following scoring rubric to guide you in *how* to approach the problem, and then to evaluate *how well* your approach solves the problem.

The *criteria*—Software Mastery, Content, Format and Layout, and Process—represent the knowledge and skills you have gained that you can apply to solving the problem. The *levels of performance*—Professional Quality, Approaching Professional Quality, or Needs Quality Improvements—help you and your instructor evaluate your result.

	Your completed project is of Professional Quality if you:	Your completed project is Approaching Professional Quality if you:	Your completed project Needs Quality Improvements if you:
1-Software Mastery	Choose and apply the most appropriate skills, tools, and features and identify efficient methods to solve the problem.	Choose and apply some appropriate skills, tools, and features, but not in the most efficient manner.	Choose inappropriate skills, tools, or features, or are inefficient in solving the problem.
2-Content	Construct a solution that is clear and well organized, contains content that is accurate, appropriate to the audience and purpose, and is complete. Provide a solution that contains no errors in spelling, grammar, or style.	Construct a solution in which some components are unclear, poorly organized, inconsistent, or incomplete. Misjudge the needs of the audience. Have some errors in spelling, grammar, or style, but the errors do not detract from comprehension.	Construct a solution that is unclear, incomplete, or poorly organized; contains some inaccurate or inappropriate content; and contains many errors in spelling, grammar, or style. Do not solve the problem.
3-Format and Layout	Format and arrange all elements to communicate information and ideas, clarify function, illustrate relationships, and indicate relative importance.	Apply appropriate format and layout features to some elements, but not others. Overuse features, causing minor distraction.	Apply format and layout that does not communicate information or ideas clearly. Do not use format and layout features to clarify function, illustrate relationships, or indicate relative importance. Use available features excessively, causing distraction.
4-Process	Use an organized approach that integrates planning, development, self-assessment, revision, and reflection.	Demonstrate an organized approach in some areas, but not others; or, use an insufficient process of organization throughout.	Do not use an organized approach to solve the problem.

Outcomes-Based Assessments

Apply a combination of
the **1A** and **1B** skills.

GO! Think | Project **1L** Student Clubs

Project Files

For Project 1L, you will need the following files:

New blank Access database
a01L_Clubs (Word file)
a01L_Student_Clubs (Excel file)
a01L_Club_Presidents (Excel file)

You will save your database as:

Lastname_Firstname_1L_Student_Clubs

Kirsten McCarty, Vice President of Student Services, needs a database that tracks information about student clubs. The database should contain two tables, one for club information and one for contact information for the club presidents.

Create a new blank database and name it **Lastname_Firstname_1L_Student_Clubs** Using the information provided in the a01L_Clubs Word document, create the first table with two records to store information about the clubs. Then import 23 records from the a01L_Student_Clubs Excel file. Create a second table by importing 25 records from the a0lL_Club_Presidents Excel file. Name the tables appropriately and include your name. Be sure the data types are correct and the records are entered correctly. Apply Best Fit to all of the columns.

Create a simple query based on the Clubs table that answers the following question: *What are the Club Name, Meeting Day, Meeting Time, and Room ID for all of the clubs?* Based on the Clubs table, create a form. Create a report based on the Presidents of the clubs that lists the Last Name (in ascending order), First Name, and Phone number of every president. Print the two tables, the seventh record in Form view, the query, and the report being sure that each object prints on one page, or submit electronically as directed. Group objects on the Navigation Pane by Tables and Related Views. On the Navigation Pane, be sure that all object names display fully.

 You have completed Project 1L _____

Apply a combination of
the **1A** and **1B** skills.

GO! Think | Project **1M** Faculty Training

Project Files

For Project 1M, you will need the following file:

New Access database using the Events template
a01M_Faculty_Training (Word file)

You will save your database as:

Lastname_Firstname_1M_Faculty_Training

Use the information provided in the a01M_Faculty_Training Word file to create a database using the Events database template. Name the database **Lastname_Firstname_1M_Faculty_ Training** Use the information in the Word file to enter the records. Training times begin at 11:30 a.m. and end at 1 p.m. Arrange the Navigation Pane by Tables and Related Views, and rename the Events table appropriately to include your name. Display the All Events report in Layout View and insert your Lastname Firstname in front of the report title *All Events*. Print the table and the All Events report or submit electronically as directed.

End You have completed Project 1M _____

Access | Chapter 1

Project 1L: Student Clubs | **Access** **113**

Outcomes-Based Assessments

You and GO! | Project 1N Personal Contacts

Project Files

For Project 1N, you will need the following file:

New blank Access database

You will save your database as:

Lastname_Firstname_1N_Personal_Contacts

Create a database that stores information about your personal contacts, such as friends and family members. Name the database **Lastname_Firstname_1N_Personal_Contacts** Include a field for a birthday. Enter at least 10 records in the table, and name the table **Lastname Firstname 1N Personal Contacts** Create a query that includes at least three of the fields in the table in the result; for example, a list of names and phone numbers. Create a report that includes the name and address for each contact. Print the table, query, and report, making sure that the data for each object prints on one page, or submit electronically as directed.

End **You have completed Project 1N** —————————————————

Sort and Query a Database

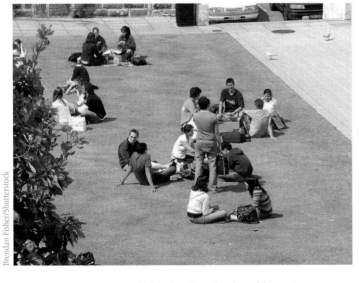

Brendan Fisher/Shutterstock

In This Chapter

In this chapter, you will sort Access database tables and create and modify queries. To convert data into meaningful information, you must manipulate your data in a way that you can answer questions. One question might be: *Which students have a grade point average of 3.0 or higher?* With such information, you could send information about scholarships or internships to selected students.

Questions can be answered by sorting the data in a table or by creating a query. Queries enable you to isolate specific data in database tables by limiting the fields that display and by setting conditions that limit the records to those that match specified conditions. You can also use a query to create a new field that is calculated by using one or more existing fields.

The projects in this chapter relate to **Capital Cities Community College**, which is located in the Washington D. C. metropolitan area. The college provides high-quality education and professional training to residents in the cities surrounding the nation's capital. Its four campuses serve over 50,000 students and offer more than 140 certificate programs and degrees at the associate's level. CapCCC has a highly acclaimed Distance Education program and an extensive Workforce Development program. The college makes positive contributions to the community through cultural and athletic programs and partnerships with businesses and non-profit organizations.

Project 2A Instructors and Courses Database

myitlab
Project 2A Training

Project Activities

In Activities 2.01 through 2.13, you will assist Carolyn Judkins, the Dean of the Business and Information Technology Division at the Jefferson Campus, in locating information about instructors and courses in the Division. Your results will look similar to Figure 2.1.

Project Files

For Project 2A, you will need the following file:

a02A_Instructors_Courses

You will save your database as:

Lastname_Firstname_2A_Instructors_Courses

Project Results

Figure 2.1
Project 2A Instructors and Courses

Objective 1 | Open an Existing Database

There will be instances in which you may want to work with a database and still keep the *original* version of the database. Like the other Microsoft Office 2010 applications, you can open a database file and save it with a new name.

Activity 2.01 | Opening and Renaming an Existing Database

1 Start **Access**. In **Backstage** view, click **Open**. Navigate to the student data files for this textbook, and then open the Access database **a02A_Instructors_Courses**.

2 Click the **File tab** to return to **Backstage** view, and then click **Save Database As.** In the **Save As** dialog box, navigate to the location where you are saving your databases for this chapter. Create a new folder named **Access Chapter 2** and then click **Open**.

3 In the **File name** box, select the file name, to which *1* has been added at the end. Edit as necessary to name the database **Lastname_Firstname_2A_Instructors_Courses** and then press **Enter**.

> Use this technique when you want to keep a copy of the original database file.

4 On the **Message Bar**, notice the **Security Warning**. In the **Navigation Pane**, notice that this database contains two table objects. Compare your screen with Figure 2.2.

Figure 2.2

- Database name in title bar
- Message Bar
- 2A Instructors table
- 2A Schedule table
- Security Warning message

Activity 2.02 | Resolving Security Alerts and Renaming Tables

The *Message Bar* is the area below the Ribbon that displays information such as security alerts when there is potentially unsafe, active content in an Office document that you open. Settings that determine the alerts that display on your Message Bar are set in the Access *Trust Center*, which is an area of Access where you can view the security and privacy settings for your Access installation.

You may or may not be able to change the settings in the Trust Center, depending upon decisions made within your organization's computing environment. You can display the Trust Center from Options, which is available in Backstage view.

1 On the **Message Bar**, click the **Enable Content** button.

> When working with the student files that accompany this textbook, repeat these actions each time you see this security warning. Databases for this textbook are safe to use on your computer.

Access | Chapter 2

2 In the **Navigation Pane**, right-click the **2A Instructors** table, and then click **Rename**. With the table name selected and using your own name, type **Lastname Firstname 2A Instructors** and then press Enter to rename the table. Using the same technique, **Rename** the **2A Schedule** table to **Lastname Firstname 2A Schedule**

> Including your name in the table enables you and your instructor to easily identify your work, because Access includes the table name in the header of printed and PDF pages.

3 Point to the right edge of the **Navigation Pane** to display the ⟷ pointer. Drag to the right to widen the pane until both table names display fully.

Objective 2 | Create Table Relationships

Access databases are relational databases because the tables in the database can relate—actually connect—to other tables through common fields. Recall that common fields are fields that contain the same data in more than one table.

After you have a table for each subject in your database, you must provide a way to connect the data in the tables when you need meaningful information. To do this, create common fields in related tables, and then define table relationships. A *relationship* is an association that you establish between two tables based on common fields. After the relationship is established, you can create a query, a form, or a report that displays information from more than one table.

Activity 2.03 | Creating Table Relationships and Enforcing Referential Integrity

In this activity, you will create a relationship between two tables in the database.

1 Double-click your **2A Instructors** table to open it in the object window and examine its contents. Then open your **2A Schedule** table and examine its contents.

> In the 2A Instructors table, *Instructor ID* is the primary key field, which ensures that each instructor will appear in the table only one time. No two instructors have the same Instructor ID.

> In the 2A Schedule table, *Schedule ID* is the primary key field. Every scheduled course section during an academic term has a unique Schedule ID. The 2A Schedule table includes the *Instructor ID* field, which is the common field between the 2A Schedule table and the 2A Instructors table.

2 In the **2A Schedule** table, scroll to the right to display the Instructor ID field, and then compare your screen with Figure 2.3.

> Because *one* instructor can teach *many* different courses, *one* Instructor ID number can be present *many* times in the 2A Schedule table. This relationship between each instructor and the courses is known as a *one-to-many relationship*. This is the most common type of relationship in Access.

Figure 2.3

Two table objects open
in the object window;
2A Schedule table active

Tables renamed

Navigation Pane width
increased so that both
table names are visible

Instructor teaches
more than one course

3 In the upper right corner of the object window, click **Close** ☒ two times to close each table. Click the **Database Tools tab**, and then in the **Relationships group**, click the **Relationships** button. Compare your screen with Figure 2.4.

> The Show Table dialog box displays in the Relationships window. In the Show Table dialog box, the Tables tab displays all of the table objects in the database. Your two tables are listed.

Figure 2.4

Relationships window

Two tables in database

4 Point to the title bar of the **Show Table** dialog box, and then drag down and to the right slightly to move the **Show Table** dialog box away from the top of the **Relationships** window.

> Moving the Show Table dialog box enables you to see the tables as they are added to the Relationships window.

5 In the **Show Table** dialog box, click your **2A Instructors** table, and then at the bottom of the dialog box, click **Add**. In the **Show Table** dialog box, double-click your **2A Schedule** table to add the table to the **Relationships** window. In the **Show Table** dialog box, click **Close**, and then compare your screen with Figure 2.5.

> You can use either technique to add a table to the Relationships window. A *field list*—a list of the field names in a table—for each of the two table objects displays, and each table's primary key is identified. Although this database currently has only two tables, larger databases can have many tables. Scroll bars in a field list indicate that there are fields that are not currently in view.

Figure 2.5

Field list for 2A Schedule table

Field list for 2A Instructors table

Primary keys

Scroll bar indicates there are fields out of view

Alert! | Are There More Than Two Field Lists in the Relationships Window?

If you double-click a table more than one time, a duplicate field list displays in the Relationships window. To remove a field list from the Relationships window, right-click the title bar of the field list, and then click Hide Table. Alternatively, click anywhere in the field list, and then on the Design tab, in the Relationships group, click the Hide Table button.

---

6 In the **2A Schedule** field list—the field list on the right—point to the title bar to display the [pointer icon] pointer. Drag the field list to the right until there is about 2 inches between the field lists.

7 In the **2A Instructors** field list—the field list on the left—point to the lower right corner of the field list to display the [pointer icon] pointer, and then drag down and to the right to increase the height and width of the field list until the entire name of the table in the title bar displays and all of the field names display.

This action enables you to see all of the available fields and removes the vertical scroll bar.

8 By using the same technique and the [pointer icon] pointer, resize the **2A Schedule** field list so that all of the field names and the table name display as shown in Figure 2.6.

Recall that *one* instructor can teach *many* scheduled courses. This arrangement of the tables on your screen displays the *one table* on the left side and the *many table* on the right side. Recall also that the primary key in each table is the field that uniquely identifies the record in each table. In the 2A Instructors table, each instructor is uniquely identified by the Instructor ID. In the 2A Schedule table, each scheduled course section is uniquely identified by the Schedule ID.

Figure 2.6

Table on *many* side of relationship

Table on *one* side of relationship

Instructor ID is common field between the two tables

Note | The Field That Is Highlighted Does Not Matter

After you rearrange the two field lists in the Relationships window, the highlighted field indicates the active field list, which is the list you moved last. This is of no consequence for completing the activity.

Another Way

On the Design tab, in the Tools group, click the Edit Relationships button. In the Edit Relationships dialog box, click Create New, and then in the Create New dialog box, designate the tables and fields that will create the relationship.

9 In the **2A Instructors** field list, point to **Instructor ID**, hold down the left mouse button, and then drag down and to the right into the **2A Schedule** field list until the 🖫 pointer's arrow is on top of **Instructor ID**. Then release the mouse button to display the **Edit Relationships** dialog box.

As you drag, a small graphic displays to indicate that you are dragging a field from one field list to another. A table relationship works by matching data in two fields—the common field. In these two tables, the common field has the same name—*Instructor ID*. Common fields are not required to have the same names; however, they must have the same data type and field size.

10 Point to the title bar of the **Edit Relationships** dialog box, and then drag the dialog box below the two field lists as shown in Figure 2.7.

Both tables include the Instructor ID field—the common field between the two tables. By dragging, you create the *one-to-many* relationship. In the 2A Instructors table, Instructor ID is the primary key. In the 2A Schedule table, Instructor ID is referred to as the ***foreign key*** field. The foreign key is the field in the related table used to connect to the primary key in another table. The field on the *one* side of the relationship is typically the primary key.

Figure 2.7

Edit Relationships dialog box

Instructor ID field common to both tables

One-To-Many indicated as Relationship Type

11 In the **Edit Relationships** dialog box, click to select the **Enforce Referential Integrity** check box.

Referential integrity is a set of rules that Access uses to ensure that the data between related tables is valid. Enforcing referential integrity ensures that an instructor cannot be added to the 2A Schedules table if the Instructor ID is *not* included in the 2A Instructors table. Similarly, enforcing referential integrity ensures that you cannot delete an instructor from the 2A Instructors table if there is a course listed in the 2A Schedule table for that instructor.

12 In the **Edit Relationships** dialog box, click the **Create** button, and then compare your screen with Figure 2.8.

A *join line*—the line joining two tables—displays between the two tables. On the join line, *1* indicates the *one* side of the relationship, and the infinity symbol (∞) indicates the *many* side of the relationship. These symbols display when referential integrity is enforced.

Figure 2.8

1 indicates one *side of the relationship*

Join line connects the two common fields, creating the relationship

∞ indicates *many* side of the relationship

Activity 2.04 | Printing a Relationship Report and Displaying Subdatasheet Records

The Relationships window provides a map of how your database tables are related, and you can print this information as a report.

1 With the **Relationships** window open, on the **Design tab**, in the **Tools group**, click the **Relationship Report** button to create the report and display it in Print Preview.

2 On the **Print Preview tab**, in the **Page Size group**, click the **Margins** button, and then click **Normal**. Compare your screen with Figure 2.9. If instructed to do so, create a paper or electronic printout of this relationship report.

Figure 2.9

Print Preview tab

Margins button

Database name and date (your date will differ)

Field lists with join lines

3 On the **Quick Access Toolbar**, click the **Save** button 🖫 to save the report. In the **Save As** dialog box, click **OK** to accept the default name.

The report name displays in the Navigation Pane under *Unrelated Objects*. Because the report is just a map of the relationships, and not a report containing actual records, it is not associated with any of the tables.

4 In the object window, **Close** ✕ the report, and then **Close** ✕ the **Relationships** window.

5 From the **Navigation Pane**, open your **2A Instructors** table, and then **Close** ⟪ the **Navigation Pane**. For the first record—*Instructor ID 1224567*—on the left side of the record, click the **plus sign** (+), and then compare your screen with Figure 2.10.

> Plus signs to the left of a record in a table indicate that *related* records exist in another table. Clicking the plus sign displays the related records in a ***subdatasheet***. In the first record, for *Deborah Fresch*, you can see that related records exist in the 2A Schedule table—she is teaching five LGL courses that are listed in the schedule. The plus sign displays because you created a relationship between the two tables using the Instructor ID field—the common field.

Figure 2.10

Course sections
from the 2A Schedule
table for *Associate
Professor Deborah Fresch*

Plus sign indicates that
related records may
exist in another table

6 For the first record, click the **minus sign** (-) to collapse the subdatasheet.

More Knowledge | **Other Types of Relationships: One-to-One and Many-to-Many**

There are other relationships you can create using the same process in the Relationships window. The type of relationship is determined by the placement of the primary key field. A one-to-one relationship exists between two tables when a record in one table is related to a single record in a second table. In this case, both tables use the same field as the primary key. This is most often used when data is placed in a separate table because access to the information is restricted.

You can also create a many-to-many relationship between tables, where many records in one table can be related to many records in another table. For example, many students can enroll in many courses. To create a many-to-many relationship, you must create a third table that contains the primary key fields from both tables. These primary key fields are then joined to their related fields in the other tables. In effect, you create multiple one-to-one relationships.

Objective 3 | Sort Records in a Table

Sorting is the process of arranging data in a specific order based on the value in a field. For example, you can sort the names in your address book alphabetically by each person's last name, or you can sort your DVD collection by the date of purchase. Initially, records in an Access table display in the order they are entered into the table. When a primary key is established, the records display in order based on the primary key field.

Activity 2.05 | Sorting Records in a Table in Ascending or Descending Order

In the following activity, you will determine the departments of the faculty in the Business and Information Technology Division by sorting the data. You can sort data in either ***ascending order*** or ***descending order***. Ascending order sorts text alphabetically (A to Z) and sorts numbers from the lowest number to the highest number. Descending order sorts text in reverse alphabetical order (Z to A) and sorts numbers from the highest number to the lowest number.

1 Notice that the records in the **2A Instructors** table are sorted in ascending order by **Instructor ID**, which is the primary key field.

Another Way

On the Home tab, in the Sort & Filter group, click the Ascending button.

2 In the field names row, click the **Department arrow**, click **Sort A to Z**, and then compare your screen with Figure 2.11.

To sort records in a table, click the arrow to the right of the field name in the column on which you want to sort, and then choose the sort order. After a field is sorted, a small arrow in the field name box indicates its sort order. The small arrow in the field name points up, indicating an ascending sort; and in the Ribbon, the Ascending button is selected.

The records display in alphabetical order by Department. Because the department names are now grouped together, you can quickly scroll the length of the table to see the instructors in each department. The first record in the table has no data in the Department field because the Instructor ID number *9999999* is reserved for Staff, a designation that is used until a scheduled course has been assigned to a specific instructor.

Figure 2.11

Ascending button selected

Small arrow indicates order by which the field is sorted

Records sorted alphabetically by Department

3 On the **Home tab**, in the **Sort & Filter group**, click the **Remove Sort** button to clear the sort and return the records to the default sort order, which is by the primary key field—*Instructor ID*.

4 Click the **Last Name arrow**, and then click **Sort Z to A**.

The records in the table are sorted by last name in reverse alphabetical order. The small arrow in the Field name box points down, indicating a descending sort. On the Ribbon, the Descending button is selected.

5 In the **Sort & Filter group**, click the **Remove Sort** button.

Activity 2.06 | Sorting Records in a Table on Multiple Fields

To sort a table on two or more fields, first identify the fields that will act as the *outermost sort field* and the *innermost sort field*. The outermost sort field is the first level of sorting, and the innermost sort field is the second level of sorting. For example, you might want to sort first by the Last Name field, which would be the outermost sort field, and then by the First Name field, which would be the innermost sort field. After you identify your outermost and innermost sort fields, sort the innermost field first, and then sort the outermost field.

In this activity, you will sort the records in descending order by the department name. Within each department name, you will sort the records in ascending order by last name.

1 In the **Last Name** field, click any record. In the **Sort & Filter group**, click the **Ascending** button.

> The records are sorted in ascending alphabetical order by Last Name—the innermost sort field.

2 Point anywhere in the **Department** field, and then right-click. From the shortcut menu, click **Sort Z to A**. Compare your screen with Figure 2.12.

> The records are sorted in descending alphabetical order first by Department—the *outermost* sort field—and then within a specific Department grouping, the sort continues in ascending alphabetical order by Last Name—the *innermost* sort field. The records are sorted on multiple fields using both ascending and descending order.

Figure 2.12

Small arrow indicates descending sort

Small arrow indicates ascending sort

Within each *Department, Last Name* sorted in ascending order

Records sorted in descending order by Department

3 Display **Backstage** view, click **Print**, and then click **Print Preview**. In the **Page Layout** group, click the **Landscape** button. In the **Zoom group**, click the **Two Pages** button, and notice that the table will print on two pages.

4 On the **Print Preview tab**, in the **Print group**, click the **Print** button. Under **Print Range**, click the **Pages** option button. In the **From** box, type **1** and then in the **To** box, type **1** to print only the first page. If directed to submit a paper copy, click OK or create an electronic copy as instructed. To create a PDF of only the first page, in the Data group, click PDF or XPS, click the Options button, and then indicate *Page 1 to 1*. In the **Close Preview group**, click the **Close Print Preview** button.

Access | Chapter 2

5 In the object window, **Close** ☒ the table. In the message box, click **Yes** to save the changes to the sort order.

6 **Open** ⟫ the **Navigation Pane**, and then open the **2A Instructors** table. Notice the table was saved with the sort order you specified.

7 In the **Sort & Filter group**, click the **Remove Sort** button. **Close** ☒ the table, and in the message box, click **Yes** to save the table with the sort removed. **Close** ⟪ the **Navigation Pane**.

> Generally, tables are not stored with the data sorted. Instead, queries are created that sort the data; and then reports are created to display the sorted data.

Objective 4 | Create a Query in Design View

Recall that a ***select query*** is a database object that retrieves (selects) specific data from one or more tables and then displays the specified data in Datasheet view. A query answers a question such as *Which instructors teach courses in the IST department?* Unless a query has already been set up to ask this question, you must create a new query.

Database users rarely need to see all of the records in all of the tables. That is why a query is so useful; it creates a ***subset*** of records—a portion of the total records—according to your specifications and then displays only those records.

Activity 2.07 | Creating a New Select Query in Design View

Previously, you created a query using the Query Wizard. To create complex queries, use Query Design view. The table or tables from which a query selects its data is referred to as the ***data source***.

1 On the Ribbon, click the **Create tab**, and then in the **Queries group**, click the **Query Design** button. Compare your screen with Figure 2.13.

> A new query opens in Design view and the Show Table dialog box displays, which lists both tables in the database.

Figure 2.13

Query1 tab

Queries group

Query Design button

Show Table dialog box

Available tables

2 In the **Show Table** dialog box, double-click **2A Instructors**, and then **Close** the **Show Table** dialog box.

> A field list for the 2A Instructors table displays in the upper area of the Query window. The Instructor ID field is the primary key field in this table. The Query window has two parts: the *table area* (upper area), which displays the field lists for tables that are used in the query, and the *design grid* (lower area), which displays the design of the query.

Alert! | **Is There More Than One Field List in the Query Window?**

If you double-click a table more than one time, a duplicate field list displays in the Query window. To remove a field list from the Query window, right-click the title bar of the field list, and then click Remove Table.

---

3 Point to the lower right corner of the field list to display the ⬚ pointer, and then drag down and to the right to expand the field list, displaying all of the field names and the table name. In the **2A Instructors** field list, double-click **Rank**, and then look at the design grid.

> The Rank field name displays in the design grid in the Field row. You limit the fields that display when the query is run by placing only the desired field names in the design grid.

4 In the **2A Instructors** field list, point to **First Name**, hold down the left mouse button, and then drag down into the design grid until the ⬚ pointer displays in the **Field** row in the second column. Release the mouse button, and then compare your screen with Figure 2.14.

> This is a second way to add field names to the design grid. As you drag the field, a small rectangular shape attaches to the mouse pointer. When you release the mouse button, the field name displays in the Field row.

Figure 2.14

2A Instructors field list expanded in table area

Two field names added to the Field row in design grid

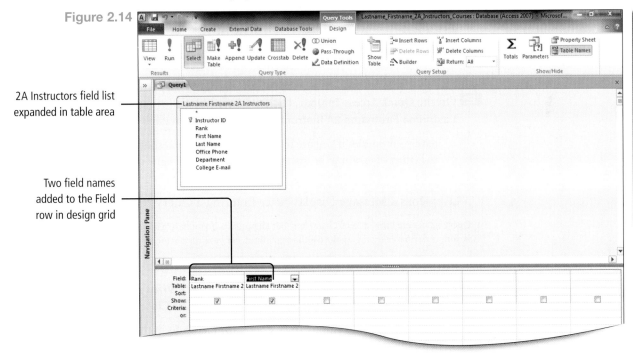

5 In design grid, in the **Field** row, click in the third column, and then click the **arrow** that displays. From the list, click **Last Name** to add the field to the design grid, which is a third way to add a field to the design grid.

6 Using one of the techniques you just practiced, add the **Office Phone** field to the fourth column and the **Department** field to the fifth column in the design grid.

Activity 2.08 | Running, Saving, Printing, and Closing a Query

After you create a query, you *run* it to display the results. When you run a query, Access looks at the records in the table (or tables) you have included in the query, finds the records that match the specified conditions (if any), and displays only those records in a datasheet. Only the fields that you have added to the design grid display in the query results. The query always runs using the current table or tables, presenting the most up-to-date information.

Another Way

On the Design tab, in the Results group, click the View button to automatically start the Run command.

1 On the **Design tab**, in the **Results group**, click the **Run** button, and then compare your screen with Figure 2.15.

This query answers the question, *What is the Rank, First Name, Last Name, Office Phone number, and Department of all of the instructors in the 2A Instructors table?* A query is a subset of the records in one or more tables, arranged in Datasheet view, using the fields and conditions that you specify. The five fields that you specified in the design grid display in columns, and the records from the 2A Instructors table display in rows.

Figure 2.15

Five fields specified in design grid

Records displayed in rows

2 On the **Quick Access Toolbar**, click the **Save** button. In the **Save As** dialog box, type **Lastname Firstname 2A Instructors Query** and then click **OK**.

Save your queries if you are likely to ask the same question again; doing so will save you the effort of creating the query again to answer the same question.

Alert! | Does a Message Display After Entering a Query Name?

Query names are limited to 64 characters. For all projects, if you have a long last name or first name that results in your query name exceeding the 64-character limit, ask your instructor how you should abbreviate your name.

---

3 Display **Backstage** view, click **Print**, and then click **Print Preview**. Create a paper or electronic printout if instructed to do so, and then **Close Print Preview**.

Queries answer questions and gather information from the data in the tables. Queries are typically created as a basis for a report, but query results can be printed like any other table of data.

4 **Close** ⊠ the query. **Open** » the **Navigation Pane**, and then notice that the **2A Instructors Query** object displays under the **2A Instructors** table object.

The new query name displays in the Navigation Pane under the table with which it is related—the 2A Instructors table. Only the design of the query is saved. The records still reside in the table object. Each time you open the query, Access runs it again and displays the results based on the data stored in the related table(s). Thus, the results of a query always reflect the latest information in the related table(s).

Objective 5 | Create a New Query from an Existing Query

You can create a new query from scratch or you can open an existing query, save it with new name, and modify the design to suit your needs. Using an existing query saves you time if your new query uses all or some of the same fields and conditions in an existing query.

Activity 2.09 | Creating a New Query from an Existing Query

1 From the **Navigation Pane**, open your **2A Instructors Query** by either double-clicking the name or by right-clicking and clicking Open.

The query runs, opens in Datasheet view, and displays the records from the 2A Instructors table as specified in the query design grid.

2 Display **Backstage** view, and then click **Save Object As**. In the **Save As** dialog box, type **Lastname Firstname 2A Instructor IDs Query** and then click **OK**. Click the **Home tab**, and then in the **Views group**, click the **View** button to switch to **Design** view.

A new query, based on a copy of the 2A Instructors Query, is created and displays in the object window and in the Navigation Pane under its data source—the 2A Instructors table.

3 **Close** « the **Navigation Pane**. In the design grid, point to the thin gray selection bar above the **Office Phone** field name until the ↓ pointer displays. Click to select the **Office Phone** column, and then press Del.

This action deletes the field from the query design only—it has no effect on the field in the underlying 2A Instructors table. The Department field moves to the left. Similarly, you can select multiple fields and delete them at one time.

4 From the gray selection bar, select the **First Name** column. In the selected column, point to the selection bar to display the ▷ pointer, and then drag to the right until a dark vertical line displays on the right side of the **Last Name** column. Release the mouse button to position the **First Name** field in the third column.

To rearrange fields in the query design, select the field to move, and then drag it to a new position in the design grid.

5 Using the technique you just practiced, move the **Department** field to the left of the **Rank** field.

6 From the field list, drag the **Instructor ID** field down to the first column in the design grid until the ▷ pointer displays, and then release the mouse button. Compare your screen with Figure 2.16.

The Instructor ID field displays in the first column, and the remaining four fields move to the right. Use this method to insert a field to the left of a field already displayed in the design grid.

Access | Chapter 2

Figure 2.16

New query created by copying the 2A Instructors Query

First Name in the last column

Five fields in the design grid

Instructor ID in the first column

Department in the second column

7 On the **Design tab**, in the **Results group**, click the **Run** button.

This query answers the question, *What is the Instructor ID, Department, Rank, Last Name, and First Name for every instructor in the 2A Instructors table?* The results of the query are a subset of the records contained in the 2A Instructors table. The records are sorted by the primary key field—Instructor ID.

8 From **Backstage** view, display the query in **Print Preview**. Create a paper or electronic printout if instructed to do so, and then **Close Print Preview**.

9 **Close** ☒ the query, and in the message box, click **Yes** to save the changes to the design—deleting a field, moving two fields, and adding a field. **Open** ☒ the **Navigation Pane**.

The query is saved and closed. The new query name displays in the Navigation Pane under the related table. Recall that when you save a query, only the *design* of the query is saved; the records reside in the related table object or objects.

Objective 6 | Sort Query Results

You can sort the results of a query in ascending or descending order in either Datasheet view or Design view. Use Design view if your query results should display in a specified sort order, or if you intend to use the sorted results in a report.

Activity 2.10 | Sorting Query Results

In this activity, you will save an existing query with a new name, and then sort the query results by using the Sort row in Design view.

1 On the **Navigation Pane**, click your **2A Instructor IDs Query**. Display **Backstage** view, and then click **Save Object As**. In the **Save As** dialog box, type **Lastname Firstname 2A Department Sort Query** and then click **OK**. Click the **Home tab**, and then drag the right edge of the **Navigation Pane** to the right to increase its width so that the names of the new query and the relationship report display fully.

Access creates a new query, based on a copy of your 2A Instructors ID Query; that is, the new query includes the same fields in the same order as the query on which it is based.

2 In the **Navigation Pane**, right-click your **2A Department Sort Query**, and then click **Design View. Close** ◄◄ the **Navigation Pane**.

3 In the design grid, in the **Sort** row, click in the **Last Name** field to display the insertion point and an arrow. Click the **Sort arrow**, and then in the list, click **Ascending**. Compare your screen with Figure 2.17.

Figure 2.17

Sort row in design grid ——

Ascending sort added to Last Name field ——

4 On the **Design tab** in the **Results group**, click the **Run** button.

In the query result, the records are sorted in ascending alphabetical order by the Last Name field, and two instructors have the same last name of *Widimer*.

5 On the **Home tab** in the **Views group**, click the **View** button to switch to **Design** view.

6 In the **Sort** row, click in the **First Name** field, click the **Sort arrow**, and then click **Ascending. Run** the query.

In the query result, the records are sorted first by the Last Name field. If instructors have the same last name, then Access sorts those records by the First Name field. The two instructors with the last name of *Widimer* are sorted by their first names.

7 Switch to **Design** view. In the **Sort** row, click in the **Department** field, click the **Sort arrow**, and then click **Descending. Run** the query; if necessary, scroll down to display the last records, and then compare your screen with Figure 2.18.

In Design view, fields with a Sort designation are sorted from left to right. That is, the sorted field on the left becomes the outermost sort field, and the sorted field on the right becomes the innermost sort field.

Thus, the records are sorted first in descending alphabetical order by the Department field—the leftmost sort field. Then, within each same department name field, the Last Names are sorted in ascending alphabetical order. And, finally, within each same last name field, the First Names are sorted in ascending alphabetical order.

If you run a query and the sorted results are not what you intended, be sure that the fields are displayed from left to right according to the groupings that you desire.

Access | Chapter 2

Figure 2.18

Department names sorted in descending order

Within each Department, Last Names sorted in ascending order

Within each Last Name, First Names sorted in ascending order

8 Display the query in **Print Preview**. Create a paper or electronic printout if instructed to do so, and then **Close Print Preview. Close** ☒ the query. In the message box, click **Yes** to save the changes to the query design.

More Knowledge | Sorting

If you add a sort order to the *design* of a query, it remains as a permanent part of the query design. If you use the sort buttons in the Datasheet view, they will override the sort order of the query design, and can be saved as part of the query. A sort order designated in Datasheet view does not display in the Sort row of the query design grid.

Objective 7 | Specify Criteria in a Query

Queries locate information in a database based on ***criteria*** that you specify as part of the query. Criteria are conditions that identify the specific records for which you are looking.

Criteria enable you to ask a more specific question; therefore, you will get a more specific result. For example, if you want to find out how many instructors are in the IST department, limit the results to that specific department, and then only the records that match the specified department will display.

Activity 2.11 | Specifying Text Criteria in a Query

In this activity, you will assist Dean Judkins by creating a query to answer the question *How many instructors are in the IST Department?*

1 Be sure that all objects are closed and that the **Navigation Pane** is closed. Click the **Create tab**, and then in the **Queries group**, click the **Query Design** button.

2 In the **Show Table** dialog box, **Add** the **2A Instructors** table to the table area, and then **Close** the **Show Table** dialog box.

3 Expand the field list to display all of the fields and the table name. Add the following fields to the design grid in the order given: **Department**, **Instructor ID**, **Rank**, **First Name**, and **Last Name**.

4 In the **Criteria** row of the design grid, click in the **Department** field, type **IST** and then press Enter. Compare your screen with Figure 2.19.

> Access places quotation marks around the criteria to indicate that this is a ***text string***—a sequence of characters. Use the Criteria row to specify the criteria that will limit the results of the query to your exact specifications. The criteria is not case sensitive; so you can type *ist* instead of IST.

Figure 2.19

Five fields added to the design grid

Criteria row in design grid

Criteria under Department—Access adds quotation marks

Note | Pressing Enter After Adding Criteria

If you press Enter or click in another column or row in the query design grid after you have added your criteria, you can see how Access alters the criteria so it can interpret what you have typed. Sometimes, there is no change, such as when you add criteria to a number or currency field. Other times, Access may capitalize a letter or add quotation marks or other symbols to clarify the criteria. Whether or not you press Enter after adding criteria has no effect on the query results. It is used here to help you see how the program behaves.

5 **Run** the query, and then compare your screen with Figure 2.20.

> Thirteen records display that meet the specified criteria—records that have *IST* in the Department field.

Figure 2.20

Thirteen records match Department *IST* criteria

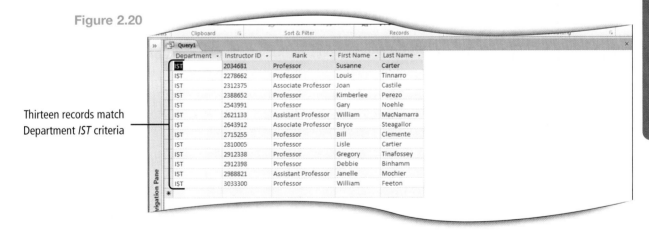

Alert! | Do Your Query Results Differ?

If you mistype the criteria, or enter it under the wrong field, or make some other error, the result will display no records. This indicates that there are no records in the table that match the criteria as you entered it. If this occurs, return to Design view and re-examine the query design. Verify that the criteria is typed in the Criteria row, under the correct field, and without typing errors. Then run the query again.

6 Save 🔲 the query as **Lastname Firstname 2A IST Query** and then display the query in **Print Preview**. Create a paper or electronic printout if instructed to do so, and then **Close Print Preview**.

7 Close ☒ the query, **Open** » the **Navigation Pane**, and then notice that the **2A IST Query** object displays under the **2A Instructors** table—its data source.

> Recall that queries in the Navigation Pane display an icon of two overlapping tables.

Activity 2.12 | Specifying Criteria Using a Field Not Displayed in the Query Results

So far, all of the fields that you included in the query design have also been included in the query results. It is not required to have every field in the query display in the results. In this activity, you will create a query to answer the question, *Which instructors have a rank of Professor?*

1 Close « the **Navigation Pane**. Click the **Create tab**, and then in the **Queries group**, click the **Query Design** button.

2 From the **Show Table** dialog box, **Add** the **2A Instructors** table to the table area, and then **Close** the dialog box. Expand the field list.

3 Add the following fields, in the order given, to the design grid: **Instructor ID**, **First Name**, **Last Name**, and **Rank**.

4 In the **Sort** row, in the **Last Name** field, click the **Sort arrow**; click **Ascending**.

5 In the **Criteria** row, click in the **Rank** field, type **professor** and then press Enter. Compare your screen with Figure 2.21.

> Recall that criteria is not case sensitive. As you start typing *professor*, a list of functions display, from which you can select if including a function in your criteria. When you press Enter, the insertion point moves to the next criteria box and quotation marks are added around the text string that you entered.

Figure 2.21

Show row; check boxes selected for every field

Last Name field sorted in Ascending order

Criteria for Rank field

6 In the design grid, in the **Show** row, notice that the check box is selected for every field. **Run** the query to view the query results.

> Nineteen records meet the criteria. In the Rank column each record displays *Professor*, and the records are sorted in ascending alphabetical order by the Last Name field.

7 Switch to **Design** view. In the design grid, under **Rank**, in the **Show** row, click to clear the check box.

> Because it is repetitive and not particularly useful to have *Professor* display for each record in the query results, clear this check box so that the field does not display. However, you should run the query before clearing the Show check box to be sure that the correct records display.

8 **Run** the query, and then notice that the *Rank* field does not display.

> The query results display the same 19 records, but the *Rank* field does not display. Although the Rank field is still included in the query criteria for the purpose of identifying specific records, it is not necessary to display the field in the results. When appropriate, clear the Show check box to avoid cluttering the query results with data that is not useful.

9 **Save** 🖫 the query as **Lastname Firstname 2A Professor Rank Query** and then display the query in **Print Preview**. Create a paper or electronic printout if instructed to do so, and then **Close Print Preview**. **Close** ⊠ the query.

Activity 2.13 | Using *Is Null* Criteria to Find Empty Fields

Sometimes you must locate records where data is *missing*. You can locate such records by using *Is Null*—empty—as the criteria in a field. Additionally, you can display only the records where a value *has* been entered in a field by using *Is Not Null* as the criteria, which will exclude records where the specified field is empty. In this activity, you will design a query to find out *Which scheduled courses have no credits listed?*

1 Click the **Create tab**. In the **Queries group**, click the **Query Design** button. Add the **2A Schedule** table to the table area, **Close** the **Show Table** dialog box, and then expand the field list.

2 Add the following fields to the design grid in the order given: **Subject**, **Catalog#**, **Section**, **Course Name**, and **Credits**.

3 In the **Criteria** row, click in the **Credits** field, type **is null** and then press [Enter].

> Access capitalizes *is null*. The criteria *Is Null* examines the field and looks for records that do *not* have any values entered in the Credits field.

4 In the **Sort** row, click in the **Subject** field, click the **Sort arrow**, and then click **Ascending**. **Sort** the **Catalog#** field in **Ascending** order, and then **Sort** the **Section** field in **Ascending** order. Compare your screen with Figure 2.22.

Figure 2.22

Three fields sorted in ascending alphabetical order

Is Null criteria in Credits field

Access | Chapter 2

5 **Run** the query, and then compare your screen with Figure 2.23.

> Five scheduled courses do not have credits listed—the Credits field is empty. The records are sorted in ascending order first by the Subject field, then by the Catalog # field, and then by the Section. Using the information displayed in the query results, a course scheduler can more easily locate the records in the table to enter the credits.

Figure 2.23

Credits field empty
(null) for five courses

Sorted first by Subject

Within Subject,
sorted by Catalog#

Within Catalog#,
sorted by Section

6 **Save** 🖫 the query as **Lastname Firstname 2A No Credits Query** and then display the query in **Print Preview**. Create a paper or electronic printout if instructed to do so, and then **Close Print Preview**.

7 **Close** ✖ the query. **Open** ≫ the **Navigation Pane**, and then notice that the **2A No Credits Query** object displays under the **2A Schedule** table object, which is the query's data source.

8 From **Backstage** view, click **Close Database**, and then click **Exit** to close the Access program. As directed by your instructor, submit your database and the eight paper or electronic printouts—relationship report, sorted table, and six queries—that are the results of this project.

End **You have completed Project 2A**

Project 2B Athletic Scholarships Database

myitlab
Project 2B Training

Project Activities

In Activities 2.14 through 2.26, you will assist Randy Shavrain, Athletic Director for Capital Cities Community College, in developing and querying his Athletic Scholarships database. Your results will look similar to Figure 2.24.

Project Files

For Project 2B, you will need the following files:

a02B_Athletes_Scholarships
a02B_Athletes (Excel file)

You will save your database as:

Lastname_Firstname_2B_Athletic_Scholarships

Project Results

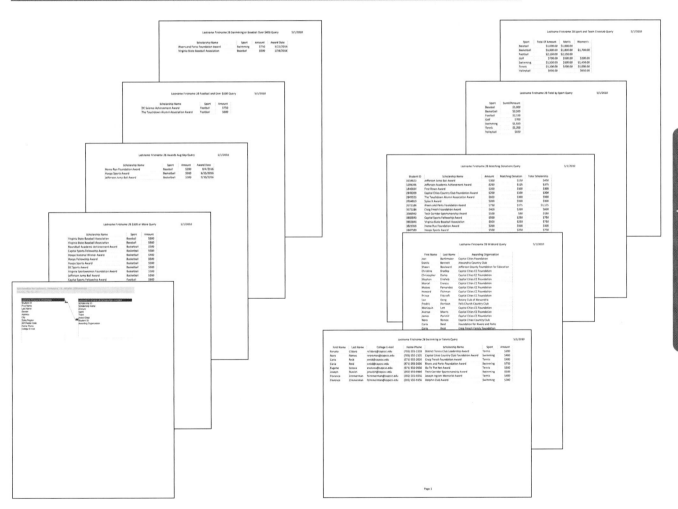

Figure 2.24
Project 2B Athletic Scholarships

Access | **Chapter 2**

Objective 8 | Specify Numeric Criteria in a Query

Criteria can be set for fields containing numeric data. When you design your table, set the appropriate data type for fields that will contain numbers, currency, or dates so that mathematical calculations can be performed.

Activity 2.14 | Opening an Existing Database and Importing a Spreadsheet

In this activity, you will open, rename, and save an existing database, and then import an Excel spreadsheet that Mr. Shavrain wants to bring into Access as a new table.

1 **Start** Access. In **Backstage** view, click **Open**. From your student files, open **a02B_Athletes_Scholarships**.

2 From **Backstage** view, click **Save Database As**. In the **Save As** dialog box, navigate to your **Access Chapter 2** folder, and then in the **File name** box, type **Lastname_Firstname_2B_Athletic_Scholarships** and then press Enter.

3 On the **Message Bar**, click the **Enable Content** button. In the **Navigation Pane**, **Rename 2B Scholarships Awarded** to **Lastname Firstname 2B Scholarships Awarded**, and then double-click to open the table. **Close** « the **Navigation Pane**, and then examine the data in the table. Compare your screen with Figure 2.25.

In this table, Mr. Shavrain tracks the names and amounts of scholarships awarded to student athletes. Students are identified only by their Student ID numbers, and the primary key is the Scholarship ID field.

Figure 2.25

Scholarship Name field

Amount field

Student ID numbers for students receiving scholarship

4 **Close** ✕ the table. On the Ribbon, click the **External Data tab**, and then in the **Import & Link group**, click the **Excel** button. In the **Get External Data – Excel Spreadsheet** dialog box, to the right of the **File name** box, click **Browse**.

5 In the **File Open** dialog box, navigate to your student data files, and then double-click **a02B_Athletes**. Be sure that the **Import the source data into a new table in the current database** option button is selected, and then click **OK**.

The Import Spreadsheet Wizard opens and displays the spreadsheet data.

6 Click **Next**. In the upper left portion of the **Import Spreadsheet Wizard** dialog box, select the **First Row Contains Column Headings** check box. Click **Next**, and then click **Next** again.

7 In the upper portion of the Wizard, click the **Choose my own primary key** option button, and then be sure that **Student ID** displays.

In the new table, Student ID will be the primary key. No two students have the same Student ID.

8 Click **Next**. In the **Import to Table** box, type **Lastname Firstname 2B Athletes** and then click **Finish**. In the **Get External Data – Excel Spreadsheet** Wizard, click **Close**, and then **Open** [»] the **Navigation Pane**. Widen the **Navigation Pane** so that the table names display fully.

9 **Open** the new **2B Athletes** table, and then on the **Home tab**, switch to **Design View**.

10 For the **Student ID** field, click in the **Data Type** box, click the **arrow**, and then click **Text**. For the **ZIP/Postal Code** field, change the **Data Type** to **Text**, and then set the **Field Size** to **5** Click in the **State/Region** field, set the **Field Size** to **2** and then switch back to **Datasheet View**, saving the changes.

Recall that numeric data that will not be used in any calculations, such as the Student ID, should have a Data Type of *Text*.

11 In the message box, click **Yes**—no data will be lost. **Close** [«] the **Navigation Pane**. Take a moment to review the imported data. Using the **Select All** button [ ], apply **Best Fit** to all of the fields. Click in any field to cancel the selection, **Save** [ ] the table, and then **Close** [×] the table.

Activity 2.15 | Creating Table Relationships

In this activity, you will create a one-to-many relationship between the 2B Athletes table and the 2B Scholarships Awarded table by using the common field—*Student ID*.

1 Click the **Database Tools tab**, and then in the **Relationships group**, click the **Relationships** button.

2 In the **Show Table** dialog box, **Add** the **2B Athletes** table, and then **Add** the **2B Scholarships Awarded** table to the table area. **Close** the **Show Table** dialog box.

3 Move and resize the two field lists to display all of the fields and the entire table name, and then position the field lists so that there is approximately one inch of space between the two field lists.

Resizing and repositioning the field lists is not required, but doing so makes it easier for you to view the field lists and the join line when creating relationships.

4 In the **2B Athletes** field list, point to the **Student ID** field. Hold down the left mouse button, drag into the **2B Scholarships Awarded** field list on top of the **Student ID** field, and then release the mouse button to display the **Edit Relationships** dialog box.

5 Point to the title bar of the **Edit Relationships** dialog box, and then drag it below the two field lists. In the **Edit Relationships** dialog box, be sure that **Student ID** is displayed as the common field for both tables.

The two tables relate in a *one-to-many* relationship—*one* athlete can have *many* scholarships. The common field between the two tables is the Student ID field. In the 2B Athletes table, Student ID is the primary key. In the 2B Scholarships Awarded table, Student ID is the foreign key.

6 In the **Edit Relationships** dialog box, select the **Enforce Referential Integrity** check box. Click **Create**, and then compare your screen with Figure 2.26.

The one-to-many relationship is established. The *1* and ∞ indicate that referential integrity is enforced, which ensures that a scholarship cannot be awarded to a student whose Student ID is not in the 2B Athletes table. Similarly, you cannot delete a student athlete from the 2B Athletes table if there is a scholarship listed for that student in the 2B Scholarships Awarded table.

Figure 2.26

Join line—symbols
indicate referential
integrity enforced

Primary key in the
one table

Foreign key in the
many table

7 On the **Design tab**, in the **Tools group**, click the **Relationship Report** button. Create a paper or electronic printout if instructed to do so.

8 Save 🖫 the report as **Lastname Firstname 2B Relationships** and then click **OK**. Close ✕ the report, and then Close ✕ the **Relationships** window.

9 Open » the **Navigation Pane**, open the **2B Athletes** table, and then Close « the **Navigation Pane**. On the left side of the table, in the first record, click the **plus sign** (+) to display the subdatasheet for the record.

> In the first record, for *Joel Barthmaier*, one related record exists in the 2B Scholarships Awarded table. The related record displays because you created a relationship between the two tables using Student ID as the common field.

10 Close ✕ the **2B Athletes** table.

Activity 2.16 | Specifying Numeric Criteria in a Query

Mr. Shavrain wants to know *Which scholarships are in the amount of $300, and for which sports?* In this activity, you will specify criteria in the query so that only the records of scholarships in the amount of $300 display.

1 Click the **Create tab**. In the **Queries group**, click the **Query Design** button.

2 In the **Show Table** dialog box, **Add** the **2B Scholarships Awarded** table to the table area, and then **Close** the **Show Table** dialog box. Expand the field list to display all of the fields and the entire table name.

3 Add the following fields to the design grid in the order given: **Scholarship Name**, **Sport**, and **Amount**.

4 In the **Sort** row, click in the **Sport** field. Click the **Sort arrow**, and then click **Ascending**.

5 In the **Criteria** row, click in the **Amount** field, type **300** and then press [Enter]. Compare your screen with Figure 2.27.

> When entering currency values as criteria, do not type the dollar sign. Include a decimal point only if you are looking for a specific amount that includes cents—for example 300.49. Access does not insert quotation marks around the criteria because the field's data type is Number.

Figure 2.27

Numeric criteria—no
quotation marks

Sort in ascending
order by *Sport*

6 On the **Design tab**, in the **Results group**, click the **Run** button to view the results.

Five scholarships were awarded in the exact amount of $300. In the navigation area, *1 of 5* displays to indicate the number of records that match the criteria.

7 On the **Home tab**, in the **Views group**, click the **View** button to switch to **Design** view.

Activity 2.17 | Using Comparison Operators

Comparison operators are symbols that evaluate each field value to determine if it is the same (=), greater than (>), less than (<), or in between a range of values as specified by the criteria.

If no comparison operator is specified, equal (=) is assumed. For example, in the previous activity, you created a query to display only records where the *Amount* is 300. The comparison operator of = was assumed, and Access displayed only records that had values equal to 300.

1 Be sure your query is displayed in **Design** view. In the **Criteria** row, click in the **Amount** field, delete the existing criteria, type **>300** and then press Enter.

2 On the **Design tab**, in the **Results group**, click the **Run** button.

Fourteen records have an Amount that is greater than $300. The results show the records for which the Amount is *greater than* $300, but do not display amounts that are *equal to* $300.

3 Switch to **Design** view. In the **Criteria** row, under **Amount**, delete the existing criteria. Type **<300** and then press Enter. **Run** the query.

Eleven records display and each has an Amount less than $300. The results show the records for which the Amount is *less than* $300, but does not include amounts that are *equal to* $300.

4 Switch to **Design** view. In the **Criteria** row, click in the **Amount** field, delete the existing criteria, type **>=300** and then press Enter.

5 **Run** the query, and then compare your screen with Figure 2.28.

Nineteen records display, including the records for scholarships in the exact amount of $300. The records include scholarships *greater than* or *equal to* $300. In this manner, comparison operators can be combined. This query answers the question, *Which scholarships have been awarded in the amount of $300 or more, and for which sports, with the Sport names in alphabetical order?*

Figure 2.28

Nineteen records with a scholarship amount of $300 or more

6 Save 🖫 the query as **Lastname Firstname 2B $300 or More Query** and then display the query in **Print Preview**. Create a paper or electronic printout if instructed to do so, and then **Close Print Preview**.

7 Close ⊠ the query. **Open** ⯈⯈ the **Navigation Pane**, and notice that the new query displays under the table from which it retrieved the records—*2B Scholarships Awarded*.

Activity 2.18 | Using the Between ... And Comparison Operator

The **Between ... And operator** is a comparison operator that looks for values within a range. It is useful when you need to locate records that are within a range of dates; for example, scholarships awarded between August 1 and September 30. In this activity, you will create a new query from an existing query, and then add criteria to look for values within a range of dates. The query will answer the question *Which scholarships were awarded between August 1 and September 30?*

1 On the **Navigation Pane**, click the **2B $300 or More Query** object to select it. Display **Backstage** view and click **Save Object As**. In the **Save As** dialog box, type **Lastname Firstname 2B Awards Aug-Sep Query** and then click **OK**.

2 Click the **Home tab**. Open the **2B Awards Aug-Sep Query** object, **Close** ⯇⯇ the **Navigation Pane**, and then switch to **Design** view. From the **2B Scholarships Awarded** field list, add the **Award Date** as the fourth field in the design grid.

3 In the **Criteria** row, click in the **Amount** field, and then delete the existing criteria so that the query is not restricted by amount. In the **Criteria** row, click in the **Award Date** field, type **between 8/1/16 and 9/30/16** and then press Enter.

4 In the selection bar of the design grid, point to the right edge of the **Award Date** column to display the ⊞ pointer, and then double-click. Compare your screen with Figure 2.29.

> The width of the Award Date column is increased to fit the longest entry, enabling you to see all of the criteria. Access places pound signs (#) around dates and capitalizes *between* and *and*. This criteria instructs Access to look for values in the Award Date field that begin with 8/1/16 and end with 9/30/16. Both the beginning and ending dates will be included in the query results.

Figure 2.29

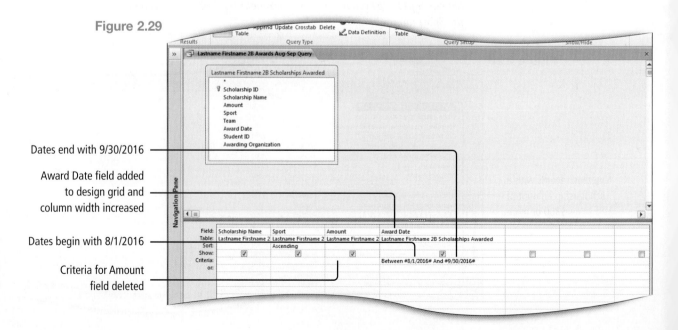

Dates end with 9/30/2016

Award Date field added to design grid and column width increased

Dates begin with 8/1/2016

Criteria for Amount field deleted

5 **Run** the query, and notice that three scholarships were awarded between 08/1/16 and 9/30/16.

6 Display the query in **Print Preview**, create a paper or electronic printout if instructed to do so, and then **Close Print Preview**.

7 **Close** ⊠ the query. In the message box, click **Yes** to save the changes to the query design. **Open** » the **Navigation Pane**, and notice that the new query displays under the table that is its data source—*2B Scholarships Awarded*.

Objective 9 | Use Compound Criteria

You can specify more than one condition—criteria—in a query; this is called *compound criteria*. Compound criteria use AND and OR *logical operators*. Logical operators enable you to enter criteria for the same field or different fields.

Activity 2.19 | Using AND Criteria in a Query

Compound criteria use an *AND condition* to display records in the query results that meet all parts of the specified criteria. In this activity, you will help Mr. Shavrain answer the question *Which scholarships over $500 were awarded for Football?*

1 **Close** « the **Navigation Pane**. On the Ribbon, click the **Create tab**. In the **Queries group**, click the **Query Design** button. **Add** the **2B Scholarships Awarded** table to the table area. **Close** the **Show Table** dialog box, and then expand the field list.

2 Add the following fields to the design grid in the order given: **Scholarship Name**, **Sport**, and **Amount**.

3 In the **Criteria** row, click in the **Sport** field, type **football** and then press ⏎.

4 In the **Criteria** row, in the **Amount** field, type **>500** and then press ⏎. Compare your screen with Figure 2.30.

> You create the AND condition by placing the criteria for both fields on the same line in the Criteria row. The results will display only records that contain *Football* AND an amount greater than *$500*.

Figure 2.30

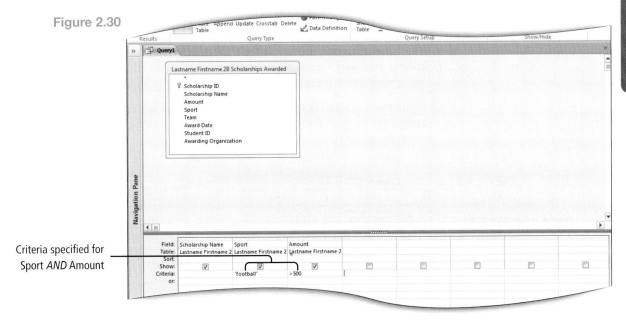

Criteria specified for Sport *AND* Amount

Access | Chapter 2

5 On the **Design tab**, in the **Results group**, click the **Run** button.

> Two records display that match both conditions—Football in the Sport field *and* greater than $500 in the Amount field.

6 **Save** 🖫 the query as **Lastname Firstname 2B Football and Over $500 Query** and then click **OK** or press Enter. **Close** ✖ the query.

7 **Open** ≫ the **Navigation Pane**, and then click one time to select the **2B Football and Over $500 Query** object. Display the query in **Print Preview**, create a paper or electronic printout if instructed to do so, and then **Close Print Preview**.

> You can print any selected object from the Navigation Pane—the object does not have to be open to print.

8 **Close** ≪ the **Navigation Pane**.

Activity 2.20 | Using OR Criteria in a Query

Use the *OR condition* to specify multiple criteria for a single field, or multiple criteria for different fields when you want to display the records that meet any of the conditions. In this activity, you will help Mr. Shavrain answer the question *Which scholarships over $400 were awarded in the sports of Baseball or Swimming, and what is the award date of each?*

1 Click the **Create tab**. In the **Queries group**, click the **Query Design** button.

2 **Add** the **2B Scholarships Awarded** table. **Close** the dialog box, expand the field list, and then add the following four fields to the design grid in the order given: **Scholarship Name**, **Sport**, **Amount**, and **Award Date**.

3 In the **Criteria** row, click in the **Sport** field, and then type **baseball**

4 In the design grid, on the **or** row, click in the **Sport** field, type **swimming** and then press Enter. **Run** the query.

> The query results display seven scholarship records where the Sport is either Baseball *or* Swimming. Use the OR condition to specify multiple criteria for a single field.

5 Switch to **Design** view. In the **or** row, under **Sport**, delete *swimming*. In the **Criteria** row, under **Sport**, delete *baseball*. Type **swimming or baseball** and then in the **Criteria** row, click in the **Amount** field. Type **>400** and then press Enter. Increase the width of the **Sport** column. Compare your screen with Figure 2.31.

> This is an alternative way to use the OR compound operator in the Sport field. Because criteria is entered for two different fields, Access selects the records that are Baseball *or* Swimming *and* that have a scholarship awarded in an amount greater than $400.

> If you enter swimming on the Criteria row and baseball on the or row, then you must enter >400 on both the Criteria row and the or row so that the correct records display when the query runs.

Figure 2.31

OR condition for two criteria in the same field

AND condition for Amount field

6 **Run** the query to display the two records that match the conditions.

7 **Close** [X] the query. In the message box, click **Yes** to save changes to the query. In the **Save As** dialog box, type **Lastname Firstname 2B Swimming or Baseball Over $400 Query** and then click **OK**.

8 **Open** [»] the **Navigation Pane**, increase the width of the **Navigation Pane** to display the full name of all objects, and then click one time to select the **2B Swimming or Baseball Over $400 Query** object. Display the query in **Print Preview**, create a paper or electronic printout if instructed to do so, and then **Close Print Preview**. **Close** [«] the **Navigation Pane**.

Objective 10 | Create a Query Based on More Than One Table

In a relational database, you can retrieve information from more than one table. Recall that a table in a relational database contains all of the records about a single topic. Tables are joined by relating the primary key field in one table to a foreign key field in another table. This common field creates a relationship, so you can include data from more than one table in a query.

For example, the Athletes table contains all of the information about the student athletes—name, address, and so on. The Scholarships Awarded table includes the scholarship name, amount, and so on. When an athlete receives a scholarship, only the Student ID field is included with the scholarship to identify who received the scholarship. It is not necessary to include any other data about the athletes in the Scholarships Awarded table; doing so would result in redundant data.

Activity 2.21 | Creating a Query Based on More Than One Table

In this activity, you will create a query that selects records from two tables. This is possible because a relationship has been created between the two tables in the database. The query will answer the questions *What is the name, e-mail address, and phone number of athletes who have received swimming or tennis scholarships, and what is the name and amount of the scholarship?*

1 Click the **Create tab**. In the **Queries group**, click the **Query Design** button. **Add** the **2B Athletes** table and the **2B Scholarships Awarded** table to the table area, and then **Close** the **Show Table** dialog box. Expand the two field lists, and then drag the **2B Scholarships Awarded** field list to the right so that there is approximately one inch of space between the field lists.

> The join line displays because you previously created a relationship between the tables. It indicates a *one-to-many* relationship—*one* athlete can have *many* scholarships.

2 From the **2B Athletes** field list, add the following fields to the design grid in the order given: **First Name**, **Last Name**, **College E-mail**, and **Home Phone**.

3 In the **Sort** row, click in the **Last Name** field. Click the **Sort arrow**, and then click **Ascending** to sort the records in alphabetical order by last name.

4 From the **2B Scholarships Awarded** field list, add the following fields to the design grid in the order given: **Scholarship Name**, **Sport**, and **Amount**.

5 In the **Criteria** row, click in the **Sport** field. Type **swimming or tennis** and then press Enter.

6 In the design grid, increase the width of the **Home Phone** and **Scholarship Name** columns to display the entire table name on the **Table** row. If necessary, scroll to the right to display the *Home Phone* and *Scholarship Name* fields in the design grid, and then compare your screen with Figure 2.32.

> When extracting data from multiple tables, the information on the Table row is helpful, especially when different tables include the same field names, such as address, but different data, such as a student's address or a coach's address.

Figure 2.32

Table row indicates data source

Criteria entered for Sport field

7 **Run** the query, and then compare your screen with Figure 2.33.

> Information for eight student athletes displays. The First Name and Last Name fields are included in the query results even though the common field—*Student ID*—is *not* included in the query design. Because Student ID is included in both tables, and a one-to-many relationship was created between the tables, the Student ID field is used to select the records in both tables by using one query. Two students—*Carla Reid* and *Florence Zimmerman*—received scholarships in both Swimming and Tennis. Recall that *one* student athlete can receive *many* scholarships.

Figure 2.33

Sport of *Tennis* or *Swimming*

Students with scholarships in both sports

8 Save the query as **Lastname Firstname 2B Swimming or Tennis Query** and then display the query in **Print Preview**. Set the **Margins** to **Normal**, and then change the orientation to **Landscape**. Create a paper or electronic printout if instructed to do so, and then **Close Print Preview**.

9 **Close** the query, **Open** the **Navigation Pane**, and then compare your screen with Figure 2.34.

> Your new query—*2B Swimming or Tennis Query*—displays under both tables from which it retrieved records.

Figure 2.34

Query displays
under data sources

Objective 11 | Use Wildcards in a Query

Wildcard characters serve as a placeholder for one or more unknown characters in the criteria. When you are unsure of the particular character or set of characters to include in criteria, use wildcard characters in place of the characters.

Activity 2.22 | Using a Wildcard in a Query

Use the asterisk (*) to represent one or more characters. For example, if you use the * wildcard in the criteria Fo*, the results will display Foster, Forrester, Forrest, Fossil, or any word beginning with *Fo*. In this activity, you will use the asterisk (*) wildcard in the criteria row to answer the question *Which athletes received scholarships from local Rotary Clubs, country clubs, or foundations?*

1 **Close** « the **Navigation Pane**. On the Ribbon, click the **Create tab**. In the **Queries group**, click the **Query Design** button.

2 **Add** both tables to the table area, **Close** the **Show Table** dialog box, and then expand the field lists.

3 Add the following fields to the design grid in the order given: from the **2B Athletes** table, **First Name** and **Last Name**; from the **2B Scholarships Awarded** table, **Awarding Organization**.

4 In the **Sort** row, click in the **Last Name** field. Click the **arrow**, and then click **Ascending**.

5 In the **Criteria** row, under **Awarding Organization**, type **rotary*** and then press Enter.

The wildcard character * is a placeholder to match one or more characters. After pressing Enter, Access adds *Like* to the beginning of the criteria.

6 **Run** the query, and then compare your screen with Figure 2.35.

Three athletes received scholarships from Rotary Clubs. The results are sorted alphabetically by the Last Name field.

Access | Chapter 2

Figure 2.35

Awarding Organization
for all records
begins with *Rotary*

First Name	·	Last Name	·	Awarding Organization	·
Ian		Geng		Rotary Club of Alexandria	
Eugene		Sotova		Rotary Club of Falls Church	
Khrystyna		Tilson		Rotary Club of Arlington	

7 Switch to **Design** view. On the **or** row, under **Awarding Organization**, type ***country club** and then press Enter.

> The * can be used at the beginning, middle, or end of the criteria. The position of the * wildcard character determines the location of the unknown characters. Here you will search for records that end in *Country Club*.

8 **Run** the query to display six records, and notice that three records begin with *Rotary*, and three records end with *Country Club*—sorted alphabetically by Last Name.

9 Switch to **Design** view. Under **Awarding Organization** and under **Like "*country club"**, type ***foundation*** and then press Enter. Compare your screen with Figure 2.36.

> The query will also display records that have the word *Foundation* anywhere—beginning, middle, or end—in the field. Three *OR* criteria have been entered for the Awarding Organization field—the query results will display students who have received scholarships from an organization name that begins with Rotary, *or* that ends in County Club, *or* that has Foundation anywhere in the middle of the name.

Figure 2.36

Three variations of
* wildcard placement

Field:	First Name	Last Name	Awarding Organizatic					
Table:	Lastname Firstname 2	Lastname Firstname 2	Lastname Firstname 2					
Sort:		Ascending						
Show:	✓	✓	✓					
Criteria:			Like "rotary*"					
or:			Like "*country club"					
			Like "*foundation*"					

10 **Run** the query to display 28 records.

> Twenty-eight scholarships were from a Country Club, *or* a Rotary Club, *or* a Foundation.

11 **Save** 🖫 the query as **Lastname Firstname 2B Wildcard Query** and then display the results in **Print Preview**. Create a paper or electronic printout if instructed to do so, and then **Close Print Preview**.

12 **Close** ✕ the query, and then **Open** » the **Navigation Pane**.

> Because the 2B Wildcard Query object retrieved data from two tables, it displays below the 2B Scholarships Awarded table *and* the 2B Athletes table—the data sources.

More Knowledge | Search for a Single Unknown Character by Using the ? Wildcard

The question mark (?) is a wildcard that is used to search for unknown single characters. For each question mark included in criteria, any character can be inserted. For example, if you use *b?d* as a criteria, the query might locate bid, bud, bed, or any three-character word beginning with *b* and ending with *d*. If *b??d* is entered as the criteria, the results could include bind, bend, bard, or any four-character word beginning with *b* and ending with *d*.

Objective 12 | Use Calculated Fields in a Query

Queries can create calculated values that are stored in a *calculated field*. A calculated field stores the value of a mathematical operation. For example, you can multiply two fields together, such as Total Credit Hours and Tuition Per Credit Hour to get a Total Tuition Due amount for each student without having to include a specific field for this amount in the table, which reduces the size of the database and provides more flexibility.

There are two steps to produce a calculated field in a query. First, name the field that will store the calculated values. Second, write the *expression*—the formula—that performs the calculation. Each field name used in the calculation must be enclosed within its own pair of square brackets, and the new field name must be followed by a colon (:).

Activity 2.23 | Using Calculated Fields in a Query

For each scholarship received by student athletes, the Capital Cities Community College Alumni Association will donate an amount equal to 50 percent of each scholarship. In this activity, you will create a calculated field to determine the additional amount each scholarship is worth. The query will answer the question *What is the value of each scholarship if the Alumni Association makes a matching 50% donation?*

1 **Close** « the **Navigation Pane**, and then click the **Create tab**. In the **Queries group**, click the **Query Design** button.

2 **Add** the **2B Scholarships Awarded** table to the table area, **Close** the **Show Table** dialog box, and then expand the field list. Add the following fields to the design grid in the order given: **Student ID**, **Scholarship Name**, and **Amount**.

3 In the **Sort** row, click in the **Student ID** field; sort **Ascending**.

4 In the **Field** row, right-click in the first empty column to display a shortcut menu, and then click **Zoom**.

The Zoom dialog box gives you more working space so that you can see the entire calculation as you type it. The calculation can also be typed directly in the empty Field box in the column.

5 In the **Zoom** dialog box, type **Matching Donation:[Amount]*0.5** and then compare your screen with Figure 2.37.

The first element, *Matching Donation*, is the new field name where the calculated values will display. Following that is a colon (:), which separates the new field name from the expression. *Amount* is enclosed in square brackets because it is an existing field name in the 2B Scholarships Awarded table; it contains the numeric data on which the calculation will be performed. Following the right square bracket is an asterisk (*), which in math calculations signifies multiplication. Finally, the percentage (0.5 or 50%) displays.

Figure 2.37

Zoom dialog box

New field name for calculated value followed by a colon (:)

Expression—formula that calculates the value

6 In the **Zoom** dialog box, click **OK**, and then **Run** the query. Compare your screen with Figure 2.38.

> The query results display three fields from the 2B Scholarships Awarded table plus a fourth field—*Matching Donation*—in which a calculated value displays. Each calculated value equals the value in the Amount field multiplied by 0.5.

Figure 2.38

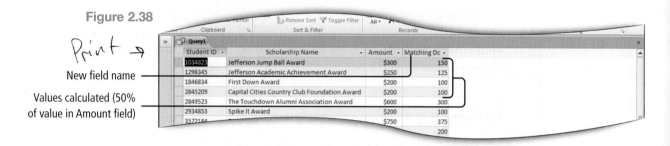

Print →

New field name

Values calculated (50% of value in Amount field)

> **Alert! | Does Your Screen Differ?**
>
> If your calculations in a query do not work, switch to Design view and carefully check the expression you typed. Spelling or syntax errors prevent calculated fields from working properly.

7 Notice the formatting of the **Matching Donation** field—there are no dollar signs, commas, or decimal places; you will adjust this formatting later.

> When using a number, such as 0.5, in an expression, the values in the calculated field may not be formatted the same as in the existing field.

8 Switch to **Design** view. In the **Field** row, in the first empty column, right-click, and then click **Zoom**. In the **Zoom** dialog box, type **Total Scholarship:[Amount]+[Matching Donation]** and then compare your screen with Figure 2.39.

> Each existing field name—*Amount* and *Matching Donation*—must be enclosed in separate pairs of brackets.

Figure 2.39

New field name followed by a colon (:)

Expression with two existing field names in separate pairs of brackets

9 In the **Zoom** dialog box, click **OK**, and then **Run** the query to view the results.

> *Total Scholarship* is calculated by adding together the Amount field and the Matching Donation field. The Total Scholarship column includes dollar signs, commas, and decimal points, which carried over from the Currency format in the Amount field.

10 Switch to **Design** view. In the **Field** row, click in the **Matching Donation** field box.

Another Way

Right-click the Matching Donation field name, and then click Properties.

11 On the **Design tab**, in the **Show/Hide group**, click the **Property Sheet** button.

> The *Property Sheet* displays on the right side of your screen. A Property Sheet is a list of characteristics—properties—for fields in which you can make precise changes to each property associated with the field. The left column displays the Property name, for example, Description. To the right of the Property name is the Property setting box.

12 In the **Property Sheet**, on the **General tab**, click in the **Format** property setting box, and then click the **arrow** that displays. Compare your screen with Figure 2.40.

> A list of formats for the Matching Donation field displays.

Figure 2.40

Property Sheet for Matching Donation field

Format arrow

List of formats for numeric field

13 In the list, click **Currency**. Click the next property, **Decimal Places**, click the **arrow**, and then click **0**.

14 In the design grid, in the **Field** row, click in the **Total Scholarship** field. On the **Property Sheet**, set the **Format** to **Currency** and the **Decimal Places** to **0**.

15 **Close** ⊠ the **Property Sheet**, and then **Run** the query. Select all of the columns and apply **Best Fit**.

> The Matching Donation and Total Scholarship fields are formatted as Currency with 0 decimal places.

16 **Save** 🖫 the query as **Lastname Firstname 2B Matching Donations Query** and then display the query results in **Print Preview**. Change the **Orientation** to **Landscape**. Create a paper or electronic printout if instructed to do so, and then **Close Print Preview**. **Close** ⊠ the query.

Access | Chapter 2

Objective 13 | Calculate Statistics and Group Data in a Query

In Access queries, you can perform statistical calculations on a group of records. Calculations that are performed on a group of records are called *aggregate functions*.

Activity 2.24 | Using the MIN, MAX, AVG, and SUM Functions in a Query

In this activity, you will use the minimum, maximum, average, and sum functions in a query to examine the amounts of scholarships awarded. The last query will answer the question *What is the total dollar amount of all scholarships awarded?*

1 On the **Create tab**, in the **Queries group**, click the **Query Design** button.

2 **Add** the **2B Scholarships Awarded** table to the table area, **Close** the **Show Table** dialog box, and then expand the field list. Add the **Amount** field to the design grid.

> Include only the field you want to summarize in the query, so that the aggregate function (minimum, maximum, average, sum, and so forth) is applied to that single field.

3 On the **Design tab**, in the **Show/Hide group**, click the **Totals** button to add a **Total** row as the third row in the design grid. Notice that in the design grid, on the **Total** row, under **Amount**, *Group By* displays.

> Use the Total row to select the aggregate function that you want to use for the field.

4 In the **Total** row, under **Amount**, click in the **Group By** box, and then click the **arrow** to display the list of aggregate functions. Compare your screen with Figure 2.41, and take a moment to review the table in Figure 2.42.

Figure 2.41

Totals button in the Show/Hide group

Total row added to the design grid

List of aggregate functions

Aggregate Functions	
Function Name	**What It Does**
Sum	Totals the values in a field.
Avg	Averages the values in a field.
Min	Locates the smallest value in a field.
Max	Locates the largest value in a field.
Count	Counts the number of records in a field.
StDev	Calculates the Standard Deviation for the values in a field.
Var	Calculates the Variance for the values in a field.
First	Displays the First value in a field.
Last	Displays the Last value in a field.
Expression	Creates a calculated field that includes an aggregate function.
Where	Limits records to those that match a condition specified in the Criteria row.

Figure 2.42

5 From the list of functions, click **Min**, and then **Run** the query. Double-click the right edge of the column heading to apply Best Fit to the column.

> Access calculates the minimum (smallest) scholarship award—*$100.00*. The field name *MinOfAmount* displays for the calculation. This query answers the question, *What is the minimum (smallest) scholarship amount awarded?*

6 Switch to **Design** view. In the **Amount** field, in the **Total** row, select the **Max** function, and then **Run** the query.

> The maximum (largest) scholarship amount is *$750.00.*

7 Switch to **Design** view, select the **Avg** function, and then **Run** the query.

> The average scholarship amount awarded is *$358.33.*

8 Switch to **Design** view. Select the **Sum** function, and then **Run** the query.

> Access sums the Amount field for all records and displays a result of *$10,750.00*. The field name, SumOfAmount, displays. This query answers the question, *What is the total dollar amount of all the scholarships awarded?*

Activity 2.25 | Grouping Data in a Query

Aggregate functions can also be used to calculate totals by groups of data. For example, to group (summarize) the amount of scholarships awarded to each student, you include the Student ID field, in addition to the Amount field, and then group all of the records for each student together to calculate a total awarded to each student. Similarly, you can calculate how much is awarded for each sport.

1 Switch to **Design** view. Drag the **Student ID** field to the first column of the design grid—**Amount** becomes the second column. On the **Total** row, under **Student ID**, notice that *Group By* displays.

This query groups—summarizes—the records by StudentID and calculates a total Amount for each student.

2 **Run** the query, and then compare your screen with Figure 2.43.

The query calculates the total amount of all scholarships for each student.

Figure 2.43

Total scholarship amount awarded to each student

3 Switch to **Design** view. In the design grid, delete the **Student ID** field, and then drag the **Sport** field to the first column—**Amount** becomes the second column.

4 In the design grid, click in the **Amount** field, and then on the **Design tab**, in the **Show/Hide group**, click the **Property Sheet** button.

5 In the **Property Sheet**, set the **Format** to **Currency**, set the **Decimal Places** to **0**, and then **Close** ☒ the **Property Sheet**.

6 **Run** the query, and then compare your screen with Figure 2.44.

Access summarizes the data by sport. Basketball scholarships are the largest total Amount—*$3,500.*

Figure 2.44

Total scholarship amount awarded for each sport

7 Save 🔲 the query as **Lastname Firstname 2B Total by Sport Query** and then display the query results in **Print Preview**. Create a paper or electronic printout if instructed to do so, and then **Close Print Preview**. **Close** ⏹ the query.

Objective 14 | Create a Crosstab Query

A *crosstab query* uses an aggregate function for data that can be grouped by two types of information and displays data in a compact, spreadsheet-like format. A crosstab query always has at least one row heading, one column heading, and one summary field. Use a crosstab query to summarize a large amount of data in a small space that is easy to read.

Activity 2.26 | Creating a Crosstab Query Using One Table

In this activity, you will create a crosstab query that displays the total amount of scholarships awarded for each sport and for each team—women's or men's.

1 On the **Create tab**, in the **Queries group**, click the **Query Wizard** button. In the **New Query** dialog box, click **Crosstab Query Wizard**, and then click **OK**.

2 In the **Crosstab Query Wizard**, click **Table: 2B Scholarships Awarded** and then click **Next**.

3 To select the row headings, under **Available Fields**, double-click **Sport** to sort the scholarship amounts by the different sports. Click **Next**, and then compare your screen with Figure 2.45.

> The sports are displayed as *row headings*; here you are prompted to select *column* headings.

Figure 2.45

Crosstab Query Wizard—
select column heading

Sport names display
as row headings

4 To select the column headings, in the field list, click **Team**. Click **Next**, and then compare your screen with Figure 2.46.

The teams will be listed as column headings; here you are prompted to select a field to summarize.

Figure 2.46

Teams display as column headings

5 Under **Fields**, click **Amount**. Under **Functions**, click **Sum**, and then click **Next**.

The crosstab query will sum the Amount field for each sport and team.

6 In the **What do you want to name your query?** box, type **Lastname Firstname 2B Sport and Team Crosstab Query** and then click **Finish**. Apply **Best Fit** to the columns, click in any field to cancel the selection, and then compare your screen with Figure 2.47.

The crosstab query displays the total amount of scholarships awarded by sport and also by men's or women's teams. For example, for the sport of Golf, a total of $700 was awarded in scholarship money; $500 to men's teams and $200 to women's teams. A crosstab query is useful to display a summary of data based on two different fields—in this case, by sport and by teams.

Figure 2.47

Grouped by Teams

Total amount of
scholarship per Sport

Grouped by Sport

7 Display the query results in **Print Preview**. Create a paper or electronic printout if instructed to do so, and then **Close Print Preview**. **Close** ☒ the query, and click **Yes** to save changes to the query layout.

8 **Open** ⟩⟩ the **Navigation Pane**. In **Backstage** view, click **Close Database**, and then click **Exit**. As directed by your instructor, submit your database and the ten paper or electronic printouts—relationship report and nine queries—that are the results of this project.

More Knowledge | Creating a Crosstab Query Using Two Related Tables

To create a crosstab query using fields from more than one table, you must first create a select query with the fields from both tables that will be included in the crosstab query.

End **You have completed Project 2B** ————————————————

Access | Chapter 2

Summary

Sorting data in a table reorders the records based on one or more fields. Use queries to ask complex questions about the data in a database in a manner that Access can interpret. Save queries so they can be run as needed against current records. Use queries to limit the fields that display, add criteria to restrict the number of records in the query results, create calculated values, include data from more than one table, and to display data grouped by two types of information.

Key Terms

Matching

Match each term in the second column with its correct definition in the first column by writing the letter of the term on the blank line in front of the correct definition.

_____ 1. The area below the Ribbon that displays information such as security alerts.

_____ 2. An area where you can view the security and privacy settings for your Access installation.

_____ 3. An association that you establish between two tables based on common fields.

_____ 4. A relationship between two tables where one record in the first table corresponds to many records in the second table.

_____ 5. A list of field names in a table.

_____ 6. The field that is included in the related table so the field can be joined with the primary key in another table for the purpose of creating a relationship.

_____ 7. A set of rules that ensures that the data between related tables is valid.

_____ 8. The line joining two tables that visually indicates the common fields and the type of relationship.

_____ 9. A format for displaying related records in a datasheet when you click the plus sign (+) next to a record in a table on the one side of a relationship.

_____ 10. The process of arranging data in a specific order based on the value in a field.

A Ascending

B Descending

C Field list

D Foreign key

E Innermost

F Join line

G Message Bar

H One-to-many relationship

I Outermost

J Referential integrity

K Relationship

L Select query

M Sorting

N Subdatasheet

O Trust Center

_____ 11. A sorting order that arranges text in alphabetical order (A to Z) or numbers from lowest to highest.

_____ 12. A sorting order that arranges text in reverse alphabetical order (Z to A) or numbers from highest to lowest.

_____ 13. When sorting on multiple fields in Datasheet view, the field that is used for the first level of sorting.

_____ 14. When sorting on multiple fields in Datasheet view, the field that is used for the second level of sorting.

_____ 15. A database object that retrieves (selects) specific data from one or more tables and then displays the results in Datasheet view.

Multiple Choice

Circle the correct answer.

1. The lower area of the Query window that displays the design of the query is the:
   A. design grid   B. property sheet   C. table area

2. The process in which Access searches the records in the table, finds the records that match specified criteria, and then displays the records in a datasheet is:
   A. select   B. run   C. sort

3. Conditions in a query that identify the specific records for which you are looking are known as:
   A. aggregate functions   B. criteria   C. expressions

4. A criteria that searches for fields that are empty is:
   A. Is Empty   B. Is Not Null   C. Is Null

5. The symbols of =, >, and < are known as:
   A. aggregate functions   B. comparison operators   C. logical operators

6. A comparison operator that looks for values within a range is:
   A. And   B. Between ... And   C. Or

7. The logical operator that requires all conditions to be met is:
   A. AND   B. Is Null   C. OR

8. A wildcard character that serves as a placeholder for one or more unknown characters is the:
   A. *   B. ?   C. /

9. A field that stores the value of a mathematical operation is:
   A. an aggregate field   B. a calculated field   C. an expression

10. A query that uses an aggregate function for data that can be grouped by two types of information is:
    A. an aggregate query   B. a calculated query   C. a crosstab query

Content-Based Assessments

Apply **2A** skills from these Objectives:

1. Open an Existing Database
2. Create Table Relationships
3. Sort Records in a Table
4. Create a Query in Design View
5. Create a New Query from an Existing Query
6. Sort Query Results
7. Specify Criteria in a Query

Skills Review | Project **2C** Music Department

In the following Skills Review, you will assist Dr. William Jinkens, the Capital Cities Community College Music Director, in using his database to answer various questions about the instruments in the Music Department's inventory. Your results will look similar to Figure 2.48.

Project Files

For Project 2C, you will need the following file:

  a02c_Music_Department

You will save your database as:

  Lastname_Firstname_2C_Music_Department

Project Results

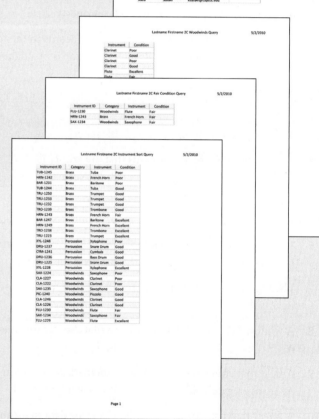

Figure 2.48

(Project 2C Music Department continues on the next page)

Content-Based Assessments

Skills Review | Project 2C Music Department (continued)

1 **Start** Access. In **Backstage** view, click **Open**. Navigate to the student files that accompany this textbook, and then open the **a02C_Music_Department** database.

  a. Click the **File tab** to return to **Backstage** view, and then click **Save Database As**. In the **Save As** dialog box, navigate to your **Access Chapter 2** folder. In the **File name** box, select the file name, and then type Lastname_Firstname_2C_Music_Department and then press [Enter]. In the **Message Bar**, click **Enable Content**.

  b. **Rename** the **2C Student Musicians** table to **Lastname Firstname 2C Student Musicians** and then **Rename** the **2C Instruments Inventory** to **Lastname Firstname 2C Instruments Inventory** Widen the **Navigation Pane** to display fully both table names.

2 **Open** both tables to examine the contents of each, **Close** the tables, and then **Close** the **Navigation Pane**.

  a. Click the **Database Tools tab**, and in the **Relationships group** click the **Relationships** button. Drag the **Show Table** dialog box down into the lower right portion of your screen.

  b. In the **Show Table** dialog box, click your **2C Student Musicians**, and then click **Add**. Double-click your **2C Instruments Inventory** to add the table to the **Relationships** window. In the **Show Table** dialog box, click **Close**.

  c. Drag the **2C Instruments Inventory** field list—the field list on the right—to the right about 3 inches. In the **2C Student Musicians** field list—the field list on the left—position your mouse pointer over the lower right corner of the field list to display the ⤡ pointer, and then drag to the right to increase the width of the field list until the entire name of the table in the title bar displays and all of the field names display. Then use the ⤡ pointer to resize the **2C Instruments Inventory** field list so that all of the field names and the table name display.

  d. In the **2C Student Musicians** field list, point to **Student ID**, hold down the left mouse button, and then drag down and to the right to the **2C Instruments Inventory** field list until your mouse pointer is on top of **Student ID**. Then release the mouse button. Drag the **Edit Relationships** dialog box to the lower portion of your screen. The relationship between the two tables is a one-to-many relationship; *one* student can play *many* instruments.

  e. In the **Edit Relationships** dialog box, click to select the **Enforce Referential Integrity** check box, and then click the **Create** button. On the **Design tab**, in the **Tools group**, click the **Relationship Report** button. On the **Print Preview tab**, in the **Page Size group**, change the **Margins** to **Normal**, and then create a paper or electronic printout as directed.

  f. **Save** the relationship report with the default name. **Close** the report, and then **Close** the **Relationships** window. From the **Navigation Pane**, open the **2C Instruments Inventory** table, and then **Close** the **Navigation Pane**.

3 In the **Condition** field, click any record. On the **Home tab**, in the **Sort & Filter group**, click the **Descending** button to sort the records from *Poor* to *Excellent*. In the field names row, click the **Category arrow**, and then click **Sort A to Z** to sort the records first by *Category* and then by *Condition*.

  a. Display **Backstage** view, click **Print**, and then click **Print Preview**. Create a paper or electronic copy as directed. **Close Print Preview**, **Close** the table, and then click **No**; you do not need to save the sort changes.

4 Click the **Create tab**, and then in the **Queries group**, click the **Query Design** button. In the **Show Table** dialog box, double-click your **2C Instruments Inventory** table, and then **Close** the **Show Table** dialog box. Expand the field list.

  a. Double-click **Instrument ID** to add the field to the design grid. Point to the **Category** field, hold down the left mouse button, and then drag the field down into the design grid until you are pointing to the **Field** row in the second column. Release the mouse button.

  b. In design grid, in the **Field** row, click in the third column, and then click the **arrow** that displays. From the list, click **Instrument** to add the field to the design grid. Using the technique of your choice, add the **Student ID** field to the fourth column and the **Condition** field to the fifth column in the design grid.

  c. On the **Design tab**, in the **Results group**, click the **Run** button. This query answers the question, *What is the Instrument ID, Category, Instrument, Student ID, and Condition of all of the instruments in the 2C Instruments Inventory table?*

  d. **Save** the query as **Lastname Firstname 2C All Instruments Query** and then click **OK**. Display the query in **Print Preview**, and then create a paper or electronic printout as directed. **Close Print Preview**.

(Project 2C Music Department continues on the next page)

Content-Based Assessments

5 Display **Backstage** view, click **Save Object As**. In the **Save As** dialog box, type **Lastname Firstname 2C Condition Query** and then click **OK** to create a new query based on an existing query. Click the **Home tab**, and then switch to **Design** view.

a. In the design grid, point to the thin gray selection bar above the **Student ID** field name until the ↓ pointer displays. Click to select the **Student ID** column, and then press Del.

b. In the gray selection bar, select the **Instrument ID** column. Point to the **selection bar** to display the ▷ pointer, and then drag to the right until a dark vertical line displays on the right side of the **Condition** column. Release the mouse button to position the **Instrument ID** field in the fourth column.

c. **Run** the query. The query results display four fields. This query answers the question, *What is the Category, Instrument, Condition, and Instrument ID for every Instrument in the 2C Instruments Inventory table?*

d. Display the query in **Print Preview**, and then create a paper or electronic printout as directed. **Close Print Preview**, **Close** the query, and in the message box, click **Yes** to save the changes to the design—you moved two fields. **Open** the **Navigation Pane**.

6 **Open** your **2C All Instruments Query**. **Save** the query object as **Lastname Firstname 2C Instrument Sort Query** and then click the **Home tab**. **Close** the **Navigation Pane**. Switch to **Design** view.

a. In the design grid, delete the **Student ID** field. In the **Sort** row, click in the **Category** field. Click the **Sort arrow**, and then in the list, click **Ascending**. In the **Sort** row, click in the **Condition** field, click the **Sort arrow**, and then click **Descending**. **Run** the query. This query answers the question, *For every Instrument ID, within each Category (with Category sorted in ascending order), what Instruments are in the inventory and what is the instrument's Condition (with Condition sorted in descending order)?*

b. Display the query in **Print Preview**. Create a paper or electronic printout if instructed to do so, and then **Close Print Preview**. **Close** the query. In the message box, click **Yes** to save the changes to the query design.

7 Click the **Create tab**, and then in the **Queries group**, click the **Query Design** button. **Add** your **2C Instruments Inventory** table to the table area, and then **Close** the **Show Table** dialog box. Expand the field list. Add the following

fields to the design grid in the order given: **Instrument ID**, **Category**, **Instrument**, and **Condition**.

a. In the design grid, on the **Criteria** row, click in the **Condition** field, type **fair** and then press Enter. **Run** the query; three records display that meet the specified criteria—records that have *fair* in the Condition field.

b. **Save** the query as **Lastname Firstname 2C Fair Condition Query** and then create a paper or electronic printout as directed. **Close Print Preview**, and then **Close** the query.

c. **Create** a new query in **Query Design** view. **Add** the **2C Instruments Inventory** table to the table area, and then expand the field list. Add the following fields, in the order given, to the design grid: **Category**, **Instrument**, and **Condition**.

d. In the **Criteria** row, click in the **Category** field, type **woodwinds** and then press Enter. Under **Category**, in the **Show** row, click to clear the check box, and then **Run** the query. Ten instruments are categorized as woodwinds. Recall that if all results use the same criteria, such as *woodwinds*, it is not necessary to display the data in the query results.

e. **Save** the query as **Lastname Firstname 2C Woodwinds Query** and then create a paper or electronic printout as directed. **Close Print Preview**. **Close** the query.

f. **Create** a new query in **Query Design** view. **Add** the **2C Student Musicians** table to the table area, and then expand the field list. Add the following fields, in the order given, to the design grid: **First Name**, **Last Name**, **E-mail Address**, and **Phone Number**.

g. In the **Criteria** row, click in the **Phone Number** field, type **is null** and then press Enter. In the **Sort** row, click in the **Last Name** field, click the **Sort arrow**, and then click **Ascending**. **Run** the query. Three student musicians do not have a phone number stored in the 2C Student Musicians table.

h. **Save** the query as **Lastname Firstname 2C Missing Phone Numbers Query** and then create a paper or electronic printout as directed. **Close Print Preview**, and then **Close** the query. **Open** the **Navigation Pane**.

i. Display **Backstage** view, click **Close Database**, and then click **Exit** to close the Access program. As directed by your instructor, submit your database and the eight paper or electronic printouts— relationship report, sorted table, and six queries— that are the results of this project.

End **You have completed Project 2C**

Content-Based Assessments

Apply **2B** skills from these Objectives:

- **8** Specify Numeric Criteria in a Query
- **9** Use Compound Criteria
- **10** Create a Query Based on More Than One Table
- **11** Use Wildcards in a Query
- **12** Use Calculated Fields in a Query
- **13** Calculate Statistics and Group Data in a Query
- **14** Create a Crosstab Query

Skills Review | Project **2D** Concerts and Sponsors

In the following Skills Review, you will assist Dr. William Jinkens, the Capital Cities Community College Music Director, in answering questions about concerts, sponsors, box office receipts, dates, and concert locations. Your results will look similar to Figure 2.49.

Project Files

For Project 2D, you will need the following files:

a02D_Concerts_Sponsors
a02D_Sponsors (Excel file)

You will save your database as:

Lastname_Firstname_2D_Concerts_Sponsors

Project Results

Figure 2.49

(Project 2D Concerts and Sponsors continues on the next page)

Content-Based Assessments

1 **Start** Access. In the **Backstage** view, click **Open**. Navigate to the student files that accompany this textbook, and then open the **a02D_Concerts_Sponsors** database.

a. Click the **File tab** to return to **Backstage** view, and then click **Save Database As**. In the **Save As** dialog box, navigate to your **Access Chapter 2** folder. In the **File name** box, select the file name, and then type Lastname_Firstname_2D_Concerts_Sponsors and then press Enter. In the **Message Bar**, click **Enable Content**. **Rename** the **2D Concerts** table to **Lastname Firstname 2D Concerts** and then widen the **Navigation Pane** to display the entire table name.

b. Click the **External Data tab**, and then in the **Import & Link group**, click the **Excel** button. In the **Get External Data – Excel Spreadsheet** dialog box, click **Browse**. Navigate to your student files, and then double-click the Excel file **a02D_Sponsors**. Be sure that the **Import the source data into a new table in the current database** option button is selected, and then click **OK**.

c. In the **Import Spreadsheet Wizard**, select the **First Row Contains Column Headings** check box, and then click **Next**. Click **Next** again. Click the **Choose my own primary key** option button, and then be sure that **Sponsor ID** displays. Click **Next**. In the **Import to Table** box, type **Lastname Firstname 2D Sponsors** and then click **Finish**. In the Wizard, click **Close**. The imported Excel spreadsheet becomes the second table in the database.

d. From the **Navigation Pane**, open your **2D Sponsors** table. Apply **Best Fit** to all columns, and then **Close** the table, saving changes to the design. Click the **Database Tools tab**, and in the **Relationships group**, click the **Relationships** button. **Add** the **2D Sponsors** table, and then **Add** the **2D Concerts** table to the table area. **Close** the **Show Table** dialog box. Expand and move the field lists as necessary.

e. In the **2D Sponsors** field list, point to the **Sponsor ID** field, hold down the left mouse button, drag into the **2D Concerts** field list, position the mouse pointer on top of the **Sponsor ID** field, and then release the mouse button. In the **Edit Relationships** dialog box, select the **Enforce Referential Integrity** check box, and then click the **Create** button. A one-to-many relationship is established; *one* sponsor organization can sponsor *many* concerts.

f. On the **Design tab**, in the **Tools group**, click the **Relationship Report** button. Create a paper or electronic printout as directed, and then **Close** the report. In the message box, click **Yes**; and then in the **Save As** dialog box, click **OK** to save the report with the default name. **Close** the **Relationships** window, and then **Close** the **Navigation Pane**.

2 Click the **Create tab**, and then in the **Queries group**, click the **Query Design** button. **Add** the **2D Concerts** table to the table area, **Close** the **Show Table** dialog box, and then expand the field list.

a. Add the following fields to the design grid in the order given: **Concert Name**, **Box Office Receipts**, and **Concert Location**. Click in the **Sort** row under **Concert Location**, click the **Sort arrow**, and then click **Ascending**. In the **Criteria** row, under **Box Office Receipts**, type >=800 press Enter, and then **Run** the query. Nine records meet the criteria. This query answers the question, *Which concerts had Box Office Receipts of $800 or more, and where was each concert held in alphabetical order by Concert Location?*

b. **Save** the query as **Lastname Firstname 2D $800 or More Query** and then create a paper or electronic printout as directed. **Close Print Preview**.

c. With the query still open, display **Backstage** view, click **Save Object As**, type **Lastname Firstname 2D Concerts Jan-Apr Query** and then click **OK**. Click the **Home tab**, and then switch to **Design** view. From the **2D Concerts** field list, add **Date** as the fourth field in the design grid.

d. In the **Criteria** row, under **Box Office Receipts**, delete the existing criteria so that the query is not restricted by receipts. Click in the **Sort** row under **Concert Location**, click the **Sort arrow**, and then click (**not sorted**). Click in the **Sort** row under **Date**, click the **Sort arrow**, and then click **Ascending**.

e. Click in the **Criteria** row under **Date**, type **between 1/1/16 and 4/30/16** and then press Enter. **Run** the query. Five records meet the criteria. This query answers the question, *What is the Concert Name, Box Office Receipts, Concert Location, and Date, in chronological order between January 1, 2016, and April 30, 2016, of concerts held?* **Print** or submit electronically as directed. **Close Print Preview**, **Close** the query, and then click **Yes** to save the changes to the query design.

(Project 2D Concerts and Sponsors continues on the next page)

Content-Based Assessments

3 **Create** a query in **Query Design** view. **Add** the **2D Concerts** table to the table area, **Close** the **Show Table** dialog box, and then expand the field list. Add the following fields to the design grid in the order given: **Concert Name, Concert Location,** and **Box Office Receipts.**

a. In the **Criteria** row, under **Concert Location,** type **Virginia Community Theater** and then press Enter. In the **Criteria** row, under **Box Office Receipts,** type **<=1000** and then press Enter. In the **Concert Location** field, clear the **Show** check box. **Run** the query; two records display. This query answers the question, *Which concerts that were held at the Virginia Community Theater had Box Office Receipts of $1,000 or less?*

b. **Save** the query as **Lastname Firstname 2D VCT Low Box Office Receipts Query** and then create a paper or electronic printout as directed. **Close** the query.

c. **Create** a query in **Query Design** view. **Add** the **2D Concerts** table to the table area, **Close** the **Show Table** dialog box, and then expand the field list. Add the following fields to the design grid: **Concert Name, Concert Location, Box Office Receipts,** and **Date.**

d. In the **Criteria** row, under **Concert Location,** type **Virginia Community Theater or DC Events Center** and press Enter. In the **Criteria** row, under **Box Office Receipts,** type **>1000** and then press Enter. In the **Sort** row, under **Date,** click the **Sort arrow,** and then click **Ascending.**

e. **Run** the query. Four records display. This query answers the question, *Which concerts held at either the Virginia Community Theater or the DC Events Center had Box Office Receipts of more than $1,000 and on what dates, in chronological order, were the concerts held?*

f. **Save** the query as **Lastname Firstname 2D VCT or DC Over $1000 Query** and then create a paper or electronic printout as directed. **Close Print Preview,** and then **Close** the query.

4 **Create** a query in **Query Design** view, **Add** both tables to the table area, and then expand the field lists. Reposition the field lists so that **2D Sponsors** is on the left side. From the **2D Sponsors** field list, add the following fields to the design grid in the order given: **Sponsor Name** and **Web Address.** Click in the **Sort** row

under **Sponsor Name,** click the **Sort arrow,** and then click **Ascending.**

a. From the **2D Concerts** field list, add the following fields to the design grid in the order give: **Concert Name, Concert Location,** and **Box Office Receipts.**

b. In the **Criteria** row, under **Concert Location,** type **Virginia Community Theater** and then click in the **or** row, under **Concert Location.** Type **DC Events Center** and then press Enter.

c. In the design grid, select the **Box Office Receipts** field, and then drag it to the first field position in the grid. **Run** the query; 12 records display. This query answers the question, *What were the Box Office Receipts, Sponsor Name, sponsor Web Address, Concert Name, and Concert Location of all concerts held at either the Virginia Community Theater or the DC Events Center, sorted alphabetically by Sponsor Name?*

d. **Save** the query as **Lastname Firstname 2D Receipts and Sponsors VCT or DC Query** and then display the query results in **Print Preview.** Change the orientation to **Landscape,** change the **Margins** to **Normal,** and then create a paper or electronic printout as directed. **Close** the query.

5 **Create** a query in **Query Design** view, **Add** both tables to the table area, **Close** the **Show Table** dialog box, and then expand the field lists. Reposition the field lists so that **2D Sponsors** is on the left side.

a. From the **2D Sponsors** field list, add the **Sponsor Name** field to the design grid. From the **2D Concerts** field list, add the **Concert Name** field to the design grid.

b. In the **Criteria** row, under **Sponsor Name,** type ***radio*** and then press Enter. In the **Criteria** row, under **Concert Name,** type ***festival** and then press Enter.

c. **Run** the query; two records have the word *Radio* somewhere in the Sponsor Name and the word *Festival* at the end of the Concert Name. This query answers the question, *Which radio stations are sponsoring Festival-type concerts?* **Save** the query as **Lastname Firstname 2D Radio Festivals Query** and then create a paper or electronic printout as directed. **Close** the query.

6 **Create** a query in **Query Design** view. **Add** both tables to the table area, **Close** the **Show Table** dialog box, and then expand the field lists. If necessary, reposition the

(Project 2D Concerts and Sponsors continues on the next page)

Access | Chapter 2

field lists so that *2D Sponsors* is on the left side. From the field lists, add the following fields to the design grid in the order given: **Concert ID**, **Sponsor Name**, and **Box Office Receipts**. Click in the **Sort** row under **Concert ID**, click the **Sort arrow**, and then click **Ascending**.

a. Sponsors have indicated that they will donate an additional amount to the Music Department based on 50 percent of the Box Office Receipts. On the **Field** row, right-click in the first empty column to display a shortcut menu, and then click **Zoom**. In the **Zoom** dialog box, type **Matching Donation:[Box Office Receipts]*0.5** and then click **OK**.

b. **Run** the query to view the new field—*Matching Donation*. Switch to **Design** view. In the **Field** row, in the first empty column, right-click, and then click **Zoom**. In the **Zoom** dialog box, type **Total Receipts: [Box Office Receipts]+[Matching Donation]** and then click **OK**. **Run** the query to view the results.

c. Switch to **Design** view. In the field row, click in the **Matching Donations** field. In the **Show/Hide group**, click the **Property Sheet** button, and then set the **Format** to **Currency** and the **Decimal Places** to **2**. **Close** the **Property Sheet**.

d. **Run** the query. This query answers the question *In ascending order by Concert ID, assuming each sponsor makes a matching 50 percent donation based on each concert's Box Office Receipts, what is the Sponsor Name, Box Office Receipts, Matching Donation, and Total Receipts for each concert?*

e. Select all of the columns, and then apply **Best Fit**. **Save** the query as **Lastname Firstname 2D Matching Donation Query** and then display the query results in **Print Preview**. Change the orientation to **Landscape**, and then create a paper or electronic printout as directed. **Close** the query.

7 Create a query in **Query Design** view. **Add** the **2D Concerts** table to the table area, **Close** the **Show Table** dialog box, and then expand the field list. Add the **Box Office Receipts** field to the design grid.

a. On the **Design tab**, in the **Show/Hide group**, click the **Totals** button, which adds a *Total* row as the third row in the design grid. On the **Total** row, under **Box Office Receipts**, click in the **Group By** box. Click the **arrow**, and then click the **Sum** function.

b. With the field still selected, display the **Property Sheet**, set the **Decimal Places** to **0**, and then **Close** the **Property Sheet**. **Run** the query. The total Box Office Receipts for all the concerts was *$17,475*. Apply **Best Fit** to the **SumOfBox Office Receipts** column.

c. Switch to **Design** view. In the design grid, add the **Concert Location** field as the first field of the design grid. **Run** the query. This query answers the question *For each Concert Location, what are the total Box Office Receipts?*

d. **Save** the query as **Lastname Firstname 2D Total Receipts by Location Query** and then create a paper or electronic printout as directed. **Close** the query.

8 Create a query using the **Query Wizard**. In the **New Query** dialog box, click **Crosstab Query Wizard**, and then click **OK**. Be sure that **2D Concerts** is selected, and then click **Next**.

a. Under **Available Fields**, double-click **Sponsor ID** so that you can display Box Office Receipts by Sponsor ID, and then click **Next**. In the field list, click **Concert Location** to add the locations as column headings, and then click **Next**.

b. Under **Fields**, click **Box Office Receipts**. Under **Functions**, click **Sum**, and then click **Next**.

c. Name the query **Lastname Firstname 2D Sponsors and Locations Crosstab Query** and then click **Finish**. Click the **Home tab**, switch to **Design** view, click in the **Box Office Receipts** column, display the **Property Sheet**, and then set the **Decimal Places** to **0**. **Close** the **Property Sheet**, **Run** the query, and apply **Best Fit** to all of the columns. This query answers the question *By Sponsor ID, what are the total Box Office Receipts for each Concert Location?*

d. Display the query results in **Print Preview**. Change the orientation to **Landscape**, change the **Margins** to **Normal**, and then create a paper or electronic printout as directed—two pages result. **Close** the query, saving changes to the design.

e. **Open** the **Navigation Pane**. Increase the width of the **Navigation Pane** to display fully all of the object names. Display **Backstage** view, click **Close Database**, and then click **Exit**. As directed by your instructor, submit your database and the ten paper or electronic printouts—relationship report and nine queries—that are the results of this project.

End You have completed Project 2D

Content-Based Assessments

Apply **2A** skills from these Objectives:

1 Open an Existing Database
2 Create Table Relationships
3 Sort Records in a Table
4 Create a Query in Design View
5 Create a New Query from an Existing Query
6 Sort Query Results
7 Specify Criteria in a Query

Mastering Access | Project 2E Grants and Organizations

In the following Mastering Access project, you will assist Susan Elkington, Director of Grants for the college, in using her database to answer questions about public and private grants awarded to the college departments. Your results will look similar to Figure 2.50.

Project Files

For Project 2E, you will need the following file:

a02E_Grants_Organizations

You will save your database as:

Lastname_Firstname_2E_Grants_Organizations

Project Results

Figure 2.50

(Project 2E Grants and Organizations continues on the next page)

1 **Start** Access. From your student files, open the **a02E_Grants_Organizations** database. Save the database in your **Access Chapter 2** folder as **Lastname_Firstname_ 2E_Grants_Organizations** and then enable the content. In the **Navigation Pane**, **Rename** the tables by adding **Lastname Firstname** to the beginning of each table name, and then widen the **Navigation Pane** to display fully both table names. **Open** both tables and examine their contents to become familiar with the data. **Close** both tables, and leave the **Navigation Pane** open.

2 Create a *one-to-many* relationship between the **2E Organizations** table and the **2E Grants Awarded** table based on the **Organization ID** field, and then **Enforce Referential Integrity**. *One* organization can award *many* grants. Create a **Relationship Report**, saving it with the default name. Create a paper or electronic printout as directed, and then **Close** all open objects, saving changes if prompted.

3 **Open** the **2E Grants Awarded** table, and then **Close** the **Navigation Pane**. **Sort** so that the records in the table are in alphabetical order by the **Department** and then in descending order by **Award Amount**. Create a paper or electronic printout as directed, being sure that the table prints on only one page by using **Landscape**, with **Normal** margins. **Close** the table, and do *not* save changes to the table.

4 **Create** a query in **Query Design** view, using the **2E Grants Awarded** table to answer the question, *What is the Grant ID, Grant Name, Award Amount, Type, and Award Date for all of the grants?* Display the fields in the order listed in the question. **Save** the query as **Lastname Firstname 2E All Grants Query** and then, with **Normal** margins, create a paper or electronic printout as directed. **Close Print Preview**, and leave the query open.

5 Use **2E All Grants Query** to create a new query. **Save** the **Object As Lastname Firstname 2E Grant Types Query** and then redesign the query to answer the question, *What is the Grant ID, Department, Type, Grant Name, and Award Amount for all grants?* Display the only the fields necessary to answer the question and in the order listed in the question. With **Normal** margins, create a paper or

electronic printout as directed. **Close** the query, saving the design changes.

6 From the **Navigation Pane**, open the **2E All Grants Query**, and then **Close** the **Navigation Pane**. **Save** the **Object As Lastname Firstname 2E Grant Sort Query** and then switch to **Design** view. Redesign the query to answer the question, *What is the Grant Name, Department, Award Amount, and Award Date for grants sorted first in alphabetical order by Department and then in descending order by Amount?* Display only the fields necessary to answer the question and in the order listed in the question. With **Normal** margins, create a paper or electronic printout as directed. **Close** the query, saving changes to the query design.

7 **Open** the **Navigation Pane**, open **2E Grant Sort Query**, and then **Close** the **Navigation Pane**. **Save** the **Object As Lastname Firstname 2E Private Grants Query** and then switch to **Design** view. Redesign the query to answer the question, *What is the Grant Name, Department, Award Amount, and Award Date for grants that have a Type of Private, sorted in alphabetical order by Grant Name?* Do *not* display the **Type** field in the query results; display the fields in the order listed in the question. With **Normal** margins, create a paper or electronic printout as directed. **Close** the query, saving changes to the query design.

8 **Create** a query in **Query Design** view, using the **2E Organizations** table to answer the question, *What is the Organization Name and Contact Name where the Contact Phone number is missing from the table, sorted in alphabetical order by the Organization Name?* Two records meet the criteria. **Save** the query as **Lastname Firstname 2E Missing Phone# Query** and then create a paper or electronic printout as directed. **Close** the query.

9 **Open** the **Navigation Pane** and widen it so that all object names display fully. In **Backstage** view, click **Close Database**, and then click **Exit**. As directed by your instructor, submit your database and the seven paper or electronic printouts—relationship report, sorted table, and five queries—that are the results of this project.

End **You have completed Project 2E**

Content-Based Assessments

Apply 2B skills from these Objectives:

- **8** Specify Numeric Criteria in a Query
- **9** Use Compound Criteria
- **10** Create a Query Based on More Than One Table
- **11** Use Wildcards in a Query
- **12** Use Calculated Fields in a Query
- **13** Calculate Statistics and Group Data in a Query
- **14** Create a Crosstab Query

In the following Mastering Access project, you will assist Hank Schwan, the Capital Cities Community College Facilities Manager, in using his database to answer questions about facilities that the college rents to community and private organizations at times when the facilities are not in use for college activities. Your results will look similar to Figure 2.51.

Project Files

For Project 2F, you will need the following files:

a02F_Events_Clients
a02F_Rental_Clients (Excel file)

You will save your database as:

Lastname_Firstname_2F_Events_Clients

Project Results

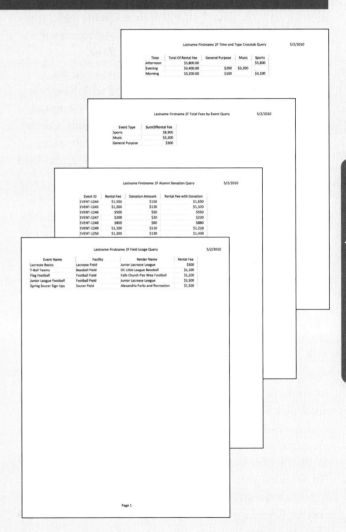

Figure 2.51

(Project 2F Events and Clients continues on the next page)

1 **Start** Access. From your student files, open the **a02F_Events_Clients** database. Save the database in your **Access Chapter 2** folder as **Lastname_Firstname_2F_ Events_Clients** and then enable the content. In the **Navigation Pane**, **Rename** the table by adding **Lastname Firstname** to the beginning of the table name.

2 **Import** the **a02F_Rental_Clients** Excel spreadsheet from the student data files that accompany this textbook into the current database as a new table. Designate the first row of the spreadsheet as column headings. Select the **Rental Client ID** field as the primary key. Name the table **Lastname Firstname 2F Rental Clients** and then widen the **Navigation Pane** to display fully the two table names. **Open** both tables and examine their contents to become familiar with the data. In the **2F Rental Clients** table, apply **Best Fit** to all of the columns. **Close** both tables, saving changes, and then **Close** the **Navigation Pane**.

3 Create a *one-to-many* relationship between the **2F Rental Clients** table and the **2F Events** table based on the **Rental Client ID** field, and then **Enforce Referential Integrity**. *One* rental client can have *many* events. Create a **Relationship Report**, saving it with the default name. Create a paper or electronic printout as directed, and then **Close** all open objects, saving changes if prompted.

4 **Create** a query in **Query Design** view using the **2F Events** table to answer the question, *What is the Event Name, Rental Client ID, and Rental Fee for events with fees greater than or equal to $500, in ascending order by Rental Client ID, and in which Facility was the event held?* Display the fields in the order listed in the question. Eleven records meet the criteria. **Save** the query as **Lastname Firstname 2F Fees $500 or More Query** Create a paper or electronic printout as directed. Leave the query open.

5 Using the **2F Fees $500 or More Query** object, create a new query, and save it as **Lastname Firstname 2F Afternoon Events Query** Redesign the query to answer the questions, *Which Events were held in the Afternoon between 7/1/16 and 8/31/16, in chronological order by date, what was the Rental Fee, and what was the Event ID?* (Hint: Open the 2F Events table to see how the Time field data is stored.). Do *not* display the **Time** field in the results, and do *not* restrict the results by **Rental Fee**. Four records meet the criteria. Create a paper or electronic printout as directed, **Close** the query, and save changes to the design.

6 **Create** a query in **Query Design** view using the **2F Events** table to answer the question, *Which Events and Event Types were held in either the White Sands Music Hall or the Theater that had Rental Fees greater than $500?* Display the fields in the order listed in the question. Three records meet the criteria. **Save** the query as **Lastname Firstname 2F WS and Theater Over $500 Query** and then create a paper or electronic printout as directed. **Close** the query.

7 **Create** a query in **Query Design** view using both tables to answer the question, *Which Events were held on one of the sports fields, for which Renter Name, and what was the Rental Fee in order of lowest fee to highest fee?* (Hint: Use a wildcard with the word *Field*.) Display the fields in the order listed in the question. Five records meet the criteria. **Save** the query as **Lastname Firstname 2F Field Usage Query** and then with **Normal** margins, create a paper or electronic printout as directed. **Close** the query.

8 The college Alumni Association will donate money to the Building Fund in an amount based on 10 percent of total facility rental fees. **Create** a query in **Query Design** view to answer the question, *In ascending order by Event ID, what will be the total of each Rental Fee if the Alumni Association donates an additional 10% of each fee?* (Hint: First compute the amount of the donation, name the new field **Donation Amount** and run the query to view the results. Then calculate the new rental fee and name the new field **Rental Fee with Donation**) **Run** the query.

Switch back to **Design** view, change the properties of the new fields to display in **Currency** format with **0** decimal places, and then **Run** the query again. For *EVENT-1244*, the *Donation Amount* is *$150* and the *Rental Fee with Donation* is *$1,650*. Apply **Best Fit** to the columns in the query results. **Save** the query as **Lastname Firstname 2F Alumni Donation Query** and then create a paper or electronic printout as directed. **Close** the query.

9 **Create** a query in **Query Design** view using the **2F Events** table and the **Sum** aggregate function to answer the question, *In descending order by Rental Fee, what are the total Rental Fees for each Event Type?* Change the properties of the appropriate field to display **Currency** format with **0** decimal places, and then **Run** the query. For a *Sports* Event Type, Rental Fees total *$8,900*. Apply **Best Fit** to the columns in the query results. **Save** the query as **Lastname Firstname 2F Total Fees by Event Query** and then create a paper or electronic printout as directed. **Close** the query.

(Project 2F Events and Clients continues on the next page)

Mastering Access | Project 2F Events and Clients (continued)

10 By using the **Query Wizard**, create a **Crosstab Query** based on the **2F Events** table. Select **Time** as the **row headings** and **Event Type** as the **column headings**. **Sum** the **Rental Fee** field. Name the query **Lastname Firstname 2F Time and Type Crosstab Query** Change the design to display **Currency** format with **0** decimal places in the appropriate column, and then apply **Best Fit** to all of the columns. This query answers the question *What are the total Rental Fees for each time of the day and for each Event Type?* Create

a paper or electronic printout as directed. **Close** the query, saving changes to the design.

11 **Open** the **Navigation Pane** and widen it so that all object names display fully. In **Backstage** view, click **Close Database**, and then click **Exit**. As directed by your instructor, submit your database and the eight paper or electronic printouts—relationship report and seven queries—that are the results of this project.

End **You have completed Project 2F** ———————————————————

Mastering Access | Project **2G** Students and Scholarships

In the following Mastering Access project, you will assist Thao Nguyen, Director of Academic Scholarships, in using her database to answer questions about scholarships awarded to students. Your results will look similar to Figure 2.52.

Project Files

For Project 2G, you will need the following file:

a02G_Students_Scholarships

You will save your database as:

Lastname_Firstname_2G_Students_Scholarships

Project Results

Figure 2.52

(Project 2G Students and Scholarships continues on the next page)

Content-Based Assessments

Mastering Access | Project 2G Students and Scholarships (continued)

1 **Start** Access. From your student files, open the **a02G_Students_Scholarships** database. Save the database in your **Access Chapter 2** folder as **Lastname_Firstname_2G_Students_Scholarships** and then enable the content. **Rename** both tables by adding **Lastname Firstname** to the beginning of the table name, and then widen the **Navigation Pane** to display fully the object names.

2 **Open** the two database tables to become familiar with the data. **Close** the tables, and then create a *one-to-many* relationship between the **2G Students** table and the **2G Scholarships Awarded** table based on the **Student ID** field, and then **Enforce Referential Integrity**; *one* student can have *many* scholarships. Create the **Relationship Report**, and create a paper or electronic printout as directed, saving it with the default name. **Close** all open objects.

3 Open the **2G Scholarships Awarded** table, and then **Sort** the appropriate fields in **Ascending** order so that the records are sorted by the **Major** field. Within each Major, the records should be sorted by **Scholarship Name**. Create a paper or electronic printout, being sure to print the results on one page. **Close** the table, and do *not* save changes to the table design. **Close** the **Navigation Pane**.

4 **Create** a query in **Query Design** view using the **2G Scholarships Awarded** table to answer the question, *In alphabetical order by Scholarship Name, what is the Amount and Major for scholarships greater than or equal to $500?* Display the fields in the order listed in the question. Ten records meet the criteria. **Save** the query as **Lastname Firstname 2G Scholarships $500 or More Query** and create a paper or electronic printout as directed. **Close Print Preview**, and leave the query open.

5 Using the **2G Scholarships $500 or More Query**, create a query. **Save** the **Object As Lastname Firstname 2G Scholarships 1st Qtr Query** and then redesign the query to answer the question *Which scholarships were awarded, in chronological order by Award Date, between 1/1/16 and 3/31/16, for what amount, and what was Student ID of the student?* Display the fields in the order listed in the question, display *only* the fields listed in the question, do not restrict the amount, and sort only by date. Eight records meet the criteria. Create a paper or electronic printout as directed. **Close** the query, saving changes.

6 **Create** a query in **Query Design** view using the **2G Scholarships Awarded** table to answer the question, *Which scholarships were awarded for either Nursing or CIS majors for amounts of more than $100, listed in descending*

order by amount? Display the fields in the order listed in the question. Four records meet the criteria. (Hint: If five records display, switch to **Design view** and combine the majors on one criteria line using OR.) **Save** the query as **Lastname Firstname 2G Nursing or CIS More Than $100 Query** and then create a paper or electronic printout as directed. **Close** the query.

7 **Create** a query in **Query Design** view. Use the **2G Students** table and a wildcard to answer the question, *In alphabetical order by City and in alphabetical order by Last Name, what are the Student ID, City, First Name, and Last Name of students from cities that begin with the letter A?* Display the fields in the order listed in the question. Four records meet the criteria. **Save** the query as **Lastname Firstname 2G Cities Query** Create a paper or electronic printout as directed. **Close** the query.

8 **Create** a query in **Query Design** view using the **2G Students** table and all of the table's fields to answer the question *For which students is the ZIP Code missing?* Three students are missing ZIP Codes. **Save** the query as **Lastname Firstname 2G Missing ZIP Query** and then with **Normal** margins, create a paper or electronic printout as directed. **Close** the query. Using the information that displays in the query results, an enrollment clerk can use a reference to look up the ZIP codes for the students and then enter the ZIP codes in the student records in the underlying table.

9 For each scholarship, the Board of Trustees of the college will donate an amount equal to 50 percent of each scholarship. **Create** a query in **Query Design** view. Use both tables and calculated fields to answer the question, *In alphabetical order by scholarship name, and including the first and last name of the scholarship recipient, what will the value of each scholarship be if the Board of Trustees makes a matching 50 percent donation?* (Hint: First compute the amount of the donation, naming the new field **Donation** and then calculate the new scholarship value, naming the new field **New Value**).

Run the query, switch back to **Design** view, and as necessary, change the properties of all the numeric fields to display in **Currency** format with **0** decimal places, and then **Run** the query. For the *Alexandria Historical Society Scholarship*, the *Donation* is *$150* and the *New Value* is *$450*. Apply **Best Fit** to the columns in the query results. **Save** the query as **Lastname Firstname 2G Trustee Donation Query** and then create a paper or electronic printout as directed, being sure to print the results on one page. **Close** the query.

(Project 2G Students and Scholarships continues on the next page)

Content-Based Assessments

Mastering Access | Project **2G** Students and Scholarships (continued)

10 **Create** a new query in **Query Design** view. Use the **2G Scholarships Awarded** table and the **Sum** aggregate function to answer the question *For each major, in descending order by amount, what are the total scholarship amounts?* Display the fields in the order listed in the question. Use the **Property Sheet** to display the sums in the **Currency** format with **0** decimal places. *History* majors received *$1,850* in scholarships. Apply **Best Fit** to the columns in the query results. **Save** the query as **Lastname Firstname 2G Total Scholarships by Major Query** and then create a paper or electronic printout as directed. **Close** the query.

11 **Create** a **Crosstab Query** using the **2G Scholarships Awarded** table. Use the **Student ID** field as row headings and the **Major** field as column headings to answer the

question *For each student or major, what is the total scholarship Amount awarded?* Name the query **Lastname Firstname 2G Student ID and Major Crosstab Query** In **Design** view, apply **0** decimal places to the appropriate fields. Apply **Best Fit** to the columns in the query results. **Save** the query, and then as directed, create a paper or electronic printout in **Landscape** orientation—the query results will print on two pages. **Close** the query.

12 **Open** the **Navigation Pane** and widen it to display all of the object names. In **Backstage** view, click **Close Database**, and then click **Exit**. As directed by your instructor, submit your database and the ten paper or electronic printouts—relationship report, sorted table, and eight queries—that are the results of this project.

End You have completed Project 2G ———————————

Content-Based Assessments

Apply a combination of
the **2A** and **2B** skills.

GO! Fix It | Project **2H** Social Sciences Division

Project Files

For Project 2H, you will need the following file:

a02H_Social_Sciences

You will save your database as:

Lastname_Firstname_2H_Social_Sciences

In this project, you will correct query design errors in a database used by the Dean of Social Sciences. From the student files that accompany this textbook, open the file a02H_Social_Sciences, and then save the database in your Access Chapter 2 folder as **Lastname_Firstname_2H_Social Sciences**

To complete the project you must find and correct errors in relationships, query design, and column widths. In addition to errors that you find, you should know:

- A relationship should be created between the 2H Social Sciences Faculty table and the 2H Anthropology Dept Course Schedule table. A relationship report should be created and named **Lastname Firstname 2H Relationship Report** One faculty member can teach many courses.

- You should add your last name and first name to each query name; do *not* rename the tables.

- Several queries do not accurately reflect the result implied in the query name. Open each query and examine and correct the design of any queries that do not accurately reflect the query name.

- Be sure that all of the object names in the Navigation Pane display fully.

- Create a paper or electronic printout of the relationship report and the four queries as directed by your instructor.

End **You have completed Project 2H**

Access | Chapter 2

Content-Based Assessments

Apply a combination of the **2A** and **2B** skills.

GO! Make It | Project 2I Faculty Awards

Project Files

For Project 2I, you will need the following file:

a02I_Faculty_Awards

You will save your database as:

Lastname_Firstname_2I_Faculty_Awards

Start Access, navigate to your student files, and then open the a02I_Faculty_Awards database file. Save the database in your Access Chapter 2 folder as **Lastname_Firstname_2I_Faculty Awards** Rename the two tables to include your name, create a relationship and relationship report. Then create two queries as shown in Figure 2.53. Create paper or electronic printouts as directed.

Project Results

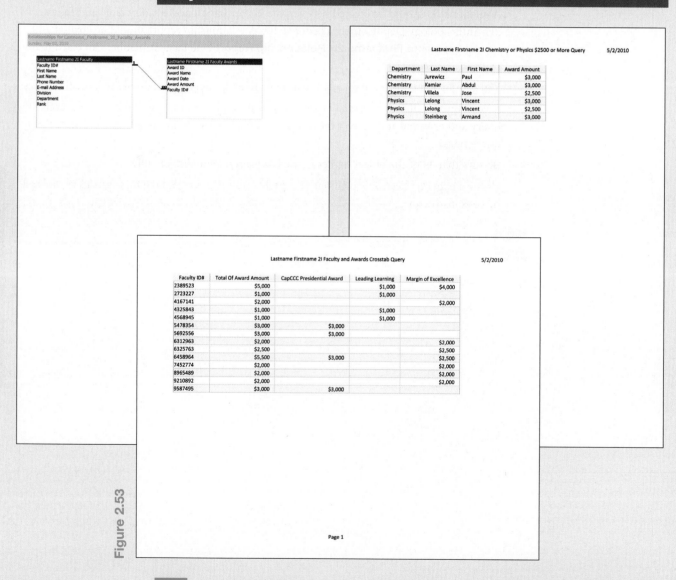

Figure 2.53

End You have completed Project 2I

Content-Based Assessments

GO! Solve It | Project 2J Student Refunds

Project Files

For Project 2J, you will need the following file:

a02J_Student_Refunds

You will save your database as:

Lastname_Firstname_2J_Student_Refunds

Start Access, navigate to your student files and open the a02J_Student_Refunds database file. Save the database in your Access Chapter 2 folder as **Lastname_Firstname_2J_Student Refunds** Rename the tables by adding **Lastname Firstname** to the beginning of each table name. Create a relationship between the tables—one student can have many refunds—and then create a relationship report.

Create and save a query to answer the question, *What is the First Name and Last Name of the students who are eligible for a refund and who live in Alexandria or Falls Church sorted alphabetically by Last Name within City?* Create and save a query to answer the question, *What is the total Refund Amount for Full Time and Part Time Students?* Create and save a query to answer the question, *In ascending order by Refund Eligibility Date, what is the Last Name and First Name of students receiving a Refund of more than $50 between the dates of 8/1/16 and 12/31/16?* Apply Best Fit to all the query results, and then create paper or electronic printouts of the report and queries as directed.

		Performance Level		
		Exemplary: You consistently applied the relevant skills	**Proficient:** You sometimes, but not always, applied the relevant skills	**Developing:** You rarely or never applied the relevant skills
Performance Element	Create relationship and relationship report	Relationship and relationship report created correctly.	Relationship and relationship report created with one error.	Relationship and relationship report created with two or more errors, or missing entirely.
	Create City query	Query created with correct name, fields, sorting, and criteria.	Query created with three elements correct and one incorrect.	Query created with two or more elements incorrect, or missing entirely.
	Create Refund query	Query created with correct name, fields, and criteria.	Query created with two elements correct and one incorrect.	Query created with two or more elements incorrect, or missing entirely.
	Create Refund Eligibility query	Query created with correct name, fields, sorting, and criteria.	Query created with three elements correct and one incorrect.	Query created with two or more two elements incorrect, or missing entirely.

End You have completed Project 2J

Content-Based Assessments

GO! Solve It | Project **2K** Leave

Project Files

For Project 2K, you will need the following file:

a02K_Leave

You will save your database as:

Lastname_Firstname_2K_Leave

Start Access, navigate to your student files, and then open the a02K_Leave database file. Save the database in your Access Chapter 2 folder as **Lastname_Firstname_2K_Leave** Rename the tables by adding **Lastname Firstname** to the beginning of each table name. Create a relationship between the tables—one employee can have many leave transactions—and a relationship report.

Create and save a query to answer the question, *Which employees, identified alphabetically by Last Name, have used Personal Leave?* Create and save a query to answer the question, *Which employees, identified alphabetically by Last Name, have no Phone Number?* Create and save a query to answer the question, *How many Leave Transactions were for Vacation leave grouped by the Employee# field?* (Hint: In the Total row of your query, use the Count function.) Create and save a crosstab query to answer the question, *What is the total number of leave transactions for each Employee # (row) by Leave Classification (column)?* Apply Best Fit to all of the query results, and then create paper or electronic printouts of the report and queries as directed by your instructor.

		Performance Level		
		Exemplary: You consistently applied the relevant skills	**Proficient:** You sometimes, but not always, applied the relevant skills	**Developing:** You rarely or never applied the relevant skills
Performance Element	Create relationship and relationship report	Relationship and relationship report created correctly.	Relationship and relationship report created with one error.	Relationship and relationship report created with two or more errors, or missing entirely.
	Create Personal Leave query	Query created with correct name, fields, sorting, and criteria.	Query created with three elements correct and one incorrect.	Query created with two or more elements incorrect, or missing entirely.
	Create Phone Number query	Query created with correct name, fields, and criteria.	Query created with two elements correct and one incorrect.	Query created with two or more elements incorrect, or missing entirely.
	Create Vacation Leave query	Query created with correct name, fields, grouping, and aggregate function.	Query created with three elements correct and one incorrect.	Query created with two or more elements incorrect, or missing entirely.
	Create Crosstab query	Query created with correct name, row headings, column headings, and aggregate function.	Query created with three elements correct and one incorrect.	Query created with two or more elements incorrect, or missing entirely.

End You have completed Project 2K

Outcomes-Based Assessments

Rubric

The following outcomes-based assessments are *open-ended assessments*. That is, there is no specific correct result; your result will depend on your approach to the information provided. Make *Professional Quality* your goal. Use the following scoring rubric to guide you in *how* to approach the problem and then to evaluate *how well* your approach solves the problem.

The *criteria*—Software Mastery, Content, Format and Layout, and Process—represent the knowledge and skills you have gained that you can apply to solving the problem. The *levels of performance*—Professional Quality, Approaching Professional Quality, or Needs Quality Improvements—help you and your instructor evaluate your result.

	Your completed project is of Professional Quality if you:	Your completed project is Approaching Professional Quality if you:	Your completed project Needs Quality Improvements if you:
1-Software Mastery	Choose and apply the most appropriate skills, tools, and features and identify efficient methods to solve the problem.	Choose and apply some appropriate skills, tools, and features, but not in the most efficient manner.	Choose inappropriate skills, tools, or features, or are inefficient in solving the problem.
2-Content	Construct a solution that is clear and well organized, contains content that is accurate, appropriate to the audience and purpose, and is complete. Provide a solution that contains no errors in spelling, grammar, or style.	Construct a solution in which some components are unclear, poorly organized, inconsistent, or incomplete. Misjudge the needs of the audience. Have some errors in spelling, grammar, or style, but the errors do not detract from comprehension.	Construct a solution that is unclear, incomplete, or poorly organized; contains some inaccurate or inappropriate content; and contains many errors in spelling, grammar, or style. Do not solve the problem.
3-Format and Layout	Format and arrange all elements to communicate information and ideas, clarify function, illustrate relationships, and indicate relative importance.	Apply appropriate format and layout features to some elements, but not others. Overuse features, causing minor distraction.	Apply format and layout that does not communicate information or ideas clearly. Do not use format and layout features to clarify function, illustrate relationships, or indicate relative importance. Use available features excessively, causing distraction.
4-Process	Use an organized approach that integrates planning, development, self-assessment, revision, and reflection.	Demonstrate an organized approach in some areas, but not others; or, use an insufficient process of organization throughout.	Do not use an organized approach to solve the problem.

Outcomes-Based Assessments

Apply a combination of the **2A** and **2B** skills.

GO! Think | Project **2L** Coaches

Project Files

For Project 2L, you will need the following file:

a02L_Coaches

You will save your database as:

Lastname_Firstname_2L_Coaches

Use the skills you have practiced in this chapter to assist Randy Shavrain, the Athletic Director, in answering questions about the coaches in your database **Lastname_Firstname_2L_Coaches** Create and save the relationship report with the default name, and save the queries you create with your name in the query title. Create paper or electronic printouts of the report and queries as directed by your instructor.

Mr. Shavrain needs to determine: 1) *In alphabetical order by Last Name, what is the Last Name and First Name of every coach involved with Dive activities?* 2) *In alphabetical order by Last Name, what is the Last Name and First Name of every coach involved with Basketball or Football activities?* 3) *In alphabetical order by Last Name, what is the Last Name and First Name of every coach with a Skill Specialty in Volleyball?*

End You have completed Project 2L ――――――――――――

Apply a combination of the **2A** and **2B** skills.

GO! Think | Project **2M** Club Donations

Project Files

For Project 2M, you will need the following file:

a02M_Club_Donations

You will save your database as:

Lastname_Firstname_2M_Club_Donations

Use the skills you have practiced in this chapter to assist Dr. Kirsten McCarty, Vice President of Student Services, in answering questions about donations collected by students to support student services in your database **Lastname_Firstname_2M_Club_Donations** Create and save the relationship report with the default name, and save the queries you create with your name in the query title. Create paper or electronic printouts of the report and queries as directed.

Dr. McCarty needs to determine: 1) *In ascending order by Last Name, what is the Last Name and First Name of donors who gave donations that are $25 or more?* 2) *What is the total of all donations grouped alphabetically by the Club Affiliation?* 3) *In alphabetical order by the student Last Name, and including the Donation ID#, what will the value of each donation be if the local sports store makes a matching 10 percent donation?* 4) *What are the total donations by Club Affiliation and Student ID?*

End You have completed Project 2M ――――――――――――

Outcomes-Based Assessments

You and GO! | Project **2N** Personal Inventory

Project Files

For Project 2N, you will need the following file:

New blank Access database

You will save your database as:

Lastname_Firstname_2N_Personal_Inventory

Create a personal database containing a household inventory of your possessions. Name the new database **Lastname_Firstname_2N_Personal_Inventory** Create one or more tables with at least 10 records. Include fields such as item, room location, value, date of purchase. Your table should have items stored in several locations. Sort the table in descending order by the value of the item. Create a paper or electronic printout. Clear all sorts, and then close the table. Create at least three queries to answer specific questions about your inventory. Name the queries to reflect the question asked. Create paper or electronic printouts of your queries.

End **You have completed Project 2N**

Forms, Filters, and Reports

PROJECT 3A
Create forms to enter and display data in a database.

1. Create and Use a Form to Add and Delete Records (p. 185)
2. Create a Form by Using the Form Wizard (p. 191)
3. Modify a Form in Layout View and in Design View (p. 193)
4. Filter Records (p. 201)

PROJECT 3B
Create reports to display database information.

5. Create a Report by Using the Report Tool (p. 207)
6. Create Reports by Using the Blank Report Tool and the Report Wizard (p. 210)
7. Modify the Design of a Report (p. 217)
8. Print a Report and Keep Data Together (p. 221)

Andresr/Shutterstock

In This Chapter

In this chapter, you will create forms to enter data and view data in database tables. Forms can display one record at a time, with fields placed in the same order to match a paper source document to make it easier to enter the new information or view existing information. Records in a form or table can be filtered to display only a portion of the total records based on matching specific values.

In this chapter, you will create reports that summarize data stored in a query or table in a professional-looking manner suitable for printing. After your report is created, you can modify the design so that the final report is laid out in a format that is useful to the person reading it.

The projects in this chapter relate to **Capital Cities Community College**, which is located in the Washington D. C. metropolitan area. The college provides high-quality education and professional training to residents in the cities surrounding the nation's capital. Its four campuses serve over 50,000 students and offer more than 140 certificate programs and degrees at the associate's level. CapCCC has a highly acclaimed Distance Education program and an extensive Workforce Development program. The college makes positive contributions to the community through cultural and athletic programs and partnerships with businesses and non-profit organizations.

Project 3A Students and Majors

Project 3A Training

Project Activities

In Activities 3.01 through 3.11, you will assist Juanita Ramirez, Director of Enrollment Services, in using an Access database to track new students and their major fields of study. Your completed forms will look similar to Figure 3.1.

Project Files

For Project 3A, you will need the following file:

a03A_Students_Majors

You will save your document as:

Lastname_Firstname_3A_Students_Majors

Project Results

Figure 3.1
Project 3A Students and Majors

Objective 1 | Create and Use a Form to Add and Delete Records

A *form* is an Access object you can use to enter new records into a table, or to edit, delete, or display existing records in a table. A form is useful to control access to the data. For example, you can design a form for college Registration Assistants who can see and enter the courses scheduled and fees paid by an individual student. However, they cannot see or enter grades in the student's record.

Some Access forms display only one record at a time; other forms display multiple records at the same time. A form that displays only one record at a time is useful not only to the individual who performs the *data entry*—typing the actual records—but also to anyone who has the job of viewing information in a database. For example, when you visit the Records Office at your college to obtain a transcript, someone displays your record on a screen. For the viewer, it is much easier to look at one record at a time, using a form, than to look at all of the student records in the database.

Activity 3.01 | Creating a Form

There are several ways to create a form in Access, but the fastest and easiest way is to use the *Form tool*. With a single mouse click, all fields from the underlying data source are placed on the form. You can use the new form immediately, or you can modify it in Layout view or in Design view.

The Form tool incorporates all of the information—both the field names and the individual records—from an existing table or query and then instantly creates the form for you. Records that you edit or create using a form automatically update the underlying table or tables. In this activity, you will create a form and then use it to add new student records to the database.

1 **Start** Access. In **Backstage** view, click **Open**. Navigate to the student data files for this textbook, and then open the **a03A_Students_Majors** database.

2 Display **Backstage** view, click **Save Database As**, and then in the **Save As** dialog box, navigate to the location where you are saving your databases for this chapter. Create a new folder named **Access Chapter 3** and then click **Open**.

3 In the **File name** box, select the file name, and then type **Lastname_Firstname_3A_ Students_Majors** and then press ⏎. On the **Message Bar**, click the **Enable Content** button. Notice that there are two tables in this database.

4 On the Ribbon, click the **Database Tools tab**. In the **Relationships group**, click the **Relationships** button. Compare your screen with Figure 3.2.

> *One* major is associated with *many* students. Thus, a one-to-many relationship has been established between the 3A Majors table and the 3A Students table using the Major ID# field as the common field.

Figure 3.2

Join line with symbols indicating one-to-many relationship and referential integrity

Major ID# is common field

---

5 **Close** ⊠ the **Relationships** window. From the **Navigation Pane**, open the **3A Students** table. Notice the ten fields—*Student ID#*, *First Name*, *MI*, *Last Name*, *Address*, *City*, *State*, *ZIP*, *Phone*, and *Major ID#*. **Close** ⊠ the table.

6 In the **Navigation Pane**, be sure the **3A Students** table is selected. Click the **Create tab**, and then in the **Forms group**, click the **Form** button. **Close** « the **Navigation Pane**, and then compare your screen with Figure 3.3.

> Access creates the form based on the currently selected object—the 3A Students table—and displays the form in *Layout view*. In Layout view, you can modify the form while it is displaying data. For example, you can adjust the size of the text boxes to fit the data.
>
> Access creates the form in a simple top-to-bottom layout, with all ten fields in the table lined up in a single column. The data for the first record in the table displays.

Figure 3.3

Layout View button active

Dotted lines indicate Layout view active

Form displays all 10 fields from the *3A Students* table

New (blank) record button

Data for Record 1 of 101 displays in form

Navigation buttons

7 In the navigation area, click the **Next record** button ▶ four times. The fifth record—*Student ID 1298345*—displays. In the navigation area, click the **Last record** button ▶|
to display the record for *Student ID 9583924*, and then click the **First record** button |◀
to display the record for *Student ID 1034823*.

You can use the navigation buttons to scroll among the records to display any single record.

8 **Save** 🖫 the form as **Lastname Firstname 3A Student Form** and then **Close** ☒ the form object.

9 **Open** ⏵⏵ the **Navigation Pane**, and then, if necessary, increase the width of the **Navigation Pane** to display the entire form name. Notice that your new form displays under the table with which it is related—the **3A Students** table.

10 In the **Navigation Pane**, click to select the **3A Majors** table. Click the **Create tab**, and then in the **Forms group**, click the **Form** button. **Close** ⏴⏴ the **Navigation Pane**, and then compare your screen with Figure 3.4. Notice that *Major ID 105*, for *Diagnostic Medical Sonography*, has five students selecting this major.

If a form's record has related records in another table, the related records display in the form because of the established one-to-many relationship between the underlying tables.

Figure 3.4

3A Majors form ———

Major ID# has related records (students declaring this major) ———

11 **Close** ☒ the **3A Majors** form. In the message box, click **Yes**. In the **Save As** dialog box, name the form **Lastname Firstname 3A Major Form** and then click **OK**.

Activity 3.02 | Adding Records to a Table by Using a Form

By using a single-record form to add and delete records, you can reduce the number of data entry errors, because the individual performing the data entry is looking at only one record at a time. Recall that your database is useful only if the information is accurate—just like your personal address book is useful only if it contains accurate addresses and phone numbers.

Forms are based on—also referred to as **bound** to—the table where the records are stored. When a record is entered in a form, the new record is added to the underlying table. The reverse is also true—when a record is added to a table, the new record can be viewed in the related form. In this activity, you will add a new record to the 3A Students table by using the form that you just created.

1 **Open** » the **Navigation Pane**, open your **3A Student Form** object, and then **Close** « the **Navigation Pane**. In the navigation area, click the **New (blank) record** button ▶* to display a new blank form.

Another Way

Press the Enter key, provided there are no special buttons on the form, such as a link to create a new form or a link to print the form.

2 In the **Student ID#** field, type **9712345** and then press Tab.

Use the Tab key to move from field to field in a form. This is known as **tab order**—the order in which the insertion point moves from one field to the next when you press the Tab key. As you start typing, the pencil icon displays in the **record selector bar** at the left—the bar used to select an entire record. This icon displays when a record is created or edited.

3 Using your own first name and last name, continue entering the data as shown in the following table, and then compare your screen with Figure 3.5.

Student ID#	First Name	MI	Last Name	Address	City	State	ZIP	Phone	Major ID#
9712345	**Firstname**	**M**	**Lastname**	**23 Park Pl**	**Arlington**	**VA**	**22226**	**(571) 555-5712**	**339**

Figure 3.5

Pencil icon in record selector bar

Be sure you have typed your own name

New record entered using the form

4 With your insertion point in the last field, press Tab to save the record and display a new blank record. **Close** ✕ the **3A Student Form** object.

5 **Open** » the **Navigation Pane**. Open the **3A Students** table. In the navigation area, click the **Last record** button ▶| to verify that the record you entered in the form is stored in the underlying table. **Close** ✕ the **3A Students** table.

6 From the **Navigation Pane**, open the **3A Major Form** object. At the bottom of your screen, in the navigation area for the form—*not* the navigation area for the subdatasheet—click the **New (blank) record** button ▶*. In the blank form, enter the information in the following table:

Major ID#	Major Name
339.555.22	**Network Security**

7 **Close** ✕ your **3A Major Form** object. From the **Navigation Pane**, open the **3A Majors** table, and then scroll down to verify that the new record for Major ID# *339.555.22 Network Security* displays in the table—records are sorted by the *Major ID#* field. **Close** ✕ the table.

Activity 3.03 | Deleting Records from a Table by Using a Form

You can delete records from a database table by using a form. In this activity, you will delete Major ID# 800.03 because the program has been discontinued.

Another Way

Press Ctrl + F.

1 From the **Navigation Pane**, open your **3A Major Form** object. On the **Home tab**, in the **Find group**, click the **Find** button to open the **Find and Replace** dialog box.

2 In the **Look In** box, notice that *Current field* displays. In the **Find What** box, type **800.03** and then click **Find Next**. Compare your screen with Figure 3.6, and confirm that the record for **Major ID# 800.03** displays.

Because you clicked in the Major ID# field before opening the dialog box, Access searches for the data in this field.

Figure 3.6

Record for *Major ID#* 800.03 displays

Find and Replace dialog box

Find What box

Look In box indicates that Access will search the Current field—*Major ID#*

3 **Close** ![×] the **Find and Replace** dialog box. On the **Home tab**, in the **Records group**, click the **Delete button arrow**, and then click **Delete Record** to delete the record for Major ID# 800.03.

> Access removes the record from the screen and displays a message alerting you that you are about to delete *1 record(s)*. If you click Yes to delete the record, you cannot use the Undo button to reverse the action. If you delete a record by mistake, you must re-create the record by reentering the data. Because no students are associated with this major, you can delete it from the table.

4 In the message box, click **Yes** to delete the record. In the navigation area for the form, notice that the number of records in the table is *70.* **Close** ![×] the form.

5 From the **Navigation Pane**, open the **3A Majors** table. Examine the table to verify that the *Major ID# 800.03* record no longer exists, and then **Close** ![×] the table.

> Adding and deleting records in a form updates the records stored in the underlying table.

Activity 3.04 | Printing a Form

Clicking the Print button while a form is displayed causes *all* of the records to print in the form layout. In this activity, you will print only *one* record.

1 From the **Navigation Pane**, open your **3A Student Form** object. Press Ctrl + F to display the **Find and Replace** dialog box. In the **Find What** box, type **9712345** and then click **Find Next** to display the record with your name. **Close** ![×] the **Find and Replace** dialog box.

2 Display **Backstage** view. Click the **Print tab**, and then in the **Print group**, click **Print**. In the **Print** dialog box, under **Print Range**, click the **Selected Record(s)** option button. In the lower left corner of the dialog box, click **Setup**.

3 In the **Page Setup** dialog box, click the **Columns tab**. Under **Column Size**, in the **Width** box, delete the existing text, and type **7.5** Compare your screen with Figure 3.7.

> Change the width of the column in this manner so that the form prints on one page. Forms are not typically printed, so the width of the column in a form may be greater than the width of the paper on which you are printing. The maximum column width that you can enter is dependent upon the printer that is installed on your system.

Figure 3.7

Column Width set to 7.5

Selected Record(s) option button selected

4 Click **OK** to close the **Page Setup** dialog box, and then, to create an electronic printout of this single form, see the instructions in the Note below. To print on paper, click **OK** to close the **Print** dialog box and to print only your record in the form layout.

> **Note** | To Print a Single Form in PDF
>
> To create a PDF electronic printout of a single record in a form, change the column width to 7.5 as described in step 3 above, and then in the Print dialog box, click Cancel. On the left edge of the form, click anywhere in the Record Selector bar so that it is black—selected. On the Ribbon, click the External Data tab. In the Export group, click the PDF or XPS button. In the Publish as PDF or XPS dialog box, navigate to the location where you are storing your files for this project. In the File name box, notice that your form name is automatically entered for you. Then, in the lower left corner of the dialog box, if necessary, select the Open file after publishing check box. In the lower right corner of the dialog box, click the Options button. In the Options dialog box, under Range, click the Selected records option button, click OK, and then click Publish. Close the Adobe Reader or Acrobat window, and then hold this file until you complete the project and submit it as directed by your instructor.

5 Close ⊠ the **3A Student Form** object. Using the techniques you just practiced, open your **3A Major Form** object, display the record for the **Major ID#** of **339.555.22**, and then print only that record, or create an electronic printout of only that record. Then Close ⊠ the **3A Major Form** object.

> If there are no related records in the subdatasheet, the empty subdatasheet does not display in the printed form.

Objective 2 | Create a Form by Using the Form Wizard

The **Form Wizard** creates a form quickly like the Form tool, but gives you more flexibility in the design, layout, and number of fields. The design of the form should be planned for the individuals who use the form—either for entering new records or viewing records. For example, when your college counselor displays information, it may be easier for the counselor to view the information if the fields are arranged in a layout that differs from the manner in which the Form Tool arranges them.

Activity 3.05 | Creating a Form by Using the Form Wizard

At Capital Cities Community College, when a student changes his or her major, the student fills out a paper form. To make it easier to change the information in the database, you will create an Access form that matches the layout of the paper form. This will make it easier for the individual who changes the data in the database.

1 In the **Navigation Pane**, click to select the **3A Students** table. On the **Create tab**, in the **Forms group**, click the **Form Wizard** button.

> The Form Wizard walks you step by step through the process of creating a form by asking questions. In the first Form Wizard dialog box, you select the fields to include on the form. The fields can come from more than one table or query.

2 Under **Tables/Queries**, in the text box, click the **arrow** to display a list of available tables and queries from which you can create the form.

> There are two tables in the database from which you can create a new form. Because you selected the 3A Students table on the Navigation Pane, the 3A Students table is the selected table.

3 Click **Table: 3A Students**, and then compare your screen with Figure 3.8.

> The field names from the 3A Students table display in the Available Fields list.

Figure 3.8

One Field button

3A Students table selected

Available Fields list

Field names in the
3A Students table

Selected Fields list

Another Way
Double-click the field
name.

4 Use the **One Field** button ![>] to move the following fields to the **Selected Fields** list: **First Name**, **Last Name**, and **Major ID#**. Compare your screen with Figure 3.9.

Three fields from the 3A Students table display in the Selected Fields list.

Figure 3.9

Three fields that will
display in the form

5 Click **Next**. Be sure **Columnar** is selected as the layout, and then click **Next**. Under **What title do you want for your form?**, select the existing text, and then type **Lastname Firstname 3A Student Major Change Form** and then click **Finish** to close the wizard and create the form. If necessary, increase the width of the Navigation Pane to display the entire form name, and then compare your screen with Figure 3.10.

The form is saved and added to the Navigation Pane under its data source. The first record in the underlying table displays in *Form view*, which is used to view, add, delete, and modify records stored in a table.

Figure 3.10

Form created using Wizard

New form displays in the
Navigation Pane under
related table

First record in the
3A Students table
displays in form

Objective 3 | Modify a Form in Layout View and in Design View

After you create a form, you can make changes to it. For example, you can group the fields, resize the fields, and change the style of the form.

Activity 3.06 | Grouping Controls and Applying a Theme to a Form in Layout View

Layout view enables you to make changes to the design of a form while displaying the data from the underlying table. Most changes to a form can be made in Layout view.

Another Way

On the Home tab, in the Views group, click the View button arrow, and then click Layout View; or, right-click the object tab, and then click Layout View.

1 **Close** ⟪ the **Navigation Pane** and be sure your **3A Student Major Change Form** object displays. In the lower right corner of your screen, on the status bar, click the **Layout View** button ▣, and then compare your screen with Figure 3.11.

The field names and data for the first record display in *controls*—objects on a form that display data, perform actions, and let you view and work with information.

The data in the first record displays in *text box controls*. The most commonly used control is the text box control, which typically displays data from the underlying table. A text box control is a *bound control*—its source data comes from a table or query.

The field names—*First Name*, *Last Name*, and *Major ID#*—display in *label controls*. Access places a label control to the left of a text box control. A label control contains descriptive information that displays on the form, usually the field name. A control that does not have a source of data, for example a label that displays the title of the form, is an *unbound control*.

Figure 3.11

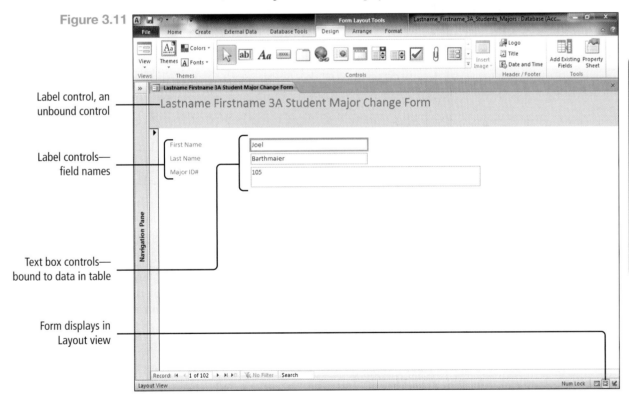

Label control, an unbound control

Label controls— field names

Text box controls— bound to data in table

Form displays in Layout view

2 Click the **First Name label control**. Hold down Shift, and then click the **Last Name label control**, the **Major ID# label control**, and the **three text box controls** to select all label and text box controls.

Alert! | Do Your Controls Change Order When Selecting?

If, when selecting controls, the controls change order, click Undo and select the controls again. Be careful not to drag the mouse when you are selecting multiple controls.

---

3 With all six controls selected—surrounded by a colored border—on the Ribbon, click the **Arrange tab**. In the **Table group**, click the **Stacked** button. Click the **First Name Label control** to deselect all of the controls and to surround the **First Name label control** with a colored border. Compare your screen with Figure 3.12.

> This action groups the controls together in the *Stacked layout* format—a layout similar to a paper form, with labels to the left of each field. Grouping the controls enables you to easily move and edit controls as you redesign your form.

> A dotted line forms a border around the field names and data. Above and to the left of the first field name—*First Name*—the **layout selector** ⊞ displays, with which you can select and move the entire group of controls.

Figure 3.12

Arrange tab

Stacked button

Layout selector

4 Click the **Design tab**, and then in the **Themes group**, click the **Themes** button. In the **Themes** gallery, locate and right-click the **Couture** theme. Click **Apply Theme to This Object Only**.

> The *Themes* button enables you to apply a predefined format to all of the database objects or to the current object. Right-click a theme so that you can apply the theme to a single object within the database. Apply a theme before performing other formatting to the text in your form.

Note | Applying a Theme to an Object and Determining the Applied Theme

If you click a theme rather than right-clicking it and selecting an option, the theme is applied to all objects in the database. To determine the applied theme, in the Themes group, point to the Themes button. The ScreenTip displays the current theme.

---

5 Click anywhere in the title *3A Student Major Change Form* to select it. Click the **Format tab**. In the **Font group**, click the **Font Size arrow**, and then click **14**. Click the **Bold** button Ⓑ to add bold emphasis to the text. Click the **Font Color button arrow**, and then under **Theme Colors**, in the last column, click the last color—**Brown, Accent 6, Darker 50%**.

Activity 3.07 | Modifying a Form in Design View

Design view presents a detailed view of the structure of your form. Because the form is not actually running when displayed in Design view, you cannot view the underlying data. However, some tasks, such as resizing sections, must be completed in Design view.

Another Way

On the Home tab, in the Views group, click the View button arrow, and then click Design View; or, right-click the object tab, and then click Design View.

1 On the status bar, click the **Design View** button. Compare your screen with Figure 3.13.

> This Design view of a form displays three sections—*Form Header*, *Detail*, and *Form Footer*—each designated by a *section bar* at the top of each section. The form header contains information, such as a form's title, that displays at the top of the screen in Form view and is printed at the top of the first page when records are printed as forms. The detail section displays the records from the underlying table, and the form footer displays at the bottom of the screen in Form view and is printed after the last detail section on the last page of a printout.

Figure 3.13

Form Header section bar

Detail section bar

Form Footer section bar

2 At the bottom of the form, point to the *lower* edge of the **Form Footer section bar** to display the pointer, and then drag downward approximately **0.5 inch** to increase the height of the Form Footer section. Compare your screen with Figure 3.14.

Figure 3.14

Form Footer section height increased 0.5 inch

3 On the **Design tab**, in the **Controls group**, click the **Label** button Aa. Move the pointer into the **Form Footer** section, and then position the plus sign of the pointer in the **Form Footer** section at approximately **0.25 inch on the horizontal ruler** and even with the lower edge of the **Form Footer section bar** as shown in Figure 3.15.

Access | Chapter 3

Figure 3.15

Button to create
a Label control

0.25 inch on
horizontal ruler

Label control pointer

4 Click one time. Using your own name, type **Created by Lastname Firstname** and then press Enter. With the label control selected, on the **Format tab**, in the **Font group**, click the **Bold** button B. Click the **Font Color arrow**, and then under **Theme Colors**, in the fourth column, click the first color—**Brown, Text 2**. If necessary, double-click the right edge of the label control to resize the control so that all of the data displays.

Another Way

On the Home tab, in the Views group, click the View button arrow, and then click Form View; or, right-click the object tab, and then click Form View.

5 On the right side of the status bar, click the **Form View** button, and then compare your screen with Figure 3.16.

Form Footer text displays on the screen at the bottom of the form and prints only on the last page if all of the forms are printed as a group. In the *Form view*, you can add, delete, or modify records stored in a table.

Figure 3.16

Title formatted,
Couture theme applied

Label control added and
formatted in Form
Footer section

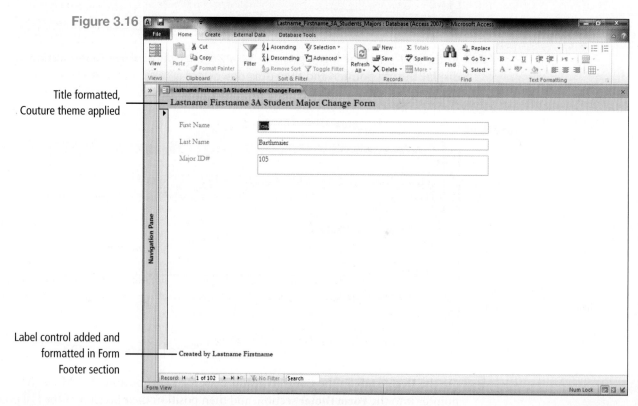

6 **Save** the changes you have made to the design of your form. Leave your **3A Student Major Change Form** open for the next activity.

Activity 3.08 | Adding, Resizing, and Moving Controls in Layout View

In Layout view, you can change the form's *control layout*—the grouped arrangement of controls.

1 At the right side of the status bar, click the **Layout View** button 🔲.

> Recall that the layout selector, which displays to the left and above the First Name label control, enables you to select and move the entire group of controls in Layout view.

2 On the **Design tab**, in the **Tools group**, click the **Add Existing Fields** button to display the **Field List** pane, which lists the fields in the underlying table—3A Students. Compare your screen with Figure 3.17.

Figure 3.17
Add Existing Fields button —
Field List pane —

3 In the **Field List** pane, click **Student ID#**, and then drag to the left until the 🔲 pointer displays above the **First Name label control** and a colored line displays above the control. Release the mouse button, and then compare your screen with Figure 3.18. If you are not satisfied with the result, click Undo and begin again.

> This action adds the Student ID# label and text box controls to the form above the First Name controls.

Figure 3.18
Student ID# label control —
Text box control for *Student ID#* field —

4 **Close** ✖ the **Field List** pane. Click the **Student ID# text box control**, which currently displays *1034823*, to surround it with a border and to remove the border from the label control.

5 Point to the right edge of the **text box control** until the ↔ pointer displays, and then drag to the left until all of the right edges of the text box controls align under the *C* in *Controls* in the Ribbon's **Controls group** above. Compare your screen with Figure 3.19.

> All four text box controls are resized simultaneously. By decreasing the width of the text box controls, you have more space in which to rearrange the form controls. In Layout view, because you can see your data, you can determine visually that the space you have allotted is adequate to display all of the data in every field.

Figure 3.19

Right edges of text box controls align under C in Controls group

Horizontal resize pointer

Drag the selected label controls to the desired location and then release the mouse button.

6 Click the **Last Name text box control**, which currently displays *Barthmaier*. Click the **Arrange tab**, and then in the **Rows & Columns group**, click the **Select Row** button. In the **Move group**, click the **Move Up** button one time to move the controls above the **First Name label control** as shown in Figure 3.20.

Figure 3.20

Select Row button

Move Up button

Last Name controls moved above *First Name* controls

7 **Save** 🖫 the changes you have made to the design of your form.

Activity 3.09 | Formatting and Aligning Controls in Layout View

Another Way

Click the first control, hold down Shift, and then click the last control.

1 With the form displayed in Layout view, click in the **Student ID# text box control**, which displays *1034823*. On the **Arrange tab**, in the **Rows & Columns group**, click the **Select Column** button to select all four text box controls.

2 With the four text box controls selected, click the **Format tab**. In the **Font group**, click the **Background Color button arrow** 🖳 ▾. Under **Theme Colors**, in the fifth column, click the second color—**Brown, Accent 1, Lighter 80%**.

> The text box controls display a background color of light brown. This formatting does not affect the label controls on the left.

3 Click the **Student ID# label control**. On the **Arrange tab**, in the **Rows & Columns group**, click the **Select Column** button. Click the **Format tab**, change the **Font Color**—*not* the Background Color—to **Brown, Text 2**—in the fourth column, the first color—and then apply **Bold** 🄱 . Click in a blank area of the screen to cancel the selection, and then compare your screen with Figure 3.21.

Figure 3.21

Text box controls—font size and background color changed

Label controls—font size and font color changed, bold applied

Another Way

Another Way

Click any control, and then on the Arrange tab, in the Rows & Columns group, click the Select Layout button.

4 Click any **label control** to display the layout selector, and then click the **layout selector** ⊞ to select all of the controls.

Clicking the layout selector enables you to edit all of the controls at one time.

5 On the **Format tab**, in the **Font group**, click the **Font Size button arrow**, and then click **12** to change the font size of the text in all of the controls.

6 With all of the controls still selected, on the Ribbon, click the **Design tab**. In the **Tools group**, click the **Property Sheet** button. In the **Property Sheet** pane, if necessary, click the **Format tab**, and then compare your screen with Figure 3.22.

The *Property Sheet* for the selected controls displays. Each control has an associated Property Sheet where precise changes to the properties—characteristics—of selected controls can be made. At the top of the Property Sheet, to the right of *Selection type:*, *Multiple selection* displays because you have more than one control selected.

Figure 3.22

Property Sheet button

Selection type

Property Sheet for selected controls

Selected controls

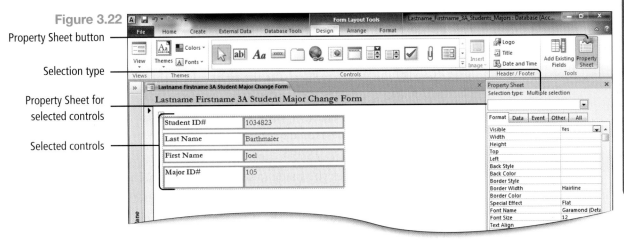

7 In the **Property Sheet**, click the word **Height**, type **0.25** and then press [Enter].

The height of each control changes to 0.25 inch.

8 Click the **Student ID# label control** to select only that label control. Click the **Arrange tab**, and then in the **Rows & Columns group**, click the **Select Column** button. In the **Property Sheet**, click **Width** to select its value to the right. Type **1.25** and then press [Enter].

The width of each selected label control changes to 1.25 inches.

9 In the **Form Footer section**, click the **label control** with your name. Hold down Shift, and then in the **Form Header section**, click the **label control** that displays the title *3A Student Major Change Form*. With these two controls selected, in the **Property Sheet**, click **Left**. Type **0.5** and then press Enter to align the left edge of the selected label controls at 0.5 inch. Compare your screen with Figure 3.23.

> The left edges of the Form Header and Form Footer label controls align at 0.5 inch. In this manner, you can place a control in a specific location on the form.

Figure 3.23

Form Header label control left aligned at 0.5 inch

Height of all controls changed to 0.25 inch; width of label controls changed to 1.25 inches

Left property setting

Form Footer label control left aligned at 0.5 inch

10 **Close** ☒ the **Property Sheet**. On the right side of the status bar, click the **Form View** button 🖿.

> The form displays in Form view, the view an individual uses when entering data in the form. By using these techniques, you can make a form attractive and easy to use for those who view and enter records.

11 **Save** 🖫 the changes you made to your form's design. In the navigation area, click the **Last record** button ▶| to display the record containing your name.

12 Display **Backstage** view, click the **Print tab**, and then on the right, click **Print**. In the **Print** dialog box, under **Print Range**, click the **Selected Record(s)** option button. Create a paper or electronic printout as directed. To create an electronic printout, follow the directions given at the end of Activity 1.04.

> Because you decreased the width of the text box controls, you do *not* have to adjust the Column Size width in the Page Setup dialog box as you did with the form you created using the Form tool.

13 With the **3A Student Major Change Form** object displayed in **Form** view, in the navigation area, click the **First record** button |◀ to prepare for the next activity.

Objective 4 | Filter Records

Filtering records in a form is the process of displaying only a portion of the total records—a *subset*—based on matching specific values. Filters are commonly used to provide a quick answer, and the result is not generally saved for future use. For example, by filtering records in a form, you can quickly display a subset of records for students majoring in Information Systems Technology, which is identified by the Major ID# of 339.

One reason that you create a form is to provide a user interface for the database. For example, the Registration Assistants at your college may not, for security reasons, have access to the entire student database. Rather, by using a form, they can access and edit only some information—the information necessary for their jobs. Filtering records within a form provides individuals who do not have access to the entire database a way to ask questions of the database without constructing a query, and also to save a filter that is used frequently.

Activity 3.10 | Filtering Data by Selection of One Field

The counselor would like to see records for students who are majoring in Information Systems Technology. In a form, you can use the *Filter By Selection* command—which retrieves only the records that contain the value in the selected field and which temporarily removes the records that do *not* contain the value in the selected field.

1 With your **3A Student Major Change Form** object displayed in **Form** view, in the first record, click in the shaded **Major ID# text box control**. On the **Home tab**, in the **Find group**, click the **Find** button. In the **Find and Replace** dialog box, in the **Find What** box, type **339** If necessary, in the Match box, click the arrow, and then click Whole Field. Click **Find Next**, and then compare your screen with Figure 3.24.

This action finds and displays a record with 339—the Major ID# for Information Systems Technology—so that you can filter the records using the selected value.

Figure 3.24

First record with *Major ID#* of 339

339 is the *Major ID#* for Information Systems Technology

2 **Close** the **Find and Replace** dialog box. In the **Sort & Filter group**, click the **Selection** button, and then click **Equals "339"**. Compare your screen with Figure 3.25.

Seven records match the contents of the selected Student Major ID# field—*339*—the ID# for the Information Systems Technology major. In the navigation area, a *Filtered* button with a funnel icon displays next to the number of records. *Filtered* also displays on the right side of the status bar to indicate that a filter is applied. On the Home tab, in the Sort & Filter group, the Toggle Filter button is active.

Figure 3.25

Toggle Filter button active

Filtered indicated
on status bar

Filtered button displays
in navigation area

Seven records match
the value *339*—the
Major ID# for Information
Systems Technology

Another Way

Click the Filtered button
in the navigation area.

3 On the **Home tab**, in the **Sort & Filter group**, click the **Toggle Filter** button to remove the filter and display all 102 records. Notice the **Unfiltered** button in the navigation area, which indicates that no filter is active.

Note | Toggle Filter Button

On the Home tab, the Toggle Filter button is used to apply or remove a filter. If no filter has been created, the button is not active—it is not highlighted. After a filter is created, this button becomes active. Because it is a toggle button used to apply or remove filters, the ScreenTip that displays for this button alternates between Apply Filter—when a filter is created but is not currently applied—and Remove Filter—when a filter is applied.

4 Be sure that the first record—for *Joel Barthmaier*—displays. On the **Home tab**, in the **Sort & Filter group**, click the **Toggle Filter** button to reapply the filter. In the navigation area, click the **Last record** button ▶︎ to display the last of the seven records that match *339*.

The record for *Student ID# 9712345* displays—the record with your name. In this manner, you can toggle a filter on or off as needed.

5 In the **Sort & Filter group**, click the **Toggle Filter** button to remove the filter and display all of the records.

6 In the navigation area, click the **Next record** button ▶︎ two times to display **Record 3**. In the **Last Name** field, select the first letter—**E**—of *Eckert*. On the **Home tab**, in the **Sort & Filter group**, click the **Selection** button. Click **Begins with "E"**.

A new filter is applied that displays three records in which the *Last Name* begins with the letter *E*.

7 In the navigation area, click the **Filtered** button to remove the filter and display all of the records.

8 **Save** 🖫 the changes to your form, and then **Close** ✕ the form.

The filter is saved with the form even though the filter is not currently applied.

Activity 3.11 | Using Filter By Form and Advanced Filter/Sort

Use the *Filter By Form* command to filter the records in a form based on one or more fields, or based on more than one value in the same field. The Filter By Form command offers greater flexibility than the Filter by Selection command and can be used to answer a question that requires matching multiple values.

In this activity, you will use filtering techniques to help Juanita Ramirez determine how many students live in Alexandria or Arlington. Then you will determine how many students live in Arlington who are majoring in Information Systems Technology.

1 **Open** ≫ the **Navigation Pane**, open your **3A Student Form** object, and then **Close** ≪ the **Navigation Pane**.

2 On the **Home tab**, in the **Sort & Filter group**, click the **Advanced** button, and then click **Filter By Form**. Compare your screen with Figure 3.26.

The Filter by Form window displays all of the field names, but without any data. In the empty text box for each field, you can type a value or choose from a list of available values. The *Look for* and *Or* tabs display at the bottom.

Figure 3.26

Filter by Form indicated

Advanced button

Look for and *Or* tabs

3 Click in the **City text box control**. At the right edge of the text box control, click the **arrow** that displays. In the list, click **Alexandria**. In the **Sort & Filter group**, click the **Toggle Filter** button.

As displayed in the navigation area, eight student records include *Alexandria* in the City field.

Another Way

Click in the text box control and type the criteria separated by the word *or*. For example, in the City text box control, type *Alexandria or Arlington*.

4 In the **Sort & Filter group**, click the **Advanced** button, and then click **Filter By Form**. At the bottom left of the window, click the **Or tab**. Click the **City text box control arrow**, and then click **Arlington**. In the **Sort & Filter group**, click the **Toggle Filter** button.

As displayed in the navigation area, eighteen student records include either Alexandria or Arlington in the City field. You have created an *OR condition*; that is, records display where, in this instance, either of two values—Alexandria *or* Arlington—is present in the selected field.

5 In the **Sort & Filter group**, click the **Advanced** button, and then click **Clear All Filters** to display all of the records.

6 Click the **Advanced** button again, and then from the list, click **Advanced Filter/Sort**. Expand the field list.

The Advanced Filter design grid displays. The design grid is similar to the query design grid.

7 From the **3A Students** field list, add the **City** field and then the **Major ID#** field to the design grid. In the **Criteria** row for the **City** field, type **Arlington** and then click in the **Criteria** row for the **Major ID#** field. Type **339** and then press Enter. Compare your screen with Figure 3.27.

Figure 3.27

Tab indicates *3A Student* Form is being filtered

Field list expanded

Design grid

Criteria for *City* field

Criteria for *Major ID#* field

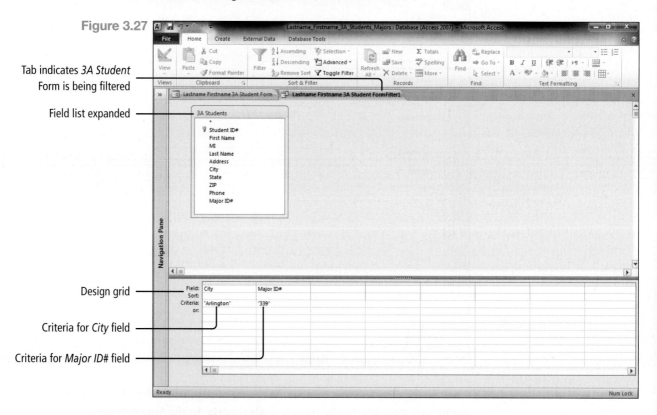

8 In the **Sort & Filter group**, click the **Toggle Filter** button.

Two records match the criteria. You have created an *AND condition*; that is, only records display where both values—Arlington *and* 339—are present in the selected fields. There are two Information Systems Technology majors who live in Arlington.

9 In the **Sort & Filter group**, click the **Toggle Filter** button to display all of the records.

In the navigation area, *Unfiltered* displays, which indicates that a filter was created for this form. Unless you Clear All Filters, the filter is saved with the form when the form is closed. When you reopen the form, you can click on the Toggle Filter button or the Unfiltered button to reapply the filter.

10 **Close** ☒ all open objects, and then **Open** ⧉ the **Navigation Pane**. Display **Backstage** view, click **Close Database**, and then click **Exit**. As directed by your instructor, submit your database and the three paper or electronic printouts that are the results of this project.

More Knowledge | Using the Filter Button

You can filter a form in a manner similar to the way you filter records in a table. Click in the text box control of the field you wish to use for the filter. On the Home tab, in the Sort & Filter group, click the Filter button to display a shortcut menu. Select the (Select All) check box to clear the option, and then select the data by which you want to filter by clicking the check boxes preceding the data. To remove the filter, redisplay the menu, and then select the (Select All) check box.

End **You have completed Project 3A** ——————————————————————

Project 3B Job Openings

myitlab
Project 3B Training

Project Activities

In Activities 3.12 through 3.19, you will assist Damon Bass, Career Center Director for Capital Cities Community College, in using an Access database to track the employers and job openings advertised for the annual Career Fair. Your completed reports will look similar to Figure 3.28.

Project Files

For Project 3B, you will need the following file:

a03B_Job_Openings

You will save your database as:

Lastname_Firstname_3B_Job_Openings

Project Results

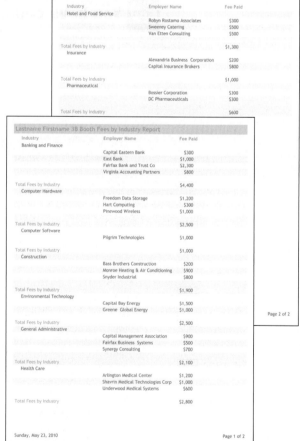

Figure 3.28
Project 3B Job Openings

Objective 5 | Create a Report by Using the Report Tool

A *report* is a database object that summarizes the fields and records from a query or from a table, in an easy-to-read format suitable for printing. A report consists of information extracted from queries or tables and also the report's design items, such as labels, headings, and graphics. The queries or tables that provide the underlying data for a report are referred to as the report's *record source*.

Activity 3.12 | Creating a Report by Using the Report Tool

The *Report tool* is the fastest way to create a report. This tool displays all of the fields and records from the record source that you select. You can use the Report tool to look at the underlying data quickly in an easy-to-read format, after which you can save the report and modify it in Layout view or in Design view. In this activity, you will use the Report tool to create a report from a query that lists all of the job openings with an annual salary of at least $40,000.

1 **Start** Access. In **Backstage** view, click **Open**. Navigate to the student data files for this textbook, and then open the **a03B_Job_Openings** database.

2 In **Backstage** view, click **Save Database As**. In the **Save As** dialog box, navigate to your **Access Chapter 3** folder. In the **File name** box, type **Lastname_Firstname_3B_Job_Openings** and then press [Enter]. On the **Message Bar**, click **Enable Content**. Notice that in this database, there are two tables and one query that uses both tables as its record source.

3 On the Ribbon, click the **Database Tools tab**. In the **Relationships group**, click the **Relationships** button. Compare your screen with Figure 3.29. If your relationships do not display, in the Relationships group, click the All Relationships button.

> *One* employer is associated with *many* job openings. Thus, a one-to-many relationship has been established between the 3B Employers table and the 3B Job Openings table by using the Employer ID# field as the common field.

Figure 3.29

Employer ID# is common field

Join line indicating a one-to-many relationship and referential integrity

4 **Close** ☒ the **Relationships** window. Open both tables, and look at the fields and data in each table. Open the query to examine the data, and then switch to **Design** view to examine the design grid. When you are finished, **Close** ☒ all objects.

> The query answers the question *What is the Job#, Position, Employer Name, and # of Openings for jobs that have an Annual Salary of $40,000 or more?*

5 In the **Navigation Pane**, click to select the **3B Salary $40,000 or More** query. Click the **Create tab**, and then in the **Reports group**, click the **Report** button. **Close** ☒ the **Navigation Pane**, and then compare your screen with Figure 3.30.

> Access creates the 3B Job Openings report and displays it in Layout view. The report includes all of the fields and all of the records in the query. In Layout view, you can see the margins and page breaks in the report.

Figure 3.30

Dotted lines indicate margins

All fields from query display in report

All records from query display in report

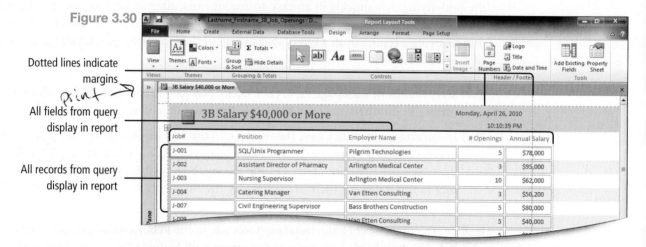

Activity 3.13 | Modifying a Report in Layout View and Printing a Report

1 On the **Design tab**, in the **Themes group**, click the **Themes** button. From the gallery of themes, scroll down, locate, and then right-click the **Waveform** theme. Click **Apply Theme to This Object Only**.

> Recall that right-clicking a theme enables you to apply a predefined format to the active object only, which is another way to give a professional look to a report. Apply a theme before performing other formatting to the text in your report.

2 Click the **Job#** field name, and then click the **Arrange tab**. In the **Rows & Columns group**, click the **Select Column** button to select both the field name and the data in the field, and then press Del to remove the field from the report.

> The Job# field is deleted, and the remaining fields move to the left. No fields extend beyond the right margin of the report.

3 Notice that for several fields, there is an extra blank line in the record. In the **Employer Name** field, click in the **text box control** that displays *Monroe Heating & Air Conditioning*. Point to the right edge of the text box control to display the ↔ pointer. Drag to the right slightly until the data in the text box control displays on one line. Scroll down to view the entire report to be sure that you have widened the column enough to accommodate all records on a single line.

> You should scroll down through the report to find the text box control that displays the most text and adjust the field width using that text box control. In this manner, you can be certain that all of the data in every text box control displays on one line.

4 Click the **Position** field name, and then click the **Home tab**. In the **Sort & Filter group**, click the **Ascending** button to sort the records in the report alphabetically by Position.

5 Scroll down to the bottom of the report, and then click the **Annual Salary calculated control**, which displays a total that is truncated at the bottom. Press `Del` to remove this total.

> Access automatically adds a calculated control to sum any field that is formatted as currency. Here, the total is not a useful number and this can be deleted.

6 At the top of the report, click the **# Openings** field name. Click the **Design tab**. In the **Grouping & Totals group**, click the **Totals** button, and then click **Sum**.

7 Scroll down to display the last line of the report. Click in the **# Openings calculated control**, point to the bottom edge of the control to display the ↕ pointer, and then double-click to resize the control. Compare your screen with Figure 3.31.

> The total number of job openings for positions with a salary equal to or greater than $40,000 is 100. Use Layout view to make quick changes to a report created with the Report tool. The Report tool is not intended to create a perfectly formatted formal report, but it is a way to summarize the data in a table or query quickly in an easy-to-read format suitable for printing and reading.

Figure 3.31

Waveform theme applied

Position field sorted in ascending order

Openings field summed

Calculated control removed from *Annual Salary* field

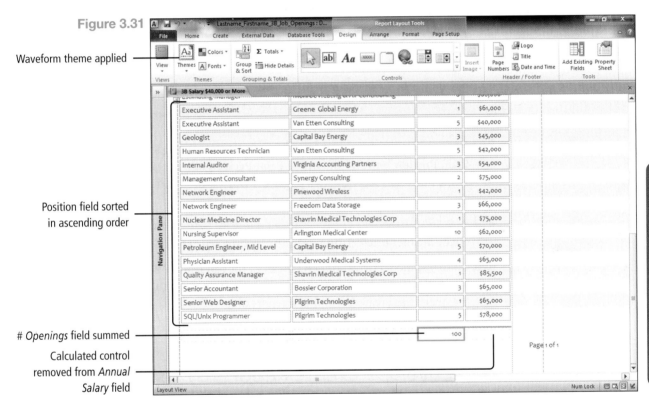

8 At the bottom of the report, notice that the **Page Number control** does not fit entirely within the margins. Click the **Page Number control** that displays *Page 1 of 1*, and then drag the pointer to the left until the page number control is visually centered between the margins of the report.

> Always look at the headers and footers to determine if the data will print on one page.

9 Scroll up to display the top of the report. In the **Report Header** section, click the label control that displays *3B Salary $40,000 or More*. Click the **Format tab**, and then in the **Font group**, change the **Font Size** to **14**. Click the **label control** again so that you can edit the title. Using your own name, add **Lastname Firstname** to the beginning of the title, and then press `Enter`. If necessary, point to the right edge of the label control to display the ↔ pointer, and then double-click to fit the width of the text in the control.

10 Click any field in the report. In the upper left corner of the report, click the **layout selector** ⊞, and then drag it slightly downward and to the right until the columns are visually centered between the margins of the report. If your columns rearrange, on the Quick Access Toolbar, click Undo and begin again. Compare your screen with Figure 3.32.

Using the layout selector, you can move the entire layout of the label controls and text box controls to horizontally center the records on the page. It is easier to control this movement if you drag downward slightly while moving the selector to the right.

Figure 3.32

Fields visually centered within margins

Your name displays in Report Header; Font Size of 14

Layout selector

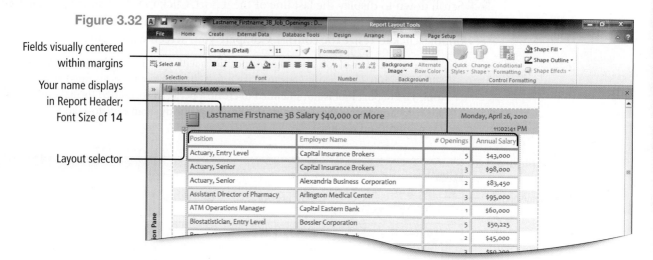

Another Way

In the object window, right-click the object tab, and then click Print Preview.

11 In the lower right corner of your screen, at the right side of the status bar, click the **Print Preview** button 🔍. On the **Print Preview tab**, in the **Zoom group**, click the **Two Pages** button to view the two pages of your report. Notice that the page number displays at the bottom of each page.

12 Save 💾 the report as **Lastname Firstname 3B Salary $40,000 or More Report** and then create a paper or electronic printout as directed. Then **Close Print Preview**.

13 Close ✕ the report, and then **Open** » the **Navigation Pane**. Expand the width of the **Navigation Pane**. Notice that the report displays under the source tables from which the query was created, and that a report object displays a small green notebook icon. **Close** « the **Navigation Pane**.

Objective 6 | Create Reports by Using the Blank Report Tool and the Report Wizard

Use the *Blank Report tool* to create a report without predefined labels and fields. This is an efficient way to create a report, especially if you plan to include only a few fields in your report.

Activity 3.14 | Creating a Report by Using the Blank Report Tool

In this activity, you will build a report that lists only the Employer Name, Contact First Name, Contact Last Name, and Phone fields, which Mr. Bass will use as a quick reference for phoning the employers to verify the details of their Career Fair participation.

1 On the **Create tab**, in the **Reports group**, click the **Blank Report** button.

A blank report displays in Layout view, and the Field List pane displays.

2 In the **Field List** pane, click **Show all tables**, and then click the **plus sign** (+) next to **3B Employers** to display the field names in the table. Compare your screen with Figure 3.33.

Figure 3.33

Field List pane ⎯

Field list for *3B Employers* table expanded ⎯

3 In the **Field List** pane, point to the **Employer Name** field, right-click, and then click **Add Field to View**.

The Employer Name field and its data display as the first column of the report. Using the Report tool, you build the report field by field in the order that you want the fields to display.

4 From the **Field List** pane, drag the **Contact First Name** field into the blank report—anywhere to the right of *Employer Name*. Double-click the **Contact Last Name** field to add it as the third field in the report. Use any technique that you just practiced to add the **Phone** field as the fourth field in the report, and then compare your screen with Figure 3.34.

Figure 3.34

Four fields added to the report ⎯

5 **Close** ☒ the **Field List** pane. On the **Design tab**, in the **Themes group**, click the **Themes** button. Right-click the **Equity** theme, and then click **Apply Theme to This Object Only**.

Recall that you should select a theme before making other formatting changes.

6 Under **Employer Name**, click in the **text box control** that displays *Monroe Heating & Air Conditioning*. Point to the right edge of the text box control to display the ⟷ pointer, and then drag to the right until the data in the text box control displays on one line and there is a small amount of space between the name and the next column. Compare your screen with Figure 3.35.

Figure 3.35

All of the records display on one line

7 On the **Design tab**, in the **Header/Footer group**, click the **Date and Time** button. In the **Date and Time** dialog box, clear the **Include Time** check box, and then click **OK**.

The current date displays in the upper right corner of the report.

8 In the **Header/Footer group**, click the **Title** button, and then using your own name, type **Lastname Firstname 3B Employer Phone List** and then press Enter. Click the **Format tab**. With the title still selected, in the **Font group**, change the **Font Size** to **14**. Point to the right edge of the title's label control to display the ⟷ pointer, and then double-click to adjust the size of the label control.

The title's label control width adjusts, and the Date control moves to the left within the margin.

Another Way

Click the first field name, and then click the Arrange tab. In the Rows & Columns group, click the Select Row button.

9 Click the **Employer Name** field name to select it. Hold down Shift, and then click the **Phone** field name to select all four field names. On the **Format tab**, in the **Font group**, click the **Center** button ☰ to center the field names over the data in the columns. Change the **Font Color** to **Automatic**, and then apply **Bold** **B**.

10 Click any one of the **Employer Name text box controls**, and then click the **Home tab**. In the **Sort & Filter group**, click the **Ascending** button to sort the records in the report alphabetically by Employer Name.

11 In the upper left corner of the report, click the **layout selector** ⊞, and then drag it downward slightly and to the right to visually center the fields between the margins. Compare your screen with Figure 3.36.

Recall that it is easier to control this movement if you drag down slightly while moving the layout selector.

Figure 3.36

Field names formatted
and centered over data

Report title added
and formatted

Layout visually centered
between the margins

Equity Theme applied

Date added
(yours will vary)

12 **Save** 🔲 the report as **Lastname Firstname 3B Employer Phone List** and then on the status bar, click the **Print Preview** button 🔲. Create a paper or electronic printout as directed.

13 **Close Print Preview**, and then **Close** ✖ the report. **Open** » the **Navigation Pane**, and notice that the report displays below the *3B Employers* table—the underlying data source. **Close** « the **Navigation Pane**.

Activity 3.15 | Creating a Report by Using the Report Wizard

Use the ***Report Wizard*** when you need flexibility and want to control the report content and design. The Report Wizard enables you to specify how the data is grouped and sorted. You can use fields from more than one table or query, assuming you have created the appropriate relationships between the tables. The Report Wizard is similar to the Form Wizard; it creates a report by asking you a series of questions and then designs the report based on your answers.

In this activity, you will prepare a report for Mr. Bass that displays the employers, grouped by industry, and the total fees paid by employers for renting a booth at the Career Fair.

1 Click the **Create tab**, and then in the **Reports group**, click the **Report Wizard** button.

Here you select the tables or queries from which you want to extract information, and then select the fields to include in the report. You can also select more than one table or query.

2 Click the **Tables/Queries arrow**, and then click **Table: 3B Employers**. Move the following fields to the **Selected Fields** list in the order given: **Industry**, **Employer Name**, and **Fee Paid** (scroll down as necessary to locate the *Fee Paid* field). Compare your screen with Figure 3.37.

Figure 3.37

Report Wizard dialog box

Fields selected from *3B Employers* table

Three fields selected

3 Click **Next**, and notice that in this dialog box, you can add grouping levels. A preview of the grouping level displays on the right side of the dialog box.

Grouping data helps to organize and summarize the data in your report.

4 With **Industry** selected, click the **One Field** button ▸, and then compare your screen with Figure 3.38.

The preview window displays how the data will be grouped in the report. Grouping data in a report places all of the records that have the same data in a field together as a group—in this instance, each *Industry* will display as a group.

Figure 3.38

Report will be grouped by *Industry* names

5 Click **Next**, and then click the **1** box **arrow**. Click **Employer Name**, and then compare your screen with Figure 3.39.

Here you indicate how you want to sort and summarize the information. You can sort on up to four fields. The Summary Options button displays because the data is grouped and contains numerical or currency data. The records in the report will sort alphabetically by Employer Name within Industry. Sorting records in a report presents a more organized report.

Figure 3.39

Sort order

Field that will be sorted

Summary options button displays because report contains numeric or currency fields

6 In the **Report Wizard** dialog box, click the **Summary Options** button, and then compare your screen with Figure 3.40.

The Summary Options dialog box displays. The Fee Paid field can be summarized by selecting one of four options—Sum, Avg, Min, or Max. You can also choose to display only summary information or to display both details—each record—and the summary information.

Figure 3.40

Aggregate functions for *Fee Paid* field

Show options

Access | Chapter 3

7 To the right of **Fee Paid**, select the **Sum** check box. Under **Show**, be sure that the **Detail and Summary** option button is selected, click **OK**, and then click **Next**.

Here you select the layout and the page orientation. A preview of the layout displays on the left.

8 Click each **Layout** option button, noticing the changes in the preview box, and then click the **Stepped** option button to select it as the layout for your report. Under **Orientation**, be sure that **Portrait** is selected. At the bottom, be sure that the **Adjust the field width so all fields fit on a page** check box is selected, and then click **Next**.

9 In the **What title do you want for your report?** box, select the existing text, type **Lastname Firstname 3B Booth Fees by Industry Report** and then click **Finish**. Compare your screen with Figure 3.41.

The report is saved and displays in Print Preview. Each of the specifications you defined in the Report Wizard is reflected in the report. The records are grouped by Industry, and then within each Industry, the Employer Names are alphabetized. Within each Industry grouping, the Fee Paid is summed or totaled—the word *Sum* displays at the end of each grouping.

Figure 3.41

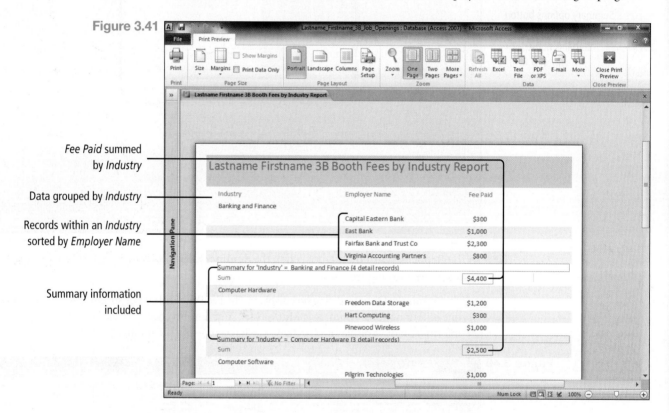

Fee Paid summed by *Industry*

Data grouped by *Industry*

Records within an *Industry* sorted by *Employer Name*

Summary information included

10 **Close Print Preview**. On the status bar, click the **Layout View** button.

Objective 7 | Modify the Design of a Report

After you create your report, you can modify its design by using tools and techniques similar to those you used to modify the design of a form. You can change the format of controls, add controls, remove controls, or change the placement of controls in the report. Most report modifications can be made in Layout view.

Activity 3.16 | Formatting and Deleting Controls in Layout View

1 With your **3B Booth Fees by Industry** report in **Layout** view, on the **Design tab**, in the **Themes group**, click the **Themes** button. In the **Themes gallery**, scroll down, and right-click the **Opulent** theme. Click **Apply Theme to This Object Only**.

2 Click the title—**3B Booth Fees by Industry Report**—to display a border around the label control, and then click the **Format tab**. In the **Font group**, change the **Font Size** to **14**, and then apply **Bold** B.

3 Within each *Industry* grouping, notice the **Summary for 'Industry'** information.

Access includes a summary line that details what is being summarized (in this case, summed) and the number of records that are included in the summary total. Now that Mr. Bass has viewed the report, he has decided this information is not necessary and can be removed.

4 Click any one of the **Summary for 'Industry' controls**.

Another Way

Right-click any of the selected controls, and then click Delete.

The control that you clicked is surrounded by a dark border, and all of the related controls are surrounded by paler borders to indicate that all are selected.

5 Press Del to remove the controls from the report. Compare your screen to Figure 3.42.

Figure 3.42

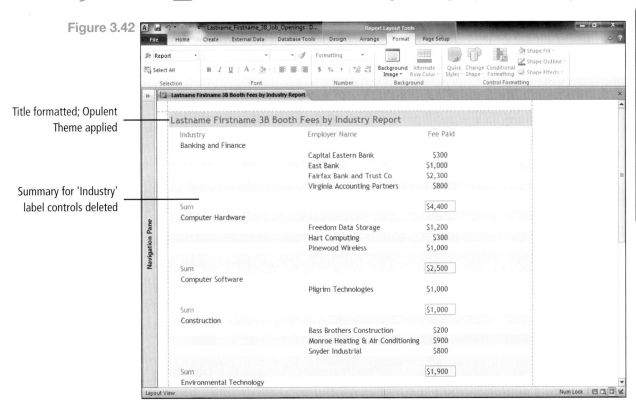

Title formatted; Opulent Theme applied

Summary for 'Industry' label controls deleted

6 **Save** 🔚 the changes you have made to the report.

Activity 3.17 | Modifying Controls in Layout View

In this activity, you will modify the text in controls, move controls, resize controls, and add a control to the report, all of which is easily accomplished in Layout view.

1 On the left side of the report, click one of the **Sum label controls** to select all of the controls, and then double-click to select the text. Type **Total Fees by Industry** and then press Enter. Compare your screen with Figure 3.43.

> The new text more clearly states what is being summed.

Figure 3.43

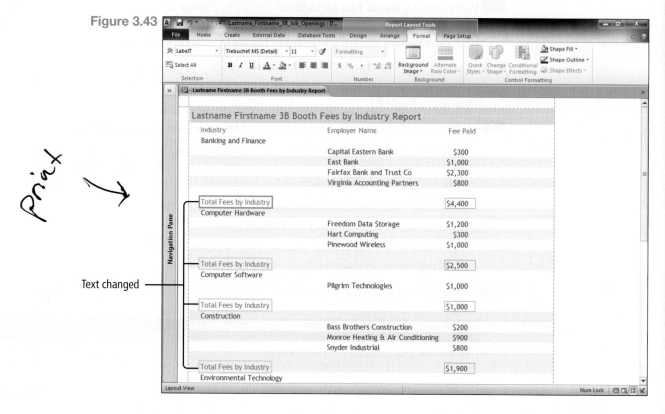

Print

Text changed ————

2 At the top of your report, click to select the **Industry label control**. Hold down Shift, click the **Employer Name label control**, and then click the **Fee Paid label control** to select all three field names. On the **Format tab**, in the **Font group**, click the **Bold** button B.

3 Scroll down to view the end of the report. Click to select the **calculated control** for the **Grand Total**, which displays *20,400*. Point to the left edge of the control to display the ↔ pointer. Drag to the left slightly and release the mouse to display **$20,400**.

> This control is an example of a ***calculated control***—a control that contains an expression, often a formula—that uses one or more fields from the underlying table or query.

4 On the left side of the report, increase the width of the right edge of the **Grand Total label control** so that all of the text displays, and then **Save** 🖫 the report.

Activity 3.18 | Aligning Controls in Design View

Design view gives you a more detailed view of the structure of your report. You can see the header and footer sections for the report, for the page, and for groups. In Design view, your report is not actually running, so you cannot see the underlying data while you are working. In the same manner as forms, you can add labels to the Page Footer section or increase the height of sections. Some tasks, such as aligning controls, can also be completed in Design view.

1 On the status bar, click the **Design View** button ![icon], and then compare your screen with Figure 3.44.

The Design view for a report is similar to the Design view for a form. You can modify the layout of the report in this view, and use the dotted grid pattern to align controls. This report contains a ***Report Header***, a ***Page Header***, a ***Group Header***, which in this instance is the *Industry* grouping, a Detail section that displays the data, a ***Group Footer*** (*Industry*), a ***Page Footer***, and a ***Report Footer***.

The Report Header displays information at the top of the *first page* of a report. The Page Header displays information at the top of *every page* of a report. The Group Header and Group Footer display the field label by which the data has been grouped—*Industry* in this instance. If you do not group data in a report, the Group Header does not display. Similarly, if you do not summarize data, the Group Footer does not display.

Figure 3.44

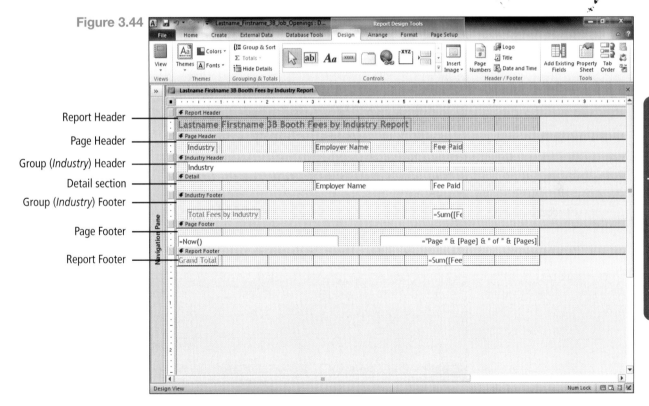

Report Header
Page Header
Group (*Industry*) Header
Detail section
Group (*Industry*) Footer
Page Footer
Report Footer

2 In the **Page Footer** section of the report, examine the two controls in this section.

The Page Footer displays information at the bottom of *every page* in the report, including the page number and the current date inserted by those controls.

The *date control* on the left side, displayed as *=Now( )*, inserts the current date each time the report is opened. The *page number control* on the right side, displayed as *="Page " & [Page] & " of " & [Pages]*, inserts the page number, for example Page 1 of 2, in the report when the report is displayed in Print Preview or when printed. Both of these are examples of functions that are used by Access to create controls in a report.

3 In the **Industry Footer** section, click the **Total Fees by Industry label control**. Hold down Shift. In the **Report Footer** section, click the **Grand Total label control** to select both controls.

4 On the **Arrange tab**, in the **Sizing & Ordering group**, click the **Align** button, and then click **Left. Save** 🖫 the report, and then compare your screen with Figure 3.45.

The left edge of the Grand Total label control is aligned with the left edge of the Total Fees by Industry label control. When using the Align Left feature, Access aligns the left edges of controls with the control that is farthest to the left in the report. Similarly, when using the Align Right feature, Access aligns the right edges of controls with the control that is farthest to the right in the report.

Figure 3.45

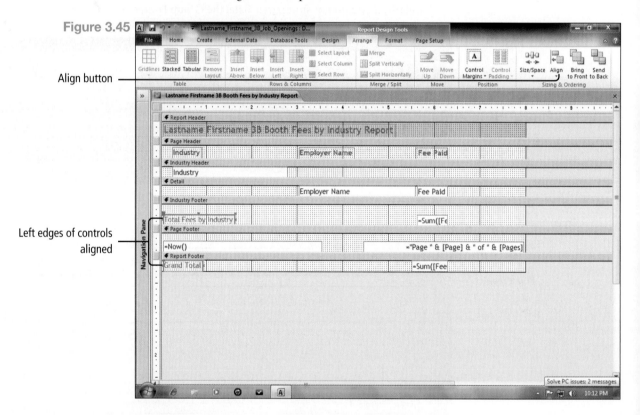

Align button

Left edges of controls aligned

5 Switch to **Layout** view to display the underlying data in the controls. Scroll down, and notice that the **Total Fees by Industry label controls** and the **Grand Total label control** are left aligned.

Objective 8 | Print a Report and Keep Data Together

Before you print a report, examine the preview of the report to ensure that all of the labels and data display fully and to make sure that all of the data is properly grouped. Sometimes a page break occurs in the middle of a group of data, leaving the labels on one page and the data or totals on another page.

Activity 3.19 | Keeping Data Together and Printing a Report

It is possible to keep the data in a group together so it does not break across a page unless, of course, the data itself exceeds the length of a page.

1 On the status bar, click the **Print Preview** button 🔲. If necessary, in the **Zoom group**, click the **Two Pages** button, and then compare your screen with Figure 3.46.

> This report will print on two pages. One record and the summary data for the *Hotel and Food Service* group display at the top of page 2, which is separated from the rest of the grouping.

Figure 3.46

Top of second page—one record and summary data

Bottom of first page—*Industry* grouping name and two records

2 Click the **Close Print Preview** button to return to **Layout** view. On the **Design tab**, in the **Grouping & Totals group**, click the **Group & Sort** button.

> At the bottom of the screen, the **Group, Sort, and Total pane** displays. Here you can control how information is grouped, sorted, or totaled. Layout view is the preferred view in which to accomplish such tasks, because you can see how the changes affect the display of the data.

3 In the **Group, Sort, and Total** pane, on the **Group on Industry bar**, click **More**. To the right of **do not keep group together on one page**, click the **arrow**, and then compare your screen with Figure 3.47.

> The *keep whole group together on one page* command keeps each industry group together, from the name in the group header through the summary in the group footer. Next to *Group on Industry, with A on top* indicates that the industry names display in ascending sort order. The default setting is *do not keep group together on one page*.

Figure 3.47

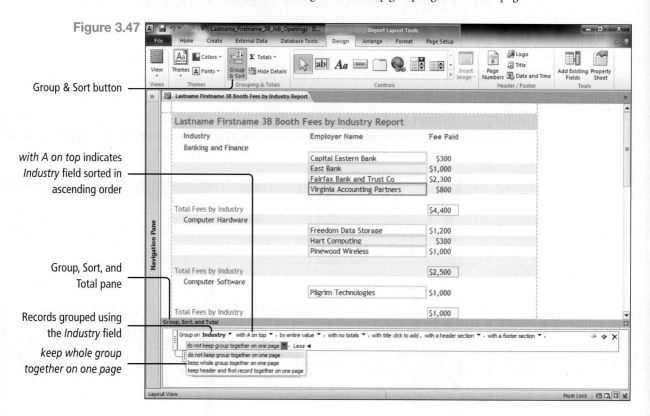

Group & Sort button

with A on top indicates *Industry* field sorted in ascending order

Group, Sort, and Total pane

Records grouped using the *Industry* field

keep whole group together on one page

4 Click **keep whole group together on one page**. In the **Grouping & Totals group**, click the **Group & Sort** button to close the **Group, Sort, and Total** pane. On the status bar, click the **Print Preview** button 🔲. If necessary, in the Zoom group, click the Two Pages button. Compare your screen with Figure 3.48.

> All the records in the *Hotel and Food Service* industry group—the group header, the three records, and the summary information—display together at the top of page 2.

Figure 3.48

Entire industry group displays together

5 **Save** 🖫 the report. Create a paper or electronic copy of the report as directed.

6 **Close Print Preview**, and then **Close** ☒ the report. **Open** ≫ the **Navigation Pane**, and, if necessary, increase the width of the pane so that all object names display fully.

7 Display **Backstage** view, click **Close Database**, and then click **Exit**. As directed by your instructor, submit your database and the three paper or electronic printouts that are the results of this project.

End **You have completed Project 3B** ———————————————

Content-Based Assessments

Summary

A form is an object for either entering or viewing information in a database—it creates a user interface for people using the database. A form is easy to use, because it can display one record at a time. Reports summarize the data in a database in a professional-looking manner suitable for printing. There are several tools for creating forms and reports, and you can modify forms and reports in Layout view or Design view.

Key Terms

Matching

Match each term in the second column with its correct definition in the first column by writing the letter of the term on the blank line in front of the correct definition.

_____ 1. The Access view in which you can make changes to a form or report while viewing the data.

_____ 2. The term used to describe objects and controls that are based on data that is stored in tables.

_____ 3. An Access view that displays the detailed structure of a query, form, or report.

_____ 4. Information, such as a form's title, that displays at the top of the screen in Form view and is printed at the top of the first page when records are printed as forms.

_____ 5. The section of a form or report that displays the records from the underlying table or query.

_____ 6. Information at the bottom of the screen in Form view that prints after the last detail section on the last page.

_____ 7. A gray bar in a form or report that identifies and separates one section from another.

_____ 8. An object on a form or report that displays data, performs actions, and lets you work with information.

_____ 9. The graphical object on a form or report that displays the data from the underlying table or query.

A Bound

B Bound control

C Calculated control

D Control

E Control layout

F Date control

G Design view

H Detail section

I Form footer

J Form header

K Label control

L Layout view

M Section bar

N Text box control

O Unbound control

Content-Based Assessments

_____ 10. A control that retrieves its data from an underlying table or query.

_____ 11. A control on a form or report that contains descriptive information, typically a field name.

_____ 12. A control that does not have a source of data, such as a title in a form or report.

_____ 13. The grouped arrangement of controls on a form or report.

_____ 14. A control that contains an expression, often a formula, that uses one or more fields from the underlying table or query.

_____ 15. A control on a form or report that inserts the current date each time the form or report is opened.

Multiple Choice

Circle the correct answer.

1. An Access object to enter new records into a table, edit or delete existing records in a table, or display existing records is a:
   A. bound control   B. form   C. report

2. The order that the insertion point moves from one field to another in a form when you press Tab is the:
   A. data entry order   B. control order   C. tab order

3. A small symbol that displays in the upper left corner of a selected control layout in a form or report that is displayed in Layout view and that is used to move an entire group of controls is the:
   A. control layout   B. label control   C. layout selector

4. A list of characteristics for controls on a form or report in which you can make precise changes to each property associated with the control is the:
   A. bound control   B. control layout   C. Property Sheet

5. The process of displaying only a portion of the total records (a subset) based on matching a specific value is:
   A. filtering   B. reporting   C. zooming

6. An Access command that filters the records in a form based on one or more fields, or based on more than one value in the field is Filter by:
   A. Form   B. Selection   C. Subset

7. A condition in which records that match at least one of the specified values are displayed is:
   A. AND   B. BOTH   C. OR

8. A database object that summarizes the fields and records from a table or query in an easy-to-read format suitable for printing is a:
   A. control   B. form   C. report

9. Information printed at the end of each group of records and that is used to display summary information for the group is called a:
   A. group footer   B. group header   C. Group, Sort, and Total pane

10. A predefined format that can be applied to the entire database or to individual objects in the database is called a:
    A. group header   B. subset   C. theme

Content-Based Assessments

1. Create and Use a
Form to Add and
Delete Records
2. Create a Form by
Using the Form
Wizard
3. Modify a Form in
Layout View and in
Design View
4. Filter Records

Skills Review | Project **3C** Student Advising

In the following Skills Review, you will assist Gerald Finn, the Dean of Information Technology, in using an Access database to track students and their faculty advisors. Your completed forms will look similar to Figure 3.49.

Project Files

For Project 3C, you will need the following file:

a03C_Student_Advising

You will save your database as:

Lastname_Firstname_3C_Student_Advising

Project Results

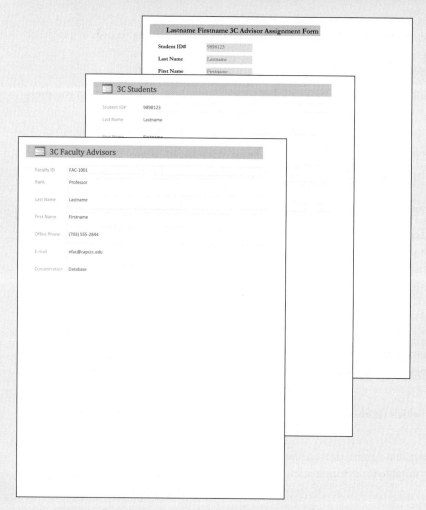

Figure 3.49

(Project 3C Student Advising continues on the next page)

1 **Start** Access. In **Backstage** view, click **Open**, and then from your student files open the **a03C_Student_Advising** database. In **Backstage** view, click **Save Database As**. Save the database in your **Access Chapter 3** folder as **Lastname_Firstname_3C_Student_Advising** On the **Message Bar**, click the **Enable Content** button.

a. On the **Database Tools tab**, in the **Relationships group**, click the **Relationships** button. Notice the one-to-many relationship between the 3C Faculty Advisors table and the 3C Students table using the Faculty ID and Faculty Advisor ID fields as the common fields. *One* faculty member can advise *many* students. Recall that common fields do not need to have the same name; they must have the same data type. **Close** the **Relationships** window.

b. In the **Navigation Pane**, select the **3C Students** table. Click the **Create tab**, and then in the **Forms group**, click the **Form** button. **Save** the form as **Lastname Firstname 3C Student Form** and then **Close** the form object.

c. In the **Navigation Pane**, select the **3C Faculty Advisors** table. Click the **Create tab**, and then in the **Forms group**, click the **Form** button. **Close** the **Navigation Pane**, and then notice that *Faculty ID FAC-2877*, for *Professor Treiman*, has been assigned one student for advising.

d. **Close** the form, saving it as **Lastname Firstname 3C Faculty Advisor Form**

2 **Open** the Navigation Pane, and increase the width to display fully the object names. Open your **3C Student Form** object, and then **Close** the Navigation Pane. In the navigation area, click the **New (blank) record** button. In the **Student ID#** field, type **9898123** and then press Tab.

a. Using your own name, continue entering the data as shown in **Table 1**.

b. In the last field, press Tab to save the record and display a new blank record. **Close** the **3C**

Student Form object, and then **Open** the Navigation Pane.

c. **Open** your **3C Faculty Advisor Form** object, and then **Close** the Navigation Pane. Notice that in the first record, your record displays in the subdatasheet for Professor Treiman. At the bottom of your screen, in the navigation area for the form—not the navigation area for the related records in the form itself—click the **New (blank) record** button. In the blank form, using your own name, enter the information in **Table 2**, being sure to press Tab after entering the data in the last field.

d. In the navigation area, click the **First record** button. Click in the **Last Name** field, and then on the **Home tab**, in the **Find group**, click the **Find** button to open the **Find and Replace** dialog box. In the **Find What** box, type **Holland** and then click **Find Next**. **Close** the **Find and Replace** dialog box.

e. On the **Home tab**, in the **Records group**, click the **Delete button arrow**, and then click **Delete Record** to delete the record for Professor Holland—because Professor Holland has no student advisees assigned, he can be deleted from the table. In the message box, click **Yes** to delete the record. In the navigation area for the form, notice that the number of records in the table is *18*.

f. Use the **Find** button to display the form for the **Faculty ID** of **FAC-1001** Display **Backstage** view. Click the **Print tab**, and then in the right panel, click **Print**. In the **Print** dialog box, under **Print Range**, click the **Selected Record(s)** option button, and then click **Setup**. In the **Page Setup** dialog box, click the **Columns tab**. Under **Column Size**, in the **Width** box, delete the existing text, type **7.5** and then click **OK** two times to print only your record in the form layout, or create an electronic printout. **Close** the **3C Faculty Advisor Form** object, and then **Open** the Navigation Pane.

Table 1

Student ID#	Last Name	First Name	Phone Number	E-mail	Concentration	Faculty Advisor ID
9898123	**Lastname**	**Firstname**	**(703) 555-1257**	**ns0001@capccc.edu**	**Network Security**	**FAC-2877**

(Return to Step 2-b)

Table 2

Faculty ID	Rank	Last Name	First Name	Office Phone	E-mail	Concentration
FAC-1001	**Professor**	**Lastname**	**Firstname**	**(703) 555-2844**	**nfac@capccc.edu**	**Database**

(Return to Step 2-d)

(Project 3C Student Advising continues on the next page)

Access | Chapter 3

Content-Based Assessments

g. Open your **3C Student Form** object, and then **Close** the **Navigation Pane**. Click in the **Last Name** field. Press Ctrl + F to display the **Find and Replace** dialog box. Enter the information to find the record where the **Last Name** field contains your **Lastname** and then **Print** only the selected record, changing the **Column Size Width** to **7.5** or create an electronic printout. **Close** the **3C Student Form** object, and then **Open** the **Navigation Pane**.

3 In the **Navigation Pane**, click to select the **3C Students** table. On the **Create tab**, in the **Forms group** click the **Form Wizard** button.

a. Under **Tables/Queries**, be sure that **Table: 3C Students** displays. Using the **One Field** button or by double-clicking, move the following fields to the **Selected Fields** list in the order specified: **First Name**, **Last Name**, and **Faculty Advisor ID**.

b. Click **Next**. Be sure **Columnar** is selected as the layout, and then click **Next**. In the box **What title do you want for your form?**, select the existing text, and then type **Lastname Firstname 3C Advisor Assignment Form** and then click **Finish** to close the wizard and create the form.

4 **Close** the **Navigation Pane**. Be sure your **3C Advisor Assignment Form** displays. In the lower right corner of your screen, click the **Layout View** button. Click the **First Name label control**. Hold down Shift, and then click the **Last Name label control**, the **Faculty Advisor ID label control**, and the **three text box controls** to select all of the controls. On the Ribbon, click the **Arrange tab**. In the **Table group**, click the **Stacked** button to group the controls. Click the **First Name label control** to deselect all of the controls and to surround the label control with a colored border.

a. On the **Design tab**, in the **Themes group**, click the **Themes** button. Right-click the **Couture** theme, and then click **Apply Theme to This Object Only**.

b. Click anywhere in the title *3C Advisor Assignment Form* to select it. On the **Format tab**, in the **Font group**, click the **Font Size button arrow**, and then click **16**. Click the **Bold** button. Click the **Font Color button arrow**, and then under **Theme Colors**, in the last column, click the last color—**Brown, Accent 6, Darker 50%**.

c. On the status bar, click the **Design View** button. Point to the *lower* edge of the **Form Footer section**

bar to display the ⊕ pointer, and then drag downward approximately **0.5 inch**. On the **Design tab**, in the **Controls group**, click the **Label** button. Position the plus sign of the ⁺ₐ pointer in the **Form Footer** section at **0.25 inch on the horizontal ruler** and even with the lower edge of the Form Footer section bar. Click one time.

d. Using your own name, type **Created by Lastname Firstname** and then press Enter. Click the **Format tab**. With the label control selected, in the **Font group**, click the **Bold** button, and then change the **Font Color** to **Brown, Text 2**—in the fourth column, the first color. Point to a sizing handle to display one of the resize pointers, and then double-click to fit the control to the text you typed.

5 **Save** the form, and then switch to **Layout** view. On the **Design tab**, in the **Tools group**, click the **Add Existing Fields** button. In the **Field List** pane, point to **Student ID#**, and then drag to the left until the pointer is above the *First Name* label control and a thick colored line displays above the control. Release the mouse button to add the Student ID# controls to the form.

a. **Close** the **Field List** pane. Click the **Last Name text box control**, which currently displays *Barthmaier*, to surround it with a border. Point to the right edge of the **text box control** until the ↔ pointer displays, and then drag to the left until there is approximately **1"** of space between *Barthmaier* and the right edge of the text box control.

b. On the **Arrange tab**, in the **Rows & Columns** group, click the **Select Row** button. In the **Move group**, click the **Move Up** button one time to move the **Last Name controls** above the **First Name controls**. **Save** the form.

6 Click the **Student ID# text box control**, which displays *1034823*. In the **Rows & Columns group**, click the **Select Column** button to select all four text box controls. On the **Format tab**, in the **Font group**, click the **Background Color button arrow**. Under **Theme Colors**, in the fifth column, click the second color—**Brown, Accent 1, Lighter 80%**.

a. Click the **Student ID# label control**. On the **Arrange tab**, in the **Rows & Columns group**, click the **Select Column** button to select all four label controls. Click the **Format tab**, change the **Font Color**—*not* the Background Color—to **Brown, Text 2**—in the fourth column, the first color. Then apply **Bold**.

(Project 3C Student Advising continues on the next page)

Content-Based Assessments

b. Click the **layout selector** ⊞ to select all of the controls. Change the **Font Size** to **12**. On the Ribbon, click the **Design tab**, and then in the **Tools group**, click the **Property Sheet** button. In the **Property Sheet**, click the word **Height**, type **0.25** and then press Enter to adjust the height of all of the controls.

c. Click the **Student ID# label control** to select only that label. Click the **Arrange tab**, and then in the **Rows & Columns group**, click the **Select Column** button. In the **Property Sheet**, click **Width**, type **1.5** and then press Enter.

d. In the **Form Footer section**, click the label control with your name. Hold down Shift, and then in the **Form Header section**, in the **label control** that displays *3C Advisor Assignment Form*, click to select both controls. In the **Property Sheet**, change the **Left** property to **0.5** and then press Enter. **Save** the form.

e. **Close** the **Property Sheet**, and then switch to **Form** view. In the navigation area, click the **Last record** button to display the record containing your name. Display **Backstage** view, click the **Print tab**, and then click **Print**. In the **Print** dialog box, under **Print Range**, click the **Selected Record(s)** option button. Create a paper or electronic printout as directed, and then **Close Print Preview**.

7 With the form displayed in **Form** view, click the **First record** button, click the **Faculty Advisor ID label control** to select the text in the text box control. On the **Home tab**, in the **Find group**, click the **Find** button. In the **Find and Replace** dialog box, in the **Find What** box, type **FAC-9119** and then click **Find Next** to find and display the record for *Amanda Bass*. **Close** the **Find and Replace** dialog box. In

the **Sort & Filter group**, click the **Selection** button, and then click **Equals "FAC-9119"**. In the navigation area, notice that two students have been assigned to the faculty member with the *FAC-9119* advisor number.

a. In the **Sort & Filter group**, click the **Toggle Filter** button to remove the filter and display all 27 records. **Close** the form, and save changes.

b. **Open** the **Navigation Pane**, open your **3C Student Form** object, and then **Close** the **Navigation Pane**. On the **Home tab**, in the **Sort & Filter group**, click the **Advanced** button, and then click **Filter By Form**. Click in the **Concentration text box control**. At the right edge of the text box control, click the **arrow** that displays. In the list, click Programming. In the **Sort & Filter group**, click the **Toggle Filter** button, and notice that two students have a *Concentration* of *Programming*.

c. In the **Sort & Filter group**, click the **Advanced** button, and then click **Filter By Form**. At the bottom left side of the window, click the **Or tab**. Click the **Concentration text box control arrow**, and then click **Networking**. In the **Sort & Filter group**, click the **Toggle Filter** button. Seven students have a Concentration of *Programming* or *Networking*. In the **Sort & Filter group**, click the **Toggle Filter** button to display all of the records. **Save** and then **Close** the form.

d. **Open** the **Navigation Pane**; be sure all object names display fully. Display **Backstage** view, click **Close Database**, and then click **Exit**. As directed by your instructor, submit your database and the three paper or electronic printouts that are the results of this project.

End You have completed Project 3C

Access | Chapter 3

Content-Based Assessments

Apply 3B skills from these Objectives:

5 Create a Report by Using the Report Tool

6 Create Reports by Using the Blank Report Tool and the Report Wizard

7 Modify the Design of a Report

8 Print a Report and Keep Data Together

Skills Review | Project **3D** Workshop Rooms

In the following Skills Review, you will assist Michelina Cortez, the Director of Workforce Development, in using an Access database to track the details about workshops offered by community members for the public and for students at the Washington Campus of Capital Cities Community College. Your completed reports will look similar to Figure 3.50.

Project Files

For Project 3D, you will need the following file:

a03D_Workshop_Rooms

You will save your database as:

Lastname_Firstname_3D_Workshop_Rooms

Project Results

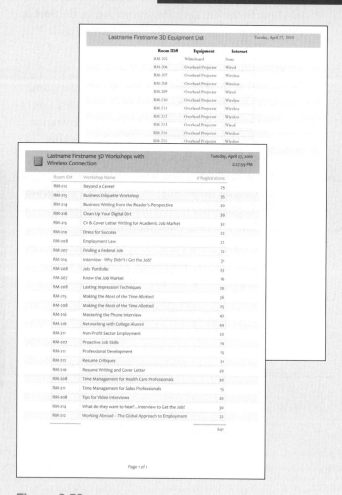

Figure 3.50

(Project 3D Workshop Rooms continues on the next page)

Content-Based Assessments

1 **Start** Access. In **Backstage** view, click **Open**. From your student files, open the **a03D_Workshop_Rooms** database. In **Backstage** view, save the database in your **Access Chapter 3** folder as **Lastname_Firstname_3D_ Workshop_Rooms** and then in the **Message Bar**, click the **Enable Content** button. On the Ribbon, click the **Database Tools tab**, and then click the **Relationships** button. If your relationships do not display, in the Relationships group, click the All Relationships button. *One* room is associated with *many* workshops. Thus, a one-to-many relationship has been established between the 3D Rooms table and the 3D Workshops table using Room ID# as the common field. **Close** the **Relationships** window.

a. Open the two tables to examine the data, and then open the query in **Design** view to examine the design grid. This query answers the question *What is the Room ID#, Workshop Name, Workshop Category, and # Registrations for workshops that have wireless Internet connections available?* **Close** all open objects. In the **Navigation Pane**, select the **3D Workshops with Wireless Connection** query. Click the **Create tab**, and then in the **Reports group**, click the **Report** button. **Close** the **Navigation Pane**.

b. On the **Design tab**, in the **Themes group**, click the **Themes** button, right-click the **Waveform** theme, and then click **Apply Theme to This Object Only**.

c. Click the **Workshop Category** field name. Click the **Arrange tab**, and then in the **Rows & Columns group**, click the **Select Column** button. Press Del to remove the field from the report.

d. Click the **Room ID#** field name, and then drag the right edge of the control to the left until there is approximately **0.5** inch of space between the room number and the right edge of the field. Scroll down the report, and then in the **Workshop Name** field—second column—click in the **text box control** that displays *What do they want to hear? . . . Interview to Get the Job!* Drag the right edge of the control to the right until the data in the control displays on one line. With the **Workshop Name** field selected, click the **Home tab**. In the **Sort & Filter group**, click the **Ascending** button.

e. Scroll down to the bottom of the report, and notice that Access counted the number of records in the report—*26* displays under the Room ID# field. Click this **calculated control**, and then press Del. At the top of the report, click the **# Registrations** field name. On

the **Design tab**, in the **Grouping & Totals group**, click the **Totals** button, and then click **Sum**. Scroll down to the bottom of the report, and then click the calculated control. Point to the bottom edge of the control to display the ↕ pointer, and then double-click to resize the control. The total number of registrations for the workshops that have a wireless connection is *641*.

f. Click the **Page number control**, and then drag the control to the left until the control is visually centered between the left and right margins of the report. At the top of the report, in the **Report Header** section, click the text *3D Workshops with Wireless Connection*. On the **Format tab**, in the **Font group**, change the **Font Size** to **14**, and then click the **label control** again to position the insertion point in the title. Using your own name, add **Lastname Firstname** to the beginning of the title. Click any field in the report. Above and to the left of the **Room ID#** field name, click the **layout selector** ⊞, and then drag it down slightly and to the right until the fields are visually centered between the margins of the report. **Save** the report as **Lastname Firstname 3D Workshops with Wireless Connection Report**

g. On the status bar, click the **Print Preview** button. On the **Print Preview tab**, in the **Zoom group**, click the **Two Pages** button, and notice that the report will print on one page. Create a paper or electronic printout as directed, and then **Close Print Preview**.

h. **Close** the report, and then **Open** the **Navigation Pane**. If necessary, increase the width of the **Navigation Pane** to display the entire report name, and then **Close** the **Navigation Pane**.

2 Click the **Create tab**, and then in the **Reports group**, click the **Blank Report** button. If the Field List pane does not display, on the Design tab, in the Tools group, click the Add Existing Fields button. In the **Field List** pane, click **Show all tables**, and then click the **plus sign** (+) next to **3D Rooms**. Point to the **Room ID#** field, right-click, and then click **Add Field to View**. From the **Field List** pane, drag the **Equipment** field into the blank report— anywhere to the right of *Room ID#*. Double-click the **Internet** field to add it as the third field in the report, and then **Close** the **Field List** pane.

a. On the **Design tab**, in the **Themes group**, click the **Themes** button, and then right-click the **Equity** theme. Click **Apply Theme to This Object Only**.

(Project 3D Workshop Rooms continues on the next page)

Under the **Equipment** field name, click in any **text box control** that displays *Overhead Projector*. Point to the right edge of the control to display the ↔ pointer, and then drag to the right until the text in the control displays on one line and there is a small amount of space between the text and the next column.

b. On the **Design tab**, in the **Header/Footer group**, click the **Date and Time** button. Clear the **Include Time** check box, and then click **OK**. In the **Header/Footer group**, click the **Title** button. Using your own name, type **Lastname Firstname 3D Equipment List** and then press Enter.

c. With the title still selected, on the **Format tab**, in the **Font group**, change the **Font Size** to **14**. On the right edge of the **label control** for the title, double-click to resize the title's label control.

d. Click the **Room ID#** field name to select it. Hold down Shift, and then click the **Internet** field name to select all three field names. On the **Format tab**, in the **Font group**, click the **Center** button to center the field names over the data in the fields. Change the **Font Color** to **Automatic**, and then apply **Bold**. Click the **layout selector** ⊞, and then drag it down slightly and to the right to visually center the fields between the margins. **Save** the report as **Lastname Firstname 3D Equipment List**

e. On the status bar, click the **Print Preview** button. Create a paper or electronic printout as directed, and then **Close Print Preview**. **Close** the report.

3 Click the **Create tab**, and then in the **Reports group**, click the **Report Wizard** button. Click the **Tables/Queries arrow**, and then click **Table: 3D Workshops**. Double-click the following fields in the order given to move them to the **Selected Fields** list: **Workshop Category**, **Workshop Name**, and **# Registrations**. Click **Next**.

a. With **Workshop Category** selected, click the **One Field** button to group the report by this field, and then click **Next**. Click the **1 box arrow**, and then click **Workshop Name** to sort the records within each Workshop Category by the Workshop Name. Click the **Summary Options** button. To the right of **# Registrations**, select the **Sum** check box. Under **Show**, be sure that the **Detail and Summary** option button is selected, click **OK**, and then click **Next**.

b. Under **Layout**, be sure that the **Stepped** option button is selected. Under **Orientation**, be sure that **Portrait** is selected, and at the bottom of the **Report Wizard** dialog box, be sure that the **Adjust the field width so all fields fit on a page** check box is selected. Click **Next**, In the **What title do you want for your report?** box, select the existing text, type **Lastname Firstname 3D Registrations by Category Report** and then click **Finish**. **Close Print Preview**, and then on the status bar, click the **Layout View** button.

4 On the **Design tab**, in the **Themes group**, click the **Themes** button, right-click the **Median** theme, and then click **Apply Theme to This Object Only**. Click the title of the report. On the **Format tab**, in the **Font group**, change the **Font Size** to **14**, and then apply **Bold**. Click one of the **Summary for 'Workshop Category' controls**, and then press Del.

a. On the left side of the report, click one of the **Sum label controls**, and then double-click to select the text inside the control. Type **Total Registrations by Workshop Category** and then press Enter.

b. At the top of your report, click the **Workshop Category label control**. Hold down Shift, click the **Workshop Name label control**, and then click the **# Registrations label control** to select all three field names. On the **Format tab**, in the **Font group**, click the **Bold** button.

c. On the status bar, click the **Design View** button. In the **Report Footer section**, click the **Grand Total label control**. Hold down Shift, and in the **Workshop Category Footer section**, click the **Total Registrations by Workshop Category label control** to select both controls. On the **Arrange tab**, in the **Sizing & Ordering group**, click the **Align** button, and then click **Left** to align the left edges of the two controls.

5 On the status bar, click the **Print Preview** button. In the **Zoom group**, click the **Two Pages** button to view how your report is currently laid out. Notice that at the bottom of Page 1 and the top of Page 2, the records in the **Keeping a Job** category are split between the two pages. Click **Close Print Preview**. On the status bar, click the **Layout View** button.

(Project 3D Workshop Rooms continues on the next page)

Content-Based Assessments

a. On the **Design tab**, in the **Grouping & Totals group**, click the **Group & Sort** button. In the **Group, Sort, and Total** pane, on the **Group on Workshop Category bar**, click **More**. Click the **do not keep group together on one page arrow**, and then click **keep whole group together on one page**. On the **Design tab**, in the **Grouping & Totals group**, click the **Group & Sort** button to close the **Group, Sort, and Total** pane. **Save** the report.

b. On the status bar, click the **Print Preview** button. Notice that the entire **Workshop Category** grouping of **Keeping a Job** displays together at the top of Page 2. Create a paper or electronic printout as directed, and then **Close Print Preview**. **Save**, and then **Close** the report. **Open** the **Navigation Pane**, and if necessary, increase the width of the Navigation Pane so that all object names display fully. In **Backstage** view, click **Close Database**, and then click **Exit**. As directed by your instructor, submit your database and the three paper or electronic printouts that are the results of this project.

End **You have completed Project 3D** ————————————————

Apply **3A** skills from these Objectives:

1 Create and Use a Form to Add and Delete Records

2 Create a Form by Using the Form Wizard

3 Modify a Form in Layout View and in Design View

4 Filter Records

Mastering Access | Project **3E** Raffle Sponsors

In the following Mastering Access project, you will assist Alina Ngo, Dean of Student Services at the Central Campus of Capital Cities Community College, in using her database to track raffle items and sponsors for the New Student Orientation sessions. Your completed forms will look similar to Figure 3.51.

Project Files

For Project 3E, you will need the following file:

a03E_Raffle_Sponsors

You will save your database as:

Lastname_Firstname_3E_Raffle_Sponsors

Project Results

Lastname Firstname 3E Sponsor Form

Sponsor ID#   SP-1211

Sponsor   Arlington Sweets

3E Raffle Items

Raffle Item ID#   RAFF-31

Item Description   Lastname Firstname Software Game

Sponsor ID#   SP-1210

Provider Item Code TG-79044

Category   Electronics

Retail Value $35

Figure 3.51

(Project 3E Raffle Sponsors continues on the next page)

Content-Based Assessments

Mastering Access | Project **3E** Raffle Sponsors (continued)

1 **Start** Access. From your student data files, **Open** the **a03E_Raffle_Sponsors** database. Save the database in your **Access Chapter 3** folder as **Lastname_Firstname_ 3E_Raffle_Sponsors** and then enable the content. View the relationship between the 3E Sponsors table and the 3E Raffle Items table. *One* sponsor can provide *many* raffle items for the New Student Orientation sessions.

2 Based on the **3E Raffle Items** table, use the **Form** tool to create a form. **Save** the form as **Lastname Firstname 3E Raffle Item Form** and then switch to **Form** view. Add the new record as shown in **Table 1**, using your own name in the **Item Description** field.

3 Display the first record, and, if necessary, click in the Raffle Item ID# field. Use the **Find** button to display the record for the **Raffle Item ID#** of **RAFF-06**, and then **Delete** the record. Display the record you entered for **RAFF-31**, and then **Print** the **Selected Record**, changing the column width to **7.5"** or create an electronic printout. **Close** the form, saving changes if prompted.

4 Based on the **3E Sponsors** table, use the **Form Wizard** tool to create a form. Include the following fields in the order given: **Sponsor**, **Contact Last Name**, **Contact First Name**, and **Phone Number**. Use a **Columnar** layout, and as the title type **Lastname Firstname 3E Sponsor Form**

5 In **Layout** view, apply the **Stacked** layout to all of the controls, and then apply the **Couture** theme to this object only. For the title of the form, change the **Font Size** to **16**, apply **Bold**, and change the **Font Color** to **Brown, Accent 6, Darker 50%**. In **Design** view, increase the height of the **Form Footer** section to approximately **0.5 inch**. In the **Form Footer** section and using your own name, add a **label control** that displays **Created by Lastname Firstname** For the **label control**, change the **Font Color** to **Brown, Text 2**, apply **Bold**, and then adjust the control to fit the text in the control.

6 **Save** the form, and then switch to **Layout** view. Display the **Field List** pane, and then add the **Sponsor ID#** field to the form above the **Sponsor** field. **Close** the **Field List** pane, and then move the **Contact First Name** controls directly above the **Contact Last Name** controls. Display **Record 5**—this record's Sponsor name is the longest entry of all records. Decrease the width of the **Sponsor text box control** until there is approximately **1 inch** between *Inc* and the right edge of the control. **Save** the form.

7 Select all five **text box controls**, set the **Background Color** to **Brown, Accent 1, Lighter 80%**. Select all of the **label controls**, set the **Font Color** to **Brown, Text 2**, and then apply **Bold**. With the controls selected, display the **Property Sheet**. For the **label controls**, set the **Width** to **1.75** Select all of the **label controls** and **text box controls**, set the **Font Size** to **12**, and the **Height** property to **0.25** In the **Form Header** and **Form Footer** sections, select the **label controls** with the title and your name. Set the **Left** property to **0.5**

8 **Close** the **Property Sheet**, **Save** the form, and then switch to **Form** view. Using your first name and last name, add the record as shown in **Table 2**, being sure to use the (Tab) key to move among fields and to save the record.

9 Display the record you just added and then **Print** the **Selected Record**, or create an electronic printout as directed. **Close** the form.

10 Open your **3E Raffle Item Form** object. Using the **Advanced Filter/Sort** tool, create a filter that displays eight records with a **Category** of **Clothing** or **Dining** After verifying that eight records display, use the **Toggle Filter** button to display all 30 records. **Save** the form.

11 **Close** all open objects. **Open** the **Navigation Pane**, and, if necessary, increase the width of the **Navigation Pane** to display fully all of the object names. Display **Backstage** view. Click **Close Database**, and then click **Exit**. As directed by your instructor, submit your database and the two paper or electronic printouts that are the results of this project.

Table 1

Raffle Item ID#	Item Description	Sponsor ID#	Provider Item Code	Category	Retail Value
RAFF-31	**Lastname Firstname Software Game**	**SP-1210**	**TG-79044**	**Electronics**	**35**

(Return to Step 3)

Table 2

Sponsor ID#	Sponsor	Contact First Name	Contact Last Name	Phone Number
SP-1211	**Arlington Sweets**	**Firstname**	**Lastname**	**(703) 555-5355**

- - -► (Return to Step 9)

End **You have completed Project 3E**

Access | Chapter 3

Project 3E: Raffle Sponsors | **Access** **235**

Mastering Access | Project **3F** Contractor Services

In the following Mastering Access project, you will assist Roger Lockheart, Director of Facilities at the Jefferson Campus of Capital Cities Community College, in using a database to track facility and contractor services for an open house for prospective college students. Your completed reports will look similar to Figure 3.52.

Project Files

For Project 3F, you will need the following file:

a03F_Contractor_Services

You will save your database as:

Lastname_Firstname_3F_Contractor_Services

Project Results

Figure 3.52

(Project 3F Contractor Services continues on the next page)

Content-Based Assessments

1 **Start** Access. From your student files, **Open** the **a03F_Contractor_Services** database. Save the database in your **Access Chapter 3** folder as **Lastname_Firstname_3F_ Contractor_Services** and then enable the content. View the relationship between the 3F Contractors table and the 3F Facility Services table. *One* contractor can provide *many* facility services. **Close** the **Relationships** window. Based on the **3F Setup and Tear Down Job Costs** query, use the **Report** tool to create a report, and then **Close** the **Navigation Pane**. This query answers the question *What is the Date, Job ID, Contractor ID, Contractor Last Name, Contractor First Name, Category, and Job Cost of setup and tear down jobs?*

2 Apply the **Waveform** theme to this object only. **Delete** the **Job ID** and **Contractor ID** fields from the report. Decrease the widths of the **Contractor Last Name**, **Contractor First Name**, and **Category** fields until there is approximately **0.25 to 0.5 inch** of space between the longest entry in each field—including the field name— and the right edge of each control. Be sure that there is enough space for *Tear Down* to display on one line. **Sort** the **Date** field in ascending order.

Scroll down to the bottom of the report, and increase the height of the **calculated control** that displays *$4,440*. Drag the **page number control** to the left to visually center it between the margins of the report. For the title, change the **Font Size** to **16**, and then using your last name and first name, add **Lastname Firstname** to the beginning of the title. Using the **layout selector** ⊞, visually center the fields between the left and right margins. **Save** the report as **Lastname Firstname 3F Setup and Tear Down Job Costs Report** and then create a paper or electronic printout as directed—two pages will print. **Close** the report. **Open** the **Navigation Pane**, and increase the width of the **Navigation Pane** to display the entire report name. **Close** the **Navigation Pane**.

3 Use the **Blank Report** tool to create a report based on the **3F Contractors** table. Add the fields to the report in the order given: **Contractor Last Name**, **Contractor First Name**, and **Phone Number**. **Close** the **Field List** pane. Apply the **Equity** theme to this object only. Increase the width of the **Contractor Last Name** field so that the field name displays fully. Add the **Date** to the Report Header section—do not include the time. Add a **Title** of **Lastname Firstname 3F Contractors Phone List** to the report, and change the **Font Size** to **14**. Decrease the width of the

title's label control to fit the text and to move the date control to the left within the right margin. Apply **Bold** to the three field names. **Sort** the **Contractor Last Name** field in **Ascending** order. Using the **layout selector** ⊞, visually center the fields between the report margins. **Save** the report as **Lastname Firstname 3F Contractors Phone List** and then create a paper or electronic printout as directed. **Close Print Preview**, and then **Close** the report.

4 Use the **Report Wizard** to create a report based on the **3F Facility Services** table. Select the following fields in the order given: **Category**, **Service Description**, and **Job Cost**. **Group** the report by **Category**, **Sort** by **Service Description**, and **Sum** the **Job Cost** field. Select the **Stepped** layout and **Portrait** orientation. For the report title, type **Lastname Firstname 3F Job Cost by Category Report** and then switch to **Layout** view.

5 Apply the **Median** theme to this object only. For the title, change the **Font Size** to **14**, and apply **Bold**. **Delete** the **Summary for 'Category' controls**. Scroll down to the bottom of the report, and click the **text box control** that displays *Wireless network for laptop lane*. Decrease the width of the control until there is approximately **0.25 inch** of space between the end of the word *lane* and the right edge of the label control. At the bottom of the report, for the last record *Wireless network for laptop lane*, to the right, click the **text box control** that displays #—the number or pound sign displays because the text box control is not wide enough to display the entire value. Hold down (Shift), and immediately below the selected control, click the **Sum calculated control**, and then under that, click the **Grand Total calculated control**. Drag the left edge of the three selected controls to the left approximately **0.5 inch** to display the amounts fully. **Save** the report.

6 Change the text in the **Sum label control** to **Total Job Cost by Category** and then at the top of the report, select the three **field names**, and apply **Bold**. **Save** the report.

7 Switch to **Design** view. Click the **label control** that displays *Total Job Cost by Category*, and then align the left edge of the control with the left edge of the **label control** that displays *Grand Total*. **Save** the report.

8 Display the report in **Print Preview** in the **Two Pages** arrangement, examine how the groupings break across pages, **Close Print Preview**, and then switch to **Layout** view. Display the **Group, Sort, and Total** pane, and then select **keep whole group together on one page**. Close the

(Project 3F Contractor Services continues on the next page)

Group, **Sort, and Total** pane. Display the report in **Print Preview** in the **Two Pages** arrangement, and then notice that the entire **Tear Down** grouping displays on Page 2. **Save** the report.

 Create a paper or electronic printout as directed, **Close Print Preview**, and then **Close** the report. **Open**

the **Navigation Pane**, and then display **Backstage** view. Click **Close Database**, and then click **Exit**. As directed by your instructor, submit your database and the three paper or electronic printouts that are the results of this project.

End **You have completed Project 3F** ─────────────

Content-Based Assessments

Apply **3A** and **3B** skills from these Objectives:

1   Create and Use a Form to Add and Delete Records

2   Create a Form by Using the Form Wizard

3   Modify a Form in Layout View and in Design View

4   Filter Records

5   Create a Report by Using the Report Tool

6   Create Reports by Using the Blank Report Tool and the Report Wizard

7   Modify the Design of a Report

8   Print a Report and Keep Data Together

Mastering Access | Project **3G** Career Books

In the following Mastering Access project, you will assist Teresa Johnson, Head Librarian at the Capital Campus of Capital Cities Community College, in using a database to track publishers and book titles to assist students in finding employment. Your completed forms and reports will look similar to Figure 3.53.

Project Files

For Project 3G, you will need the following file:

    a03G_Career_Books

You will save your database as:

    Lastname_Firstname_3G_Career_Books

Project Results

Figure 3.53

(Project 3G Career Books continues on the next page)

Content-Based Assessments

1 **Start** Access. From your student files, open the **a03G_Career_Books** database. **Save** the database in your **Access Chapter 3** folder as **Lastname_Firstname_3G_Career_Books** and then enable the content. Review the relationship between the 3G Publishers table and the 3G Career Book Titles table. *One* publisher can publish *many* books.

2 Based on the **3G Career Book Titles** table, use the **Form** tool to create a form. Switch to **Form** view, and then using your own name, add the record as shown in **Table 1**.

3 **Save** the form as **Lastname Firstname 3G Career Book Form** and then display the first record. Use the **Find** button to display the record for the **Title ID** of **T-18**, and then **Delete** the record. Display the record you entered for **T-34**, and then **Print** the **Selected Record**, changing the column width to **7.5"** or create an electronic printout. **Close** the form, saving changes if prompted.

4 Use the **Form Wizard** to create a form based on the **3G Publishers** table. Include the following fields: **Company Name**, **Rep Last Name**, **Rep First Name**, **Job Title**, and **Phone Number**. Use a **Columnar** layout, and as the title, type **Lastname Firstname 3G Publisher Form**

5 In **Layout** view, select all of the controls, and then apply the **Stacked** layout. Apply the **Couture** theme to this object only. For the title, change the **Font Size** to **16**, apply **Bold**, and change the **Font Color** to **Brown, Accent 6, Darker 50%**—in the last column, the last color. In **Design** view, increase the height of the **Form Footer** section approximately **0.5 inch**. In the **Form Footer** section, add a **label control** that displays **Created by Lastname Firstname** and then change the **Font Color** to **Brown, Text 2**—in the fourth column, the first color. Apply **Bold**, and then adjust the control to fit the data in the control. **Save** the form.

6 In **Layout** view, display the **Field List** pane, and then add the **Publisher ID** field to the form above the **Company Name** field. **Close** the **Field List** pane. Move the **Rep First Name** field directly above the **Rep Last Name** field. Click the **Job Title text box control**, and then drag the right edge of the control to the left until there is approximately **1 inch** of space between *Representative* and the right edge of the control. **Save** the form.

7 Select all of the **text box controls**, set the **Background Color** to **Brown, Accent 1, Lighter 80%**—in the fifth column, the second color. Select all of the **label controls**. Set the **Font Color** to **Brown, Text 2**, apply **Bold**, and then set the **Width** property to **1.5** Select all of the **label controls** and **text box controls**, set the **Font Size** to **12**, and then set the **Height** property to **0.25** For the **form header label control** and the **form footer label control**, set the **Left** property to **0.5**

8 **Close** the **Property Sheet**, **Save** the form, and switch to **Form** view. Using your own name, add a new record as shown in **Table 2**.

9 Display the record you just added and then **Print** the **Selected Record** or create an electronic printout as directed. **Close** the form.

10 **Open** your **3G Career Book Form** object. Using the **Filter By Form** tool, filter the records to display the **Category** of **Resumes** or **Job Search**. Twenty books meet the criteria. Click the **Toggle Filter** button to display all 31 records. **Save** the form, and then **Close** the form.

11 Use the **Report** tool to create a report based on the **3G Resume or Interview Books** query. Apply the **Waveform** theme to this object only. **Delete** the **Publisher ID**, **Category**, and **Company Name** fields from the report.

Table 1

Title ID	Title	Author Last Name	Author First Name	Publisher ID	Category	Copies On Hand	Value of Books
T-34	Effective Networking	Lastname	Firstname	PUB-100	Job Search	6	180

(Return to Step 3)

Table 2

Publisher ID	Company Name	Rep First Name	Rep Last Name	Job Title	Phone Number
PUB-111	Associated Publishers	Firstname	Lastname	Sales Associate	(703) 555-0857

(Return to Step 9)

(Project 3G Career Books continues on the next page)

Decrease the widths of the **Author Last Name** and **Author First Name** fields so that there is approximately **0.5 inch** between the word *Name* in the field name and the right edge of the label controls. Increase the width of the **Title** field until each title displays on one line. **Sort** the **Title** field in **Ascending** order.

Click the **Title** field name, and then on the **Design tab**, click the **Totals** button. Add a control that counts the number of records, and then increase the height of the control so that *14* displays fully in the calculated control. Drag the **page number control** to the left to visually center it between the report margins. For the title of the report, change the **Font Size** to **14**, and then using your own name, add **Lastname Firstname** to the beginning of the title. Using the **layout selector** ⊞, visually center the fields between the left and right margins. **Save** the report as **Lastname Firstname 3G Resume or Interview Books Report** and then create a paper or electronic printout as directed. **Close** the report.

12 Use the **Blank Report** tool to create a report based on the **3G Publishers** table. Add the following fields to the report in the order listed: **Company Name**, **Rep First Name**, **Rep Last Name**, and **Phone Number**. **Close** the **Field List** pane, and then apply the **Equity** theme to this object only. Increase the width of the **Company Name** field so that the text in each record displays on one line. Add the **Date** to the report, add a **Title** of **Lastname Firstname 3G Reps Phone List** For the title, change the **Font Size** to **14**, and then adjust the width of the title's label control, being sure that the date displays within the right margin of the report. Apply **Bold** to all of the field names, and then **Center** the field names over the data. **Sort** the **Company Name** field in **Ascending** order. Using the **layout selector**, visually center the fields between the left and right margins. **Save** the report as **Lastname Firstname 3G Reps Phone List** and then create a paper or electronic printout as directed. **Close** the report.

13 Use the **Report Wizard** to create a report based on the **3G Career Book Titles** table, Select the following fields: **Category**, **Title**, and **Value of Books**. **Group** the report by **Category**, **Sort** by **Title**, and **Sum** the **Value of Books** field. Select the **Stepped** layout, and **Portrait** orientation as the report title, type **Lastname Firstname 3G Book Values by Category Report** and then switch to **Layout** view.

14 Apply the **Opulent Theme** to this object only. For the title of the report, change the **Font Size** to **14** and then apply **Bold**. **Delete** the **Summary for 'Category' controls**. Scroll down to the bottom of the report, and in the **Title** field, click the **text box control** that displays *Interview Techniques and Resume Tips*, which is the longest entry in the field. Point to the right edge of the **text box control**, and then drag the pointer to the left until there is approximately **0.25 inch** between *Tips* and the right edge of the text box control. Scroll to the top of the report, and then click in the **Value of Books label control**. Double-click the left edge of the **label control** to increase the width of the label control and to display fully the text in the label control. **Save** the report.

15 Scroll down to the bottom of the report, and then on the right side of the report, increase the width of the **Sum calculated controls** and the **Grand Total calculated control** so that the entire figure, including the dollar sign, displays—the Grand Total is *$8,810*. Change the text in the **Sum label controls** to **Total Value of Books by Category** and then increase the width of the **Grand Total label control** to display fully the text in the control. **Save** the report.

16 At the top of the report, apply **Bold** to the three field names. Select any of the **Title text box controls**. Display the **Property Sheet**, set the **Height to 0.25**. **Close** the **Property Sheet**. In **Design** view, align the left edge of the **label control** that displays *Total Value of Books by Category* with the left edge of the **label control** that displays *Grand Total*. **Save** the report.

17 Display the report in **Print Preview** in the **Two Pages** arrangement, examine how the groupings break across pages, and then **Close Print Preview**. In **Layout** view, display the **Group, Sort, and Total** pane, and then click **keep whole group together on one page**. Close the **Group, Sort, and Total** pane. **Save** the report. Display the report in **Print Preview** in the **Two Pages** arrangement, and then notice that the entire **Resumes** grouping displays on Page 2. Create a paper or electronic printout as directed, and then **Close Print Preview**.

18 **Close** the report, and then **Open** the **Navigation Pane**. If necessary, increase the width of the Navigation Pane to display all of the object names fully. In **Backstage** view, click **Close Database**, and then click **Exit**. As directed by your instructor, submit your database and the five paper or electronic printouts that are the results of this project.

End You have completed Project 3G

Content-Based Assessments

GO! Fix It | Project 3H Resume Workshops

Project Files

For Project 3H, you will need the following file:

a03H_Resume_Workshops

You will save your database as:

Lastname_Firstname_3H_Resume_Workshops

In this project, you will make corrections to and update an Access database that stores information about resume workshops that are scheduled for students. Start Access, navigate to the student files that accompany this textbook, and then open the a03H_Resume_Workshops database. Save the database in your Access Chapter 3 folder as **Lastname_Firstname_3H_Resume_Workshops** and enable the content.

To complete the project, you should know that:

- In the Participant Form object, all the field heights should be the same, and your name and 3H should display in the title. Create a filter that finds records where the Workshop Fee is $35—five records meet the criteria. Toggle the filter off, and then save the form. In the first record, enter your first name and last name in the appropriate fields. Then, as directed, create a paper or electronic printout of only this record.

- In the Resume Workshop Form object, in the header, change Lastname Firstname to your own last name and first name. Add a label control to the Form Footer section. Using your own name, type **Created by Lastname Firstname** and then bold the text. Save the form. Find the record for Workshop ID# R-002, and then, as directed, create a paper or electronic printout of only this record.

- In the Participant Input Form object, you should adjust the height and width of the controls so that the text in the controls displays on one line. The font sizes for the label controls and text box controls should match. Add your name and 3H to the title, and be sure that the title displays on one line. For the title, change the font size so that the title does not extend to the right of the text box controls beneath it. In the Form Footer section, create a label typing **Created by Lastname Firstname** and then bold the text in the label. Add a light blue background color to the text box controls, and then save the form. Display the record with your name and then, as directed, create a paper or electronic printout of only this record.

- For the Participant Fees Report, apply the Opulent theme to this object only. Add a title to the report that includes your name and 3H. Adjust the font size and the width of the label control, and be sure that the date control displays within the right margin of the report. Center the data in the Workshop ID text box controls. Center the layout between the margins, and add a total for the Workshop Fee column that sums the fees. Sort the Date Fee Received field in ascending order. Save the report, and then create a paper or electronic printout as directed.

- In the Participants by Workshop Name report, apply the Equity theme to this object only. Add your name and 3H to the title, and reduce the Font Size. Adjust controls so that all of the data displays fully. Delete the Summary for 'Workshop ID#' control. Change the text in the Sum label controls so that they reflect what is being summed. Align the left edges of the Sum and Grand Total label controls. Add the date to the Report Header section. Be sure that the groupings are kept together when printed. Create a paper or electronic printout as directed.

End You have completed Project 3H

Content-Based Assessments

GO! Make It | Project 3I Study Abroad

Project Files

For Project 3I, you will need the following file:

a03I_Study_Abroad

You will save your database as:

Lastname_Firstname_3I_Study_Abroad

From the student files that accompany this textbook, open the a03I_Study_Abroad database, and then save the database in your Access Chapter 3 folder as **Lastname_Firstname_3I_Study_Abroad** Using the Blank Report tool, create the report shown in Figure 3.54. Apply the Slipstream theme, and then create a paper or electronic printout as directed.

Project Results

Lastname Firstname 3I Trip Dates and Cost Report

Destination	Cost of Trip	Departure Date	Return Date
Costa Rica	$3,000	2/15/2016	2/25/2016
Egypt	$4,300	2/16/2016	2/26/2016
Great Britain	$6,000	3/22/2016	4/4/2016
Greece	$6,000	5/5/2016	5/15/2016
Ireland	$5,000	5/23/2016	6/2/2016
Italy	$4,500	5/1/2016	5/8/2016
Mexico	$2,000	2/8/2016	2/18/2016
Panama	$2,900	4/30/2016	5/5/2016
Paris	$7,580	5/6/2016	5/17/2016
Rome	$7,250	5/2/2016	5/12/2016
Singapore	$5,000	4/12/2016	4/20/2016
South Africa	$4,780	3/3/2016	3/10/2016
Switzerland	$5,400	2/25/2016	3/3/2016
Tokyo	$4,950	3/4/2016	3/12/2016
Tuscan Valley	$5,600	2/4/2016	2/14/2016

Figure 3.54

End You have completed Project 3I

Content-Based Assessments

GO! Solve It | Project **3J** Job Offers

Project Files

For Project 3J, you will need the following file:

a03J_Job_Offers

You will save your database as:

Lastname_Firstname_3J_Job_Offers

From the student files that accompany this textbook, open the a03J_Job_Offers database file, save the database in your Access Chapter 3 folder as **Lastname_Firstname_3J_Job_Offers** and then enable the content.

Kevin Bodine, coordinator of the Student Employment Office, would like one form and two reports created from the Job Offers database. Using the skills you have practiced in this chapter, create an attractive form that can be used to update student candidate records. Using your own information, add a new record as Student ID# **9091246** with a College Major of **Business** and a Phone Number of **(703) 555-9876** Leave the Internship Completed field blank. Save the form as **Lastname Firstname 3J Candidate Update Form** and then create a paper or electronic printout of only your record.

Mr. Bodine wants an attractive report listing the Organization Name and the Offer Amount of each job offered to a student, grouped by the Student ID#, sorted in ascending order by the Organization Name. The Offer Amount field should display the maximum amount offered. Create and save the report as **Lastname Firstname 3J Job Offers by Student ID# Report** and then create a paper or electronic printout as directed.

Mr. Bodine also wants an attractive report of the names, college majors, and phone numbers of the student candidates, grouped by college majors and then sorted by the Last Name field. Save the report as **Lastname Firstname 3J Student Candidates by Major Report** and then create a paper or electronic printout as directed.

	Performance Level		
	Exemplary You consistently applied the relevant skills	**Proficient** You sometimes, but not always, applied the relevant skills	**Developing** You rarely or never applied the relevant skills
Create 3J Candidate Update Form	Form created with correct fields in easy-to-follow format and record entered for student.	Form created with no more than two missing elements.	Form created with more than two missing elements.
Create 3J Job Offers by Student ID# Report	Report created with correct fields, grouped and sorted correctly, and in an attractive format.	Report created with no more than two missing elements.	Report created with more than two missing elements.
Create 3J Student Candidates by Major Report	Report created with correct fields, grouped and sorted correctly, and in an attractive format.	Report created with no more than two missing elements.	Report created with more than two missing elements.

Performance Criteria

End You have completed Project 3J ——————

Content-Based Assessments

GO! Solve It | Project 3K Financial Aid

Project Files

For Project 3K, you will need the following file:

a03K_Financial_Aid

You will save your database as:

Lastname_Firstname_3K_Financial_Aid

From the student files that accompany this textbook, open the a03K_Financial_Aid database file, and then save the database in your Access Chapter 3 folder as **Lastname_Firstname_3K_Financial_Aid**

Marguerite Simons, the Financial Aid Director, wants an attractive, easy-to-follow form that can be used to update the Financial Aid Students table. Using your first name and last name, add a new record with the following information:

Student ID#	Financial Aid ID	Home Phone#	College E-mail
1472589	FA-07	(703) 555-3874	ns589@capccc.edu

Save the form as **Lastname Firstname 3K FA Student Update Form** and then create a paper or electronic printout of only your record.

Ms. Simons also wants an attractively formatted report listing the Award Name, the Student ID# and the Award Amount for financial aid offered to students, grouped by the Award name and sorted in ascending order by the Student ID# field (Hint: Use data from both tables). The Award Amount should be summed. Save the report as **Lastname Firstname 3K Amount by Award Name Report** and then create a paper or electronic printout of the report.

Performance Criteria	Performance Level		
	Exemplary You consistently applied the relevant skills	**Proficient** You sometimes, but not always, applied the relevant skills	**Developing** You rarely or never applied the relevant skills
Create 3K FA Student Update Form	Form created with correct fields in easy-to-follow format and record entered for student.	Form created with no more than two missing elements.	Form created with more than two missing elements.
Create 3K Amount by Award Name Report	Report created with correct fields, grouped and sorted correctly, and in an attractive format.	Report created with no more than two missing elements.	Report created with more than two missing elements.

End You have completed Project 3K

Outcomes-Based Assessments

Rubric

The following outcomes-based assessments are *open-ended assessments*. That is, there is no specific correct result; your result will depend on your approach to the information provided. Make *Professional Quality* your goal. Use the following scoring rubric to guide you in *how* to approach the problem, and then to evaluate *how well* your approach solves the problem.

The *criteria*—Software Mastery, Content, Format and Layout, and Process—represent the knowledge and skills you have gained that you can apply to solving the problem. The *levels of performance*—Professional Quality, Approaching Professional Quality, or Needs Quality Improvements—help you and your instructor evaluate your result.

	Your completed project is of Professional Quality if you:	Your completed project is Approaching Professional Quality if you:	Your completed project Needs Quality Improvements if you:
1-Software Mastery	Choose and apply the most appropriate skills, tools, and features and identify efficient methods to solve the problem.	Choose and apply some appropriate skills, tools, and features, but not in the most efficient manner.	Choose inappropriate skills, tools, or features, or are inefficient in solving the problem.
2-Content	Construct a solution that is clear and well organized, contains content that is accurate, appropriate to the audience and purpose, and is complete. Provide a solution that contains no errors in spelling, grammar, or style.	Construct a solution in which some components are unclear, poorly organized, inconsistent, or incomplete. Misjudge the needs of the audience. Have some errors in spelling, grammar, or style, but the errors do not detract from comprehension.	Construct a solution that is unclear, incomplete, or poorly organized; contains some inaccurate or inappropriate content; and contains many errors in spelling, grammar, or style. Do not solve the problem.
3-Format and Layout	Format and arrange all elements to communicate information and ideas, clarify function, illustrate relationships, and indicate relative importance.	Apply appropriate format and layout features to some elements, but not others. Overuse features, causing minor distraction.	Apply format and layout that does not communicate information or ideas clearly. Do not use format and layout features to clarify function, illustrate relationships, or indicate relative importance. Use available features excessively, causing distraction.
4-Process	Use an organized approach that integrates planning, development, self-assessment, revision, and reflection.	Demonstrate an organized approach in some areas, but not others; or, use an insufficient process of organization throughout.	Do not use an organized approach to solve the problem.

Outcomes-Based Assessments

Apply a combination of the 3A and 3B skills.

GO! Think | Project 3L Food Services

Project Files

For Project 3L, you will need the following file:

> a03L_Food_Services

You will save your database as:

> Lastname_Firstname_3L_Food_Services

Use the skills you have practiced in this chapter to assist Luciano Perez, the Hospitality Director, in creating a form and a report to assist him with the staff scheduling of food services for a two-day student orientation workshop. Create an attractive form that he can use to update the 3L Staff table saving the form as **Lastname Firstname 3L Staff Update Form** Using your own name, add a new record with the following information:

Staff ID: **STAFF-1119** Phone Number: **(703) 555-0845** Title: **Server**

Create a paper or electronic printout of only your record. Create an attractive, easy-to-read report for calling staff members when the schedule changes. Name the report **Lastname Firstname 3L Staff Phone List** and then create a paper or electronic printout of the report as directed.

End You have completed Project 3L ————————————————

Apply a combination of the 3A and 3B skills.

GO! Think | Project 3M Donors and Gifts

Project Files

For Project 3M, you will need the following file:

> a03M_Donors_Gifts

You will save your database as:

> Lastname_Firstname_3M_Donors_Gifts

Use the skills you have practiced in this chapter to assist the Dean of Information Technology in using her database to create attractive forms and reports. The Dean would like an attractive form that would enable her work study student to enter the information in the Donors table. Create and save a form naming it **Lastname Firstname 3M Donor Update Form** Using your own name, add a new record with the following information:

Donor ID: **DNR-1212** Donor: **Lastname Foundation** Phone Number: **(703) 555-6091**

Create a paper or electronic printout of only your record. Create a donor list with the donor, contact names, and phone numbers so that the Dean can call the donors to thank them for donating gifts that will be distributed during the high school recruitment tours. Save the report as **Lastname Firstname 3M Donor Phone List** and then create a paper or electronic printout as directed.

Create a report grouped by Category and sorted by Item Description that includes the Retail Value totals and a Grand Total of the Retail Value of the gift items. Create a page footer control that displays **Created by Lastname Firstname** and then save the report as **Lastname Firstname 3M Gift Amounts by Category Report** and then create a paper or electronic printout as directed.

End You have completed Project 3M ————————————————

Outcomes-Based Assessments

You and GO! | Project **3N** Personal Inventory

Project Files

For Project 3N, you will need the following file:

Lastname_Firstname_2N_Personal_Inventory (your file from Chapter 2)

You will save your database as:

Lastname_Firstname_3N_Personal_Inventory

If you have your database from Project 2N, save it in your Access Chapter 3 folder as **Lastname_Firstname_3N_Personal_Inventory** If you do not have the database from Project 2N, create a new database, saving it in your Access Chapter 3 folder with the same name given above. In the database, create one table with at least 18 records. Include fields such as item, room location, value, and date of purchase. Your table should have items stored in several locations.

Using the table, create an attractive form, naming it **Lastname Firstname 3N Inventory Update Form** Using the form, enter at least three records and then create a paper or electronic printout of one of the new records. Using the table, create an attractive report including fields for the room location, item name, and value or purchase price of the item—you may add more fields if you desire. Group the report by the room location, and sort by the value or purchase price of the item, summarizing the values. Name the report **Lastname Firstname 3N Room Values Report** and then create a paper or electronic printout as directed.

End **You have completed Project 3N** _____

Business Running Case

This project relates to **Front Range Action Sports**, which is one of the country's largest retailers of sports gear and outdoor recreation merchandise. The company has large retail stores in Colorado, Washington, Oregon, California, and New Mexico, in addition to a growing online business. Major merchandise categories include fishing, camping, rock climbing, winter sports, action sports, water sports, team sports, racquet sports, fitness, golf, apparel, and footwear.

In this project, you will apply skills you practiced from the Objectives in Access Chapters 1 through 3. You will create a database for Frank Osei, Vice President of Finance, that contains inventory and supplier information. In addition, you will create queries that answer specific questions relating to the inventory items and suppliers, forms for entering and updating information, and reports. Your printed results will look similar to Figure 1.1.

Project Files

For Project BRC1, you will need the following files:

New blank Access database
aBRC1_Inventory (Excel workbook)
aBRC1_Suppliers (Excel workbook)

You will save your database as:

Lastname_Firstname_BRC1_Inventory_Suppliers

Project Results

Figure 1.1

Business Running Case

Front Range Action Sports

1 **Start** Access to create a new **Blank database**. In the location where you are storing your projects, create a new folder named **Front Range Action Sports** or navigate to this folder if you have already created it. **Save** the database as **Lastname_Firstname_BRC1_Inventory_Suppliers**

a. Rename the **ID** field to **Item ID#** and change the **Data Type** to **Text**. Then create the fields as shown in **Table 1**.

b. Enter the two records as shown in **Table 2**.

c. **Close** the table, **Save** it as **Lastname Firstname BRC1 Inventory** and then increase the width of the **Navigation Pane** to display the entire table name. On the **External Data tab**, in the **Import & Link group**, click the **Excel** button. Navigate to your student files, double-click **aBRC1_Inventory**, and then **Append a copy of the records** to the **BRC1 Inventory** table. From the **Navigation Pane**, open the **BRC1 Inventory** table and verify that there are 116 records in the table. Apply **Best Fit** to all of the fields—scroll down to be sure that all of the data in the **Item Name** field displays. Display the table in **Print Preview**, and then create a paper or electronic printout of the first page. **Close Print Preview, Close** the table, and **Save** changes to the layout of the table.

d. On the **External Data tab**, in the **Import & Link group**, click the **Excel** button. Navigate to your student files, double-click **aBRC1_Suppliers**, and then **Import the source data into a new table in the current database**. Click **First Row Contains Column Headings** and set the primary key to **Supplier ID**. Name the table **Lastname Firstname BRC1 Suppliers** and then **Open** the table. **Delete** the **Fax Number** field, and then apply **Best Fit** to all of the fields. Display the table in **Print Preview**, change the orientation to **Landscape**, change the **Margins** to **Normal**, and then create a paper or electronic printout as directed. **Close Print Preview, Close**

the table, and save changes to the layout of the table. On the **Navigation Pane**, click the **Navigation Pane arrow**, and then click **Tables and Related Views**.

e. Click the **Database Tools tab**, and then in the **Relationships group**, click the **Relationships** button. In the **Show Table** dialog box, double-click **BRC1 Suppliers**, double-click **BRC1 Inventory**, and then **Close** the dialog box. Expand the field lists, and then in the **BRC1 Suppliers** field list, point to **Supplier ID**. Drag to the right into the **BRC1 Inventory** field list on top of the **Supplier ID** field, release the mouse button, click **Enforce Referential Integrity**, and then click **Create**. *One* supplier can supply *many* inventory items. Create a **Relationship Report**, **Save** the report with the default name, and then create a paper or electronic printout as directed. **Close Print Preview**, and then **Close** any open objects. Increase the width of the **Navigation Pane** to display the entire report name, and then **Close** the **Navigation Pane**.

2 Create a query in **Query Design** view, based on the **BRC1 Inventory** table to answer the question, *What is the Item Name (in alphabetical order), Retail Price, and Category for the Sport of Hiking?* Do not display the **Sport** field in the query results. Forty records meet the criteria. **Save** the query as **Lastname Firstname BRC1 Hiking Query** and then create a paper or electronic printout as directed. **Close Print Preview**, and then **Close** the query.

a. Create a copy of the **BRC1 Hiking Query**, saving the object as **Lastname Firstname BRC1 Hiking or Biking Shoes Query** Redesign the query to answer the question, *What is the Sport, Item Name, Retail Price, and Supplier ID for the Category of Shoes where the Sport is Hiking or Biking?* **Sort** the records by the **Sport** field and by the **Item Name** field. Do not display the **Category** field in the query results. Nine records meet the criteria. Create a paper or electronic

Table 1

Data Type	Text	Text	Currency	Text	Text	Text
Field Name	Item ID#	Item Name	Retail Price	Category	Sport	Supplier ID

(Return to Step 1-b)

Table 2

Item#	Item Name	Retail Price	Category	Sport	Supplier ID#
106555	Snowboard	256.99	Equipment	Skiing	SUPP-06
106556	Wool Socks	12.59	Socks and Gloves	Skiing	SUPP-04

(Business Running Case: Front Range Action Sports continues on the next page)

(Return to Step 1-c)

printout as directed. **Close Print Preview**, and **Close** the query.

b. Create a query in **Query Design** view, based on the **BRC1 Suppliers** table and the **BRC1 Inventory** table to answer the question, *What is the Item Name, Category, Company, and Business Phone for Categories that begin with the letter S, and sorted by Category, for the Sport of Fitness?* Do not display the **Sport** category in the query results. Eighteen records meet the criteria. **Save** the query as **Lastname Firstname BRC1 S Category Query** and then create a paper or electronic printout as directed. **Close Print Preview**, and **Close** the query.

c. Create a query in **Query Design** view, based on the **BRC1 Suppliers** table and the **BRC1 Inventory** table to answer the question, *What is the Company, Item Name, Category, Sport, and Retail Price for items that have a retail price of $100 or greater sorted in ascending order by Sport and then in descending order by Retail Price?* Twenty records meet the criteria. **Save** the query as **Lastname Firstname BRC1 Price $100 or Over Query** and then create a paper or electronic printout as directed, changing the margins to **Normal**. **Close Print Preview**, and **Close** the query.

d. Create a query in **Query Design** view, based on the **BRC1 Inventory** table to answer the question, *For Supplier ID of SUPP-01, for each Item Name and Retail Price, what is the markup of each item if marked up 10%, and what is the final price?* All numeric fields should be formatted as **Currency**, **2 Decimal** places. Apply **Best Fit** to all of the fields, **Save** the query as **Lastname Firstname BRC1 10 Percent Markup Query** and then create a paper or electronic printout as directed. **Close Print Preview**, and then **Close** the query.

3 Based on the **BRC1 Suppliers** table, use the **Form** tool to create a form. Switch to **Form** view, and then using your own first name and last name for the **Company** field, add a new record as shown in **Table 3**.

a. Save the form as **Lastname Firstname BRC1 Supplier Form** and then create a paper or electronic printout of only the record you just created in the form, changing the **Column Width** to **7.5"** **Close Print Preview**, and then **Close** the form.

4 Based on the **BRC1 Suppliers** table, use the **Report** tool to create a new report. **Delete** the following fields from the report: **Supplier ID**, **Address**, **City**, **State**, and **ZIP**. Apply the **Paper** theme to this object only. **Sort** the **Company** field in **Ascending** order. Decrease the width of the **Business Phone** field to accommodate the longest entry in the field. **Bold** the field names, and **Center** the **Company** and **E-mail Address** field names over the data. Use the **layout selector** to visually center the layout between the left and right margins, and then visually center the **page number control** between the left and right margins. (Hint: scroll to the right to display the control.) **Save** the report as **Lastname Firstname BRC1 Suppliers Contact List** Display the report in **Print Preview**, and then create a paper or electronic printout as directed. **Close Print Preview**, and then **Close** the report.

5 Using the **Report Wizard**, create a report based on the **BRC1 Inventory** table. Add the following fields to the report: **Category**, **Item Name**, and **Retail Price**. **Group** by **Category**. **Sort** in **Ascending** order by **Item Name**. Find the **Average** of the **Retail Price** field. Select the **Stepped Layout**, and then as the report title, type **Lastname Firstname BRC1 Avg Price by Category Report**

a. In **Print Preview**, display the report by **Two Pages** and notice how the groupings are split between pages, that the **Retail Price** field name displays only *Price*, and that the prices in the text box and calculated controls display ###. **Close Print Preview**, and then switch to **Layout** view. Apply the **Oriel** theme to the report and no other objects.

b. Click the **Item Name** field name, hold down Shift, and then click the **text box control** that displays *Snowboard*. Decrease the width of the field until there is approximately **2** inches between **Item Name** and the right edge of the text box control. Scroll down the

Table 3

Supplier ID	Company	E-mail Address	Business Phone	Address	City	State	ZIP
SUPP-12	Lastname Firstname Inc	info@watersports.biz	(305) 555-6543	14 South Beach Rd	Miami	FL	33125

(Business Running Case: Front Range Action Sports continues on the next page)

(Return to Step 3-a)

Front Range Action Sports (continued)

report to be sure that all Item Names display fully. Scroll to the top of the report, and then click the **Retail Price** field name, which displays only a portion of the word *Price*. Hold down Shift, click the **text box control** below the field name, which displays ###, and then click the **calculated control** that also displays ###. Increase the width of the controls by pointing to the left edge of any one of the selected controls and dragging it to the left until the entire field name—**Retail Price**—displays as the field name.

c. Delete the **Summary for 'Category' label controls**. Change the text in the **Avg label control** from *Avg* to **Average Retail Price Per Category** and then move the **label control** to the right until the right edge of the control is approximately **0.25 inch** from the left edge of its associated calculated control.

d. Click in the **title** of the report, and then change the **Font Size** to **16**. Visually center the title between the left and right margins of the report. Select all of the field names, and then apply **Bold** and **Italic**.

e. On the **Design tab**, in the **Grouping & Totals** group, click the **Group & Sort** button. In the **Group, Sort, and Total** pane, click **More**. Click the **do not keep group together on one page arrow**, and then click **keep whole group together on one page**. In the **Grouping & Totals group**, click the **Group & Sort** button to close the **Group, Sort, and Total** pane. **Save** the report.

f. Display the report in **Print Preview** by **Two Pages**, and notice how the groupings are kept together on one page. On the **Print Preview tab**, in the **Print group**, click the **Print** button. In the **Print** dialog box, under **Print Range**, click **Pages**. In the **From** box, type **1** and in the **To** box, type **2** and then click **OK** to create a paper printout—or create an electronic printout as directed. **Close Print Preview**, and then **Close** the report.

6 **Open** the **Navigation Pane**, and if necessary, widen the pane to display fully all object names. Display **Backstage** view, click **Close Database**, and then click **Exit**.

End **You have completed Business Running Case 1** ——————————

Glossary

Address bar The bar at the top of a folder window with which you can navigate to a different folder or library, or go back to a previous one.

Aggregate functions Calculations such as MIN, MAX, AVG, and SUM that are performed on a group of records.

Alignment The placement of paragraph text relative to the left and right margins.

All Programs An area of the Start menu that displays all the available programs on your computer system.

AND condition A condition in which only records where all of the values are present in the selected fields.

Append To add on to the end of an object; for example, to add records to the end of an existing table.

Application Another term for a program.

Ascending order A sorting order that arranges text in alphabetical order (A to Z) or numbers from the lowest to highest number.

AutoNumber data type A data type that describes a unique sequential or random number assigned by Access as each record is entered and that is useful for data that has no distinct field that can be considered unique.

AutoPlay A Windows feature that displays when you insert a CD, a DVD, or other removable device, and which lets you choose which program to use to start different kinds of media, such as music CDs, or CDs and DVDs containing photos.

Back and Forward buttons Buttons at the top of a folder window that work in conjunction with the address bar to change folders by going backward or forward one folder at a time.

Backstage tabs The area along the left side of Backstage view with tabs to display various pages of commands.

Backstage view A centralized space for file management tasks; for example, opening, saving, printing, publishing, or sharing a file. A navigation pane displays along the left side with tabs that group file-related tasks together.

Best Fit An Access command that adjusts the width of a column to accommodate the column's longest entry.

Between ... And operator A comparison operator that looks for values within a range.

Blank database A database that has no data and has no database tools—you must create the data and the tools as you need them.

Blank Report tool An Access tool with which you can create a report from scratch by adding the fields you want in the order in which you want them to display.

Bound The term used to describe objects and controls that are based on data that is stored in tables.

Bound control A control that retrieves its data from an underlying table or query; a text box control is an example of a bound control.

Calculated control A control that contains an expression, often a formula, that uses one or more fields from the underlying table or query.

Calculated field A field that stores the value of a mathematical operation.

Caption A property setting that displays a name for a field in a table, query, form, or report other than that listed as the field name.

Center alignment The alignment of text or objects that is centered horizontally between the left and right margin.

Click The action of pressing the left button on your mouse pointing device one time.

Command An instruction to a computer program that causes an action to be carried out.

Common dialog boxes The set of dialog boxes that includes Open, Save, and Save As, which are provided by the Windows programming interface, and which display and operate in all of the Office programs in the same manner.

Common field A field in one or more tables that stores the same data.

Comparison operator Symbols that evaluate each value to determine if it is the same (=), greater than (>), less than (<), or in between a range of values as specified by the criteria.

Compound criteria Multiple conditions in a query or filter.

Compressed file A file that has been reduced in size and thus takes up less storage space and can be transferred to other computers quickly.

Context sensitive command A command associated with activities in which you are engaged.

Contextual tabs Tabs that are added to the Ribbon automatically when a specific object, such as a picture, is selected, and that contain commands relevant to the selected object.

Control An object on a form or report that displays data, performs actions, and lets you view and work with information.

Control layout The grouped arrangement of controls on a form or report.

Copy A command that duplicates a selection and places it on the Clipboard.

Criteria (Access) Conditions in a query that identify the specific records for which you are looking.

Crosstab query A query that uses an aggregate function for data that can be grouped by two types of information and displays the data in a compact, spreadsheet-like format.

Currency data type An Access data type that describes monetary values and numeric data that can be used in mathematical calculations involving data with one to four decimal places.

Cut A command that removes a selection and places it on the Clipboard.

Data Facts about people, events, things, or ideas.

Data entry The action of typing the record data into a database form or table.

Data source (Access) The table or tables from which a form, query, or report retrieves its data.

Data type The characteristic that defines the kind of data that can be entered into a field, such as numbers, text, or dates.

Database An organized collection of facts about people, events, things, or ideas related to a specific topic or purpose.

Database management system Database software that controls how related collections of data are stored, organized, retrieved, and secured; also known as a *DBMS*.

Database template A preformatted database designed for a specific purpose.

Datasheet view The Access view that displays data organized in columns and rows similar to an Excel worksheet.

Date control A control on a form or report that inserts the current date each time the form or report is opened.

DBMS An acronym for *database management system.*

Default The term that refers to the current selection or setting that is automatically used by a computer program unless you specify otherwise.

Descending order A sorting order that arranges text in reverse alphabetical order (Z to A) or numbers from the highest to lowest number.

Deselect The action of canceling the selection of an object or block of text by clicking outside of the selection.

Design grid The lower area of the Query window that displays the design of the query.

Design view An Access view that displays the detailed structure of a query, form, or report; for forms and reports, may be the view in which some tasks must be performed, and only the controls, and not the data, display in this view.

Desktop In Windows, the opening screen that simulates your work area.

Destination table (Access) The table to which you import or append data.

Detail section The section of a form or report that displays the records from the underlying table or query.

Details pane The area at the bottom of a folder window that displays the most common file properties.

Dialog box A small window that contains options for completing a task.

Dialog Box Launcher A small icon that displays to the right of some group names on the Ribbon, and which opens a related dialog box or task pane providing additional options and commands related to that group.

Document properties Details about a file that describe or identify it, including the title, author name, subject, and keywords that identify the document's topic or contents; also known as *metadata.*

Double-click The action of clicking the left mouse button two times in rapid succession.

Drag The action of holding down the left mouse button while moving your mouse.

Edit The actions of making changes to text or graphics in an Office file.

Ellipsis A set of three dots indicating incompleteness; when following a command name, indicates that a dialog box will display.

Enhanced ScreenTip A ScreenTip that displays more descriptive text than a normal ScreenTip.

Expression A formula.

Extract To decompress, or pull out, files from a compressed form.

Field A single piece of information that is stored in every record and formatted as a column in a database table.

Field list A list of the field names in a table.

Field properties Characteristics of a field that control how the field displays and how data can be entered in the field.

File A collection of information stored on a computer under a single name, for example a Word document or a PowerPoint presentation.

File list In a folder window, the area on the right that displays the contents of the current folder or library.

Fill The inside color of an object.

Filter by Form An Access command that filters the records in a form based on one or more fields, or based on more than one value in the field.

Filter by Selection An Access command that retrieves only the records that contain the value in the selected field.

Filtering The process of displaying only a portion of the total records (a subset) based on matching a specific value.

First principle of good database design A principle of good database design stating that data is organized in tables so that there is no redundant data.

Flat database A simple database file that is not related or linked to any other collection of data.

Folder A container in which you store files.

Folder window In Windows, a window that displays the contents of the current folder, library, or device, and contains helpful parts so that you can navigate.

Font A set of characters with the same design and shape.

Font styles Formatting emphasis such as bold, italic, and underline.

Footer A reserved area for text or graphics that displays at the bottom of each page in a document.

Foreign key The field that is included in the related table so the field can be joined with the primary key in another table for the purpose of creating a relationship.

Form (Access) An Access object you can use to enter new records into a table, edit or delete existing records in a table, or display existing records.

Form footer Information at the bottom of the screen in Form view that is printed after the last detail section on the last page.

Form header Information, such as a form's title, that displays at the top of the screen in Form view and is printed at the top of the first page when records are printed as forms.

Form tool The Access tool that creates a form with a single mouse click, which includes all of the fields from the underlying data source (table or query).

Form view The Access view in which you can view the records, but you cannot change the layout or design of the form.

Form Wizard The Access tool that creates a form by asking a series of questions.

Format Painter An Office feature that copies formatting from one selection of text to another.

Formatting The process of establishing the overall appearance of text, graphics, and pages in an Office file—for example, in a Word document.

Formatting marks Characters that display on the screen, but do not print, indicating where the Enter key, the Spacebar, and the Tab key were pressed; also called *nonprinting characters.*

Gallery An Office feature that displays a list of potential results instead of just the command name.

Group footer Information printed at the end of each group of records; used to display summary information for the group.

Group header Information printed at the beginning of each new group of records, for example, the group name.

Group, Sort, and Total pane A pane that displays at the bottom of the screen in which you can control how information is sorted and grouped in a report; provides the most flexibility for adding or modifying groups, sort orders, or totals options on a report.

Groups On the Office Ribbon, the sets of related commands that you might need for a specific type of task.

Header A reserved area for text or graphics that displays at the top of each page in a document.

Icons Pictures that represent a program, a file, a folder, or some other object.

Import The process of copying data from another file, such as a Word table or an Excel workbook, into a separate file, such as an Access database.

Info tab The tab in Backstage view that displays information about the current file.

Information Data that is organized in a useful manner.

Innermost sort field When sorting on multiple fields in Datasheet view, the field that will be used for the second level of sorting.

Insertion point A blinking vertical line that indicates where text or graphics will be inserted.

Is Not Null A criteria that searches for fields that are not empty.

Is Null A criteria that searches for fields that are empty.

Join line In the Relationships window, the line joining two tables that visually indicates the related field and the type of relationship.

Keyboard shortcut A combination of two or more keyboard keys, used to perform a task that would otherwise require a mouse.

KeyTips The letter that displays on a command in the Ribbon and that indicates the key you can press to activate the command when keyboard control of the Ribbon is activated.

Label control A control on a form or report that contains descriptive information, typically a field name.

Landscape orientation A page orientation in which the paper is wider than it is tall.

Layout selector A small symbol that displays in the upper left corner of a selected control layout in a form or report that is displayed in Layout view or Design view; used to move an entire group of controls.

Layout view The Access view in which you can make changes to a form or report while the object is running—the data from the underlying data source displays.

Library In Windows, a collection of items, such as files and folders, assembled from various locations that might be on your computer, an external hard drive, removable media, or someone else's computer.

Link A connection to data in another file.

Live Preview A technology that shows the result of applying an editing or formatting change as you point to possible results—*before* you actually apply it.

Location Any disk drive, folder, or other place in which you can store files and folders.

Logical operators Operators that combine criteria using AND and OR. With two criteria, AND requires that both conditions be met and OR requires that either condition be met.

Message Bar The area directly below the Ribbon that displays information such as security alerts when there is potentially unsafe, active content in an Office 2010 document that you open.

Metadata Details about a file that describe or identify it, including the title, author name, subject, and keywords that identify the document's topic or contents; also known as *document properties*.

Microsoft Access A database program, with which you can collect, track, and report data.

Microsoft Communicator An Office program that brings together multiple modes of communication, including instant messaging, video conferencing, telephony, application sharing, and file transfer.

Microsoft Excel A spreadsheet program, with which you calculate and analyze numbers and create charts.

Microsoft InfoPath An Office program that enables you to create forms and gather data.

Microsoft Office 2010 A Microsoft suite of products that includes programs, servers, and services for individuals, small organizations, and large enterprises to perform specific tasks.

Microsoft OneNote An Office program with which you can manage notes that you make at meetings or in classes.

Microsoft Outlook An Office program with which you can manage e-mail and organizational activities.

Microsoft PowerPoint A presentation program, with which you can communicate information with high-impact graphics.

Microsoft Publisher An Office program with which you can create desktop publishing documents such as brochures.

Microsoft SharePoint Workspace An Office program that enables you to share information with others in a team environment.

Microsoft Word A word processing program, also referred to as an authoring program, with which you create and share documents by using its writing tools.

Mini toolbar A small toolbar containing frequently used formatting commands that displays as a result of selecting text or objects.

Multiple Items form A form that enables you to display or enter multiple records in a table.

Navigate The process of exploring within the organizing structure of Windows.

Navigation area An area at the bottom of the Access window that indicates the number of records in the table and contains controls (arrows) with which you can navigate among the records.

Navigation Pane (Access) An area of the Access window that displays and organizes the names of the objects in a database; from here, you open objects for use.

Nonprinting characters Characters that display on the screen, but do not print, indicating where the Enter key, the Spacebar, and the Tab key were pressed; also called *formatting marks*.

Normalization The process of applying design rules and principles to ensure that your database performs as expected.

Object window An area of the Access window that displays open objects, such as tables, forms, queries, or reports; by default, each object displays on its own tab.

Objects The basic parts of a database that you create to store your data and to work with your data; for example, tables, forms, queries, and reports.

Office Clipboard A temporary storage area that holds text or graphics that you select and then cut or copy.

One-to-many relationship A relationship between two tables where one record in the first table corresponds to many records in the second table—the most common type of relationship in Access.

Open dialog box A dialog box from which you can navigate to, and then open on your screen, an existing file that was created in that same program.

Option button A round button that allows you to make one choice among two or more options.

Options dialog box A dialog box within each Office application where you can select program settings and other options and preferences.

OR condition A condition in which records that match at least one of the specified values are displayed.

Outermost sort field When sorting on multiple fields in Datasheet view, the field that will be used for the first level of sorting.

Page footer Information printed at the end of every page in a report; used to print page numbers or other information that you want to display at the bottom of every report page.

Page header (Access) Information printed at the top of every page of a report.

Page number control A control on a form or report that inserts the page numbers when displayed in Print Preview or when printed.

Paragraph symbol The symbol ¶ that represents a paragraph.

Paste The action of placing text or objects that have been copied or moved from one location to another location.

Paste Options Icons that provide a Live Preview of the various options for changing the format of a pasted item with a single click.

PDF (Portable Document Format) file A file format that creates an image that preserves the look of your file, but that cannot be easily changed; a popular format for sending documents electronically, because the document will display on most computers.

Point The action of moving your mouse pointer over something on your screen.

Pointer Any symbol that displays on your screen in response to moving your mouse.

Points A measurement of the size of a font; there are 72 points in an inch, with 10-12 points being the most commonly used font size.

Populate The action of filling a database table with records.

Portrait orientation A page orientation in which the paper is taller than it is wide.

Preview pane button In a folder window, the button on the toolbar with which you can display a preview of the contents of a file without opening it in a program.

Primary key The field that uniquely identifies a record in a table; for example, a Student ID number at a college.

Print Preview A view of a document as it will appear when you print it.

Program A set of instructions that a computer uses to perform a specific task, such as word processing, accounting, or data management; also called an *application*.

Program-level control buttons In an Office program, the buttons on the right edge of the title bar that minimize, restore, or close the program.

Property Sheet A list of characteristics—properties—for fields or controls on a form or report in which you can make precise changes to each property associated with the field or control.

Protected view A security feature in Office 2010 that protects your computer from malicious files by opening them in a restricted environment until you enable them; you might encounter this feature if you open a file from an e-mail or download files from the Internet.

Pt. The abbreviation for *point*; for example when referring to a font size.

Query A database object that retrieves specific data from one or more database objects—either tables or other queries—and then, in a single datasheet, displays only the data you specify.

Quick Access Toolbar In an Office program, the small row of buttons in the upper left corner of the screen from which you can perform frequently used commands.

Quick Commands The commands Save, Save As, Open, and Close that display at the top of the navigation pane in Backstage view.

Read-Only A property assigned to a file that prevents the file from being modified or deleted; it indicates that you cannot save any changes to the displayed document unless you first save it with a new name.

Record All of the categories of data pertaining to one person, place, thing, event, or idea, and which is formatted as a row in a database table.

Record selector bar The bar at the left edge of a record when it is displayed in a form, and which is used to select an entire record.

Record selector box The small box at the left of a record in Datasheet view that, when clicked, selects the entire record.

Record source The tables or queries that provide the underlying data for a form or report.

Redundant In a database, information that is repeated in a manner that indicates poor database design.

Referential integrity A set of rules that Access uses to ensure that the data between related tables is valid.

Relational database A sophisticated type of database that has multiple collections of data within the file that are related to one another.

Relationship An association that you establish between two tables based on common fields.

Report A database object that summarizes the fields and records from a table or query in an easy-to-read format suitable for printing.

Report footer Information printed once at the end of a report; used to print report totals or other summary information for the entire report.

Report header Information printed once at the beginning of a report; used for logos, titles, and dates.

Report tool The Access tool that creates a report with one mouse click, which displays all of the fields and records from the record source that you select—a quick way to look at the underlying data.

Report Wizard An Access feature with which you can create a report by answering a series of questions; Access designs the report based on your answers.

Ribbon The user interface in Office 2010 that groups the commands for performing related tasks on tabs across the upper portion of the program window.

Ribbon tabs The tabs on the Office Ribbon that display the names of the task-oriented groups of commands.

Right-click The action of clicking the right mouse button one time.

Run The process in which Access searches the records in the table(s) included in the query design, finds the records that match the specified criteria, and then displays the records in a datasheet; only the fields that have been included in the query design display.

Sans serif A font design with no lines or extensions on the ends of characters.

ScreenTip A small box that that displays useful information when you perform various mouse actions such as pointing to screen elements or dragging.

Scroll bar A vertical or horizontal bar in a window or a pane to assist in bringing an area into view, and which contains a scroll box and scroll arrows.

Scroll box The box in the vertical and horizontal scroll bars that can be dragged to reposition the contents of a window or pane on the screen.

Search box In a folder window, the box in which you can type a word or a phrase to look for an item in the current folder or library.

Second principle of good database design A principle stating that appropriate database techniques are used to ensure the accuracy of data entered into a table.

Section bar A gray bar in a form or report that identifies and separates one section from another; used to select the section and to change the size of the adjacent section.

Select To highlight, by dragging with your mouse, areas of text or data or graphics, so that the selection can be edited, formatted, copied, or moved.

Select query A type of Access query that retrieves (selects) data from one or more tables or queries, displaying the selected data in a datasheet; also known as a *simple select query*.

Serif font A font design that includes small line extensions on the ends of the letters to guide the eye in reading from left to right.

Shortcut menu A menu that displays commands and options relevant to the selected text or object.

Simple select query Another name for a select query.

Single-record form A form that enables you to display or enter one record at a time in a table.

Sort The process of arranging data in a specific order based on the value in each field.

Source file When importing a file, refers to the file being imported.

Split button A button divided into two parts and in which clicking the main part of the button performs a command and clicking the arrow opens a menu with choices.

Stacked layout A control layout format that is similar to a paper form, with label controls placed to the left of each textbox control. The controls are grouped together for easy editing.

Start button The button on the Windows taskbar that displays the Start menu.

Start menu The Windows menu that provides a list of choices and is the main gateway to your computer's programs, folders, and settings.

Status bar The area along the lower edge of an Office program window that displays file information on the left and buttons to control how the window looks on the right.

Structure In Access, the underlying design of a table, including field names, data types, descriptions, and field properties.

Subdatasheet A format for displaying related records when you click the plus sign (+) next to a record in a table on the *one* side of a relationship.

Subfolder A folder within a folder.

Subset A portion of the total records available.

Tab order The order in which the insertion point moves from one field to another in a form when you press the Tab key.

Table (Access) The database object that stores data organized in an arrangement of columns and rows, and which is the foundation of an Access database.

Table area The upper area of the Query window that displays field lists for the tables that are used in the query.

Tables and Related Views An arrangement in the Navigation Pane that groups objects by the table to which they are related.

Tabs On the Office Ribbon, the name of each activity area in the Office Ribbon.

Tags Custom file properties that you create to help find and organize your own files.

Task pane A window within a Microsoft Office application in which you can enter options for completing a command.

Text box control The graphical object on a form or report that displays the data from the underlying table or query; a text box control is known as a bound control.

Text data type An Access data type that describes text, a combination of text and numbers, or numbers that are not used in calculations, such as a number that is an identifier like a Student ID.

Text string A sequence of characters.

Theme A predefined format that can be applied to the entire database or to individual objects in the database.

Theme A predesigned set of colors, fonts, lines, and fill effects that look good together and that can be applied to your entire document or to specific items.

Title bar The bar at the top edge of the program window that indicates the name of the current file and the program name.

Toggle button A button that can be turned on by clicking it once, and then turned off by clicking it again.

Toolbar In a folder window, a row of buttons with which you can perform common tasks, such as changing the view of your files and folders or burning files to a CD.

Triple-click The action of clicking the left mouse button three times in rapid succession.

Truncated Refers to data that is cut off or shortened.

Trust Center An area of the Access program where you can view the security and privacy settings for your Access installation.

Trusted Documents A security feature in Office 2010 that remembers which files you have already enabled; you might encounter this feature if you open a file from an e-mail or download files from the Internet.

Unbound control A control that does not have a source of data, such as a title in a form or report.

USB flash drive A small data storage device that plugs into a computer USB port.

Views button In a folder window, a toolbar button with which you can choose how to view the contents of the current location.

Wildcard character In a query, a character that serves as a placeholder for one or more unknown characters in your criteria; an asterisk (*) represents one or more unknown characters, and a question mark (?) represents a single unknown character.

Window A rectangular area on a computer screen in which programs and content appear, and which can be moved, resized, minimized, or closed.

Windows Explorer The program that displays the files and folders on your computer, and which is at work anytime you are viewing the contents of files and folders in a window.

Windows taskbar The area along the lower edge of the Windows desktop that contains the Start button and an area to display buttons for open programs.

Wizard A feature in Microsoft Office that walks you step by step through a process.

Zoom The action of increasing or decreasing the viewing area on the screen.

Index

SINGLE PC LICENSE AGREEMENT AND LIMITED WARRANTY

READ THIS LICENSE CAREFULLY BEFORE OPENING THIS PACKAGE. BY OPENING THIS PACKAGE, YOU ARE AGREEING TO THE TERMS AND CONDITIONS OF THIS LICENSE. IF YOU DO NOT AGREE, DO NOT OPEN THE PACKAGE. PROMPTLY RETURN THE UNOPENED PACKAGE AND ALL ACCOMPANYING ITEMS TO THE PLACE YOU OBTAINED THEM. *THESE TERMS APPLY TO ALL LICENSED SOFTWARE ON THE DISK EXCEPT THAT THE TERMS FOR USE OF ANY SHAREWARE OR FREEWARE ON THE DISKETTES ARE AS SET FORTH IN THE ELECTRONIC LICENSE LOCATED ON THE DISK:*

1. GRANT OF LICENSE and OWNERSHIP: The enclosed computer programs ("Software") are licensed, not sold, to you by Prentice-Hall, Inc. ("We" or the "Company") and in consideration of your purchase or adoption of the accompanying Company textbooks and/or other materials, and your agreement to these terms. We reserve any rights not granted to you. You own only the disk(s) but we and/or our licensors own the Software itself. This license allows you to use and display your copy of the Software on a single computer (i.e., with a single CPU) at a single location for academic use only, so long as you comply with the terms of this Agreement. You may make one copy for back up, or transfer your copy to another CPU, provided that the Software is usable on only one computer.

2. RESTRICTIONS: You may not transfer or distribute the Software or documentation to anyone else. Except for backup, you may not copy the documentation or the Software. You may not network the Software or otherwise use it on more than one computer or computer terminal at the same time. You may not reverse engineer, disassemble, decompile, modify, adapt, translate, or create derivative works based on the Software or the Documentation. You may be held legally responsible for any copying or copyright infringement which is caused by your failure to abide by the terms of these restrictions.

3. TERMINATION: This license is effective until terminated. This license will terminate automatically without notice from the Company if you fail to comply with any provisions or limitations of this license. Upon termination, you shall destroy the Documentation and all copies of the Software. All provisions of this Agreement as to limitation and disclaimer of warranties, limitation of liability, remedies or damages, and our ownership rights shall survive termination.

4. DISCLAIMER OF WARRANTY: THE COMPANY AND ITS LICENSORS MAKE NO WARRANTIES ABOUT THE SOFTWARE, WHICH IS PROVIDED "AS-IS." IF THE DISK IS DEFECTIVE IN MATERIALS OR WORKMANSHIP, YOUR ONLY REMEDY IS TO RETURN IT TO THE COMPANY WITHIN 30 DAYS FOR REPLACEMENT UNLESS THE COMPANY DETERMINES IN GOOD FAITH THAT THE DISK HAS BEEN MISUSED OR IMPROPERLY INSTALLED, REPAIRED, ALTERED OR DAMAGED. THE COMPANY DISCLAIMS ALL WARRANTIES, EXPRESS OR IMPLIED, INCLUDING WITHOUT LIMITATION, THE IMPLIED WARRANTIES OF MERCHANTABILITY AND FITNESS FOR A PARTICULAR PURPOSE. THE COMPANY DOES NOT WARRANT, GUARANTEE OR MAKE ANY REPRESENTATION REGARDING THE ACCURACY, RELIABILITY, CURRENTNESS, USE, OR RESULTS OF USE, OF THE SOFTWARE.

5. LIMITATION OF REMEDIES AND DAMAGES: IN NO EVENT, SHALL THE COMPANY OR ITS EMPLOYEES, AGENTS, LICENSORS OR CONTRACTORS BE LIABLE FOR ANY INCIDENTAL, INDIRECT, SPECIAL OR CONSEQUENTIAL DAMAGES ARISING OUT OF OR IN CONNECTION WITH THIS LICENSE OR THE SOFTWARE, INCLUDING, WITHOUT LIMITATION, LOSS OF USE, LOSS OF DATA, LOSS OF INCOME OR PROFIT, OR OTHER LOSSES SUSTAINED AS A RESULT OF INJURY TO ANY PERSON, OR LOSS OF OR DAMAGE TO PROPERTY, OR CLAIMS OF THIRD PARTIES, EVEN IF THE COMPANY OR AN AUTHORIZED REPRESENTATIVE OF THE COMPANY HAS BEEN ADVISED OF THE POSSIBILITY OF SUCH DAMAGES. SOME JURISDICTIONS DO NOT ALLOW THE LIMITATION OF DAMAGES IN CERTAIN CIRCUMSTANCES, SO THE ABOVE LIMITATIONS MAY NOT ALWAYS APPLY.

6. GENERAL: THIS AGREEMENT SHALL BE CONSTRUED IN ACCORDANCE WITH THE LAWS OF THE UNITED STATES OF AMERICA AND THE STATE OF NEW YORK, APPLICABLE TO CONTRACTS MADE IN NEW YORK, AND SHALL BENEFIT THE COMPANY, ITS AFFILIATES AND ASSIGNEES. This Agreement is the complete and exclusive statement of the agreement between you and the Company and supersedes all proposals, prior agreements, oral or written, and any other communications between you and the company or any of its representatives relating to the subject matter. If you are a U.S. Government user, this Software is licensed with "restricted rights" as set forth in subparagraphs (a)-(d) of the Commercial Computer-Restricted Rights clause at FAR 52.227-19 or in subparagraphs (c)(1)(ii) of the Rights in Technical Data and Computer Software clause at DFARS 252.227-7013, and similar clauses, as applicable.

Should you have any questions concerning this agreement or if you wish to contact the Company for any reason, please contact in writing:

Multimedia Production,
Higher Education Division,
Prentice-Hall, Inc.,
1 Lake Street,
Upper Saddle River NJ 07458.